A Korean War Diary

A Historian in a War

By Kim Sungchil
Translated by Kibong Kim

IMPRIMATUR

Uijeongbu, die 9 Mensis November. 2021

+ Petrus K. H. LEE

Episcopus Uijeongbuensis

© Kim Sungchil
Translated by Kibong Kim
Final manuscript editing by Yoon Yeo Ick
Typesetting by Jang Eunhee

Printed in the United States of America

All rights reserved. This book or any portion thereof may not be reproduced or used in any manner whatsoever without the express written permission of the publisher except for the use of brief quotations in a book review.
First Printing, December 15, 2021
Published by Catholic Institute of Northeast Asia Peace
(publ-cinap@hanmail.net)
ISBN : 979-8-78609-895-3

A refugee line in the winter ©Wikimedia Commons

August 16, 1950.

I think this may be the real strength of the People's Republic (North Korea). Everybody is in a near-death situation with hunger, so they need to dance to its Party's music to survive. Everybody has a certain amount of (*unknown but probable*) fear, so they must endorse unconditionally whatever the Party does. This may be the perfect political technique when it comes to governing by fear.

Oct 5, 1950.

Those --- defeated North Korean soldiers who stayed at our house a couple of weeks ago --- and --- these South Korean soldiers sitting in front of me now… they should not be enemies against each other, they must be on the same side. *What did they do wrong, other than having bad leaders?*

They said… "At the front, the two sides got into hand-to-hand combat. When I was just about to thrust a knife into an enemy soldier, I realized he was my second elder brother! As I called out, "Brother!", and threw away my knife, I started crying."

Nov 10, 1950.

He said …. "What disappointed me more than anything was not that my identity was blown or that the People's Republic Army was defeated and ran away, but that the People's Republic lost the hearts of the people through and through. I see that citizens of Seoul now abominate North Koreans from the depth of their heart."

Dec 19, 1950.

"A young woman with a baby on her back was trying to climb to the top of a train with all of her might, but as her hands were frozen, she could not protect the baby much. After a while, when she tried to feed her baby, the baby was already dead from the cold. The young mother went mad right there."

Dec 30, 1950.

Whatever hardships and struggles arise in our nation's future, we will overcome them all with our power of sheer survival………

Preface

A diary of my father, Kim[1] Sungchil, describes a life of a scholar during the Korean War. He recorded his family's trials and tribulations, what took place around him as much as he could understand and his thoughts on various events. As a historian by profession, he recorded events that he encountered dutifully.

He started the diary on the day when the Korean War started (25 June 1950). He recognized the need to record the events of the war, almost as a public record. It records vivid encounters of an ordinary citizen during a war that devastated the entire country.

The Democratic People's Republic of Korea (DPRK, the North Korea) came down upon the South on 25 June 1950, nearly pushing the Republic of Korea (ROK, the South Korea) out of the Korean peninsula before the United Nations (UN) troops arrived. The UN and ROK troops pushed the North Koreans back to the north, almost to the Chinese border. Then a massive contingent of Chinese troops came down to push the fighting lines back South below the 38th Parallel around where a ceasefire was agreed upon three years later. See Appendix A for more details about the war.

At the beginning of the war, some privileged people were able to escape Seoul while the bulk of Seoul citizens were

---

1 Kim is the family name. Family names appear first in Korean names.

left stranded in Seoul. Once the North occupied Seoul, they turned the whole system upside down and there was a purposeful 'clean-up' of people with democratic ideologies. Ordinary citizens endured extreme hardships as their jobs vanished, their possessions were taken away, their family members were lost, and their lives were threatened. Many people perished of starvation.

It was not a garden of paradise either when the UN and ROK forces recovered Seoul three months later. There were reckless and never-ending 'counter-clean-up' operations against communist sympathizers and even some who passively endured the communist regime.

When China intervened in the war, pushing the UN and ROK forces south, people who were able to escape Seoul during the cold winter with meager possessions were in a severe hardship.

The author despaired at the harshness of the war, suffering of people and mean and cruel acts of both sides. He started out looking at communism and democracy together while trying to identify strong and weak points in each. Within a couple of months of the war, he was totally disappointed by communism.

People like him, the leading young intellectuals of his time, had been divided into the two ideologies long before the war. Even before the war, he had lost many friends who chose communism over democracy and moved north. Some of his most heart-wrenching agonies came in the form of losing some of his closest friends to the North during the war.

The diary describes his observations on communism in action in Seoul and how people suffered under it, events after the recovery of Seoul and some experiences in Busan[2] as a refugee. He had to make sure that he and his family were safe on the one hand, but he also wanted to make right decisions in his actions and thoughts in the challenging times. In a way, the diary describes his search for his own identity.

Throughout this period of turmoil, he tried to view things objectively and act accordingly. As a son translating his diary, I am quite taken by his ability to see things through and make decisions correctly most of the times, with paltry information available to him.

He maintained a love for his fellow countrymen and tried his best not to commit wrongs and encouraged others to do rights. He respected people on a person-to-person basis, while maintaining critical eyes on both sides of the politics. He was a people person. He interacted with many sorts of people: teachers, colleagues, friends, neighbors, students, relatives, and family members. He learned from their actions and sought to be a positive influence on them.

Korea, a small country and one of the poorest in the world at the time of the war, had been subjected to mistreatment by stronger and more aggressive neighbors throughout its history spanning thousands of years. Its survival had been a continuous challenge.

Prof. Kim observed, despite its people's naiveté, blind allegiance, irrationality, self-righteousness, stupidity, ruth-

---

[2] Busan is located at the Southeasternmost part and the second largest city of South Korea.

lessness, deceit, greed and corruption as described in the diary, that Korea had survived and had sometimes prospered thanks to their resilience, determination, aspiration, hardwork, enterprise, cooperation and good-heartedness of the same people.

Within just 70 years following the war, South Korea transformed itself from a beggar country that was totally leveled by the war, into one of the most advanced countries in the world, with Samsungs, K-pops and what-nots. The achievements are breathtaking. One wonders, "How did they do it?"

On the other hand, there still lurks the danger to the country from outside (North Korea, perhaps China, etc.) and from within (new ideological infightings, etc.). The Korean peninsula still is one of the more dangerous places in the world. One worries, "Where is it going now?"

Kibong Kim, son and translator.
Vienna, VA, United States
September 2021

Korean War Map and Diary Map of Seoul

June 1950 through July 1953
Copied from Google Chrome

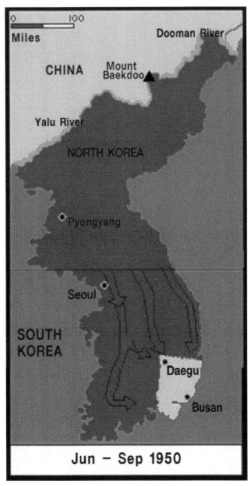

1st map: The straight horizontal line in the middle of the map (the 38th Parallel) is the original boundary between South Korea and North Korea before the war. The small lighter-shaded area in the Southeast corner of the peninsula shows how far the North Korean army came down in August 1950.

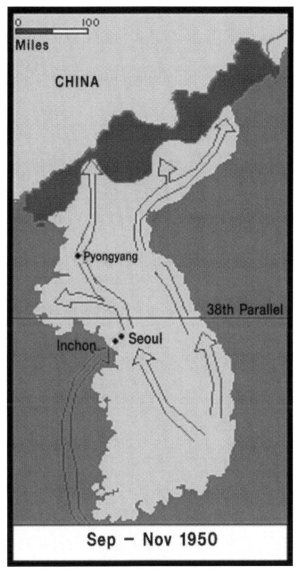

2nd map: The arrow on the left (on the sea) toward Inchon, East of Seoul, shows where the UN Forces landed in September 1950. The arrows on land show how far the UN forces went up North, almost to Yalu River, when the Chinese army crossed the river and came down south.

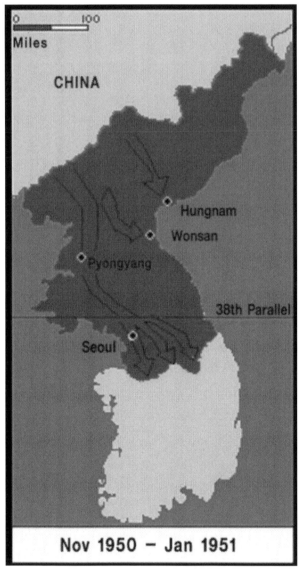

3rd map: The map shows how far south the Chinese Army came down.

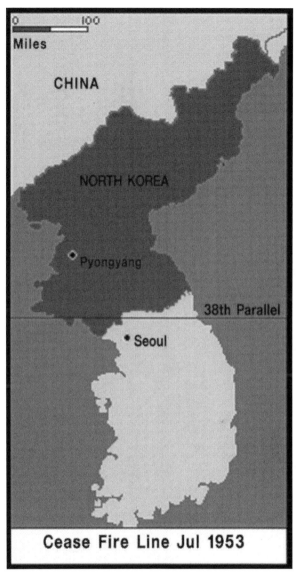

4th map: The map shows where the Armistice Line was drawn in July 1953.

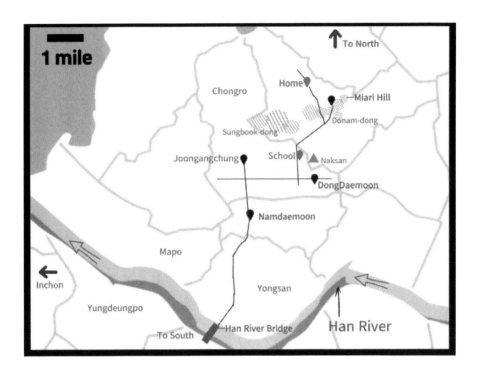

Contents

Preface 1

Korean War Map and Diary Map of Seoul 6

The War Diary 13

Three Months under North Koreans 14

    June 1950 14

    July 1950 39

    August 1950 121

    September 1950 172

Recovery of Seoul, and Escape to the South 226

    October 1950 226

    November 1950 263

    December 1950 292

Life in Busan 317

    March 1951 317

    April 1951 327

Appendix A: A Short History of the Korean War .. 329

Appendix B: My Parents 332

Epilogue 340

The War Diary

In the diary, some relevant information deemed useful are given by the translator in footnotes or in short parentheses with *Italicized* comments. Un-Italicized words in parentheses are those of the author.

A few Korean words without adequate corresponding English words are phonetically spelled out in English alphabets and *Italicized*. Their meanings will be explained in footnotes or otherwise.

Occasionally, musings of Prof. Kim appear in the diary, and they are also *Italicized*.

Most proper nouns for people, places, organizations, etc. are not *Italicized*, except for book titles.

Three Months under North Koreans

June 1950

25 June 1950[3]

When I went out to the vegetable field[4] around noon, Mr. Kang, the owner of the next-door store, said he was just coming back from downtown and relayed the news to me that the North Koreans had come down across the 38th parallel[5] this morning. Fierce fighting broke out everywhere and there was an emergency summons for military personnel in the city. The mood in the streets was all very tense.

I am not sure whether it is another one of the repeating conflicts along the cursed 38th parallel, or if it is indeed a large invasion. But this must be at least an emergency event, as indicated by the way Mr. Kang scurries about.

This may be a well-planned series of actions by the North, considering that this happened very soon after The Motherland Unification Democratic Front of the North[6] sent

---

3 It is the day when the Korean War started. The war is called the 6.25 War or the 6.25 Incident by Koreans.
4 A small vegetable field by a stream, of perhaps a couple of acres.
5 The boundary between the South Korea and the North Korea.
6 The political organization of the Democratic People's Republic

'an appeal' letter to the South. The South government arrested three people who carried the letter as soon as they crossed the 38th parallel, thus giving an excuse to the North: "We called for a peaceful unification, but as you guys are so unyielding, we have to resort to military actions - -."

As it was not officially announced, I do not know all the details of the appeal letter, but what newspapers reported seemed highly absurd: To demand that President Rhee[7] and nine other top officials in the South be excluded from the unification process. There may be some faults with President Rhee and those people, but that is a different matter.

What if the South behaved this way towards the North? Would the North listen to a proposal from the South for a unification that excludes Premier Kim Ilsung[8] and many important officials of the North? After such a proposal, if the North refused to come to the table, will the South be justified to invade the North?

I do not think the response of the South to the so-called Motherland Unification Call was proper either. Shouldn't the government have sent back the three people who were carrying the letter while publicizing the irrationality of the proposal to the nation? Fumbling and keeping the contents

---

of Korea, DPRK, the North Korea.
7 The president Rhee Syngman of the Republic of Korea, the South Korea.
8 General Kim Ilsung was the leader of Democratic People's Republic of Korea. He started the Korean War in 1950. He was and still is revered by North Koreans almost as if he is a deity. He is the grandfather of the current (2021) North Korean leader, Kim Jong-un.

of the call a secret, while announcing the 'conversion' of the arrested people, is not the right thing to do.

However irrational the proposal was, it is against common sense and decency to arrest and coerce the messengers. It is ridiculous to announce that these messengers were so overwhelmed by what they saw in the South that they decided to betray the North. People would wonder what kind of clever torture techniques have been used to convert those people so quickly who crossed the border, with resolve and without personal concerns.

Anyway, how will the people cope through a war when the price of a bushel of rice is approaching the 6,000 *won*[9] level and people everywhere are suffering in poverty?

26 June 1950.

I went out early in the morning and waited for a bus to come. It didn't. Even though it was getting late, there weren't many people waiting for the bus today. I finally came to see that they have commandeered buses to use in

---

9 Won is the Korean monetary unit. His monthly salary at the university was 20,000 won. See the diary input on Sept 4. In other words, a university assistant professor was paid about three and half bushels of rice monthly. Fortunately, he had other income from book royalties (See Appendix B, My Parents) and two small pieces of land where he grew vegetables and peaches. It is hard for the translator to understand how people made a living with the low salaries.

fights that started yesterday. I walked to the school[10] and felt the unsettled air in the streets. Since last night, we could hear muted booming sounds, like distant thunder. People say that the North Koreans have crossed the 38th parallel already and are coming down toward Euijungboo[11].

In my study were two students, Kang[12] and Kim, who came and studied just like any other day. They are helping me in a research project of mine as core members, so I opened my study to them. Both students are sincere and diligent. Kang has shown no ideological inclinations and focuses on his studies only. Kim is on the watch list as a leftist by the Students Homeland Protection League (Hakdo Hokook Dae)[13] because he had objected to the National University Plan (Kookdaean)[14]. I see him as a pure liberalist, and nothing more.

---

10 Seoul National University in which Prof. Kim worked.
11 A small city directly north of Seoul. Seoul is only 60 miles away from the 38th Parallel.
12 Kang is Kang Sinhang who would later become a professor at Sungkyoonkwan University. He was very helpful after the war when Prof. Kim's family was struggling to cope with the post-war confusion.
13 A rightist students' watchdog organization.
14 After the liberation from Japan in 1945 until 1948 when a South Korean government was set up, a United States Military Government governed South Korea. A proposal was made by this government, in 1946, to consolidate several colleges in the Seoul area into a single national university. It caused vehement protests among professors and students from many colleges. Academic activities in the South were paralyzed, and many prominent scholars went to the North as a result.

Regarding the National University Plan, I am one of those who ardently dislike it. Perhaps I may be seen as biased, but I still believe it is wrong to label them as 'leftists' just because they opposed the National University Plan. It may have been easy to brand the opposition members as leftists because there had been a suspicion that the leftists controlled opposition efforts to the plan.

Our view is that the leftists took advantage of the complaints against the plan and incited people against it. Still, it may not be in the best national interest to keep persecuting those students who, with pure hearts, had opposed the symbol of contradiction and irrationality. My statement here is not necessarily confined to the students who opposed to the National University Plan. In general, the rightists insist too much on their own prejudices, pushing many conscientious neutralists to the left. This would be counterproductive for the right.

Kang *koon*[15] and Kim *koon* suggested that we all attend the morning school assembly as it is Monday today. It is held every Monday morning and there have been repeated requests that professors be present too, but I have never been to any of them. It is firstly because my house is too far away to make it to the school early on Monday mornings when I don't have any classes; and secondly, I heard too many unpleasant stories about them. For example, a rumor has it that rightist students collect teachers' attendance records

---

15 The title 'koon', of which no comparable English word is available, is used for people who are generally close friends or juniors of the author. It implies a certain amount of affection and respect. This word will appear often in the dairy.

and report them directly to the ROK education minister[16]. Also, there was an incident where many professors got upset at a meeting when a gymnastics teacher stood up and hinted at forced attendance to these assemblies.

For one reason or another, I have not been to any of them. When the students suggested that I attend, thinking that it may be the last such assembly, I felt like going to watch one. Perhaps I am reading too much into the students' minds, but they seemed to suggest to me that, during this dangerous period, I may have to go there to show a certain willingness to cooperate.

The dean started with an admonitory lecture to the students, but it lacked both scholarly depth and patriotic fervor. He mentioned a little about the current international political situation and concluded that young students should be spiritually ready to face this extraordinary situation. But he did not give any hints regarding what this spiritual readiness should entail. Can I just blame this on the inadequacy of one school dean? Rather, I think it is a good example of today's educated elites bent on self-protection only. I wonder if I am not just another of those as well. This can be considered an unfortunate outcome of our current standing, torn between the grips of the American and Soviet superpowers.

In the afternoon, Mr. Lee Keunmoo came by. He was looking for a recommendation for a candidate for a home mathematics tutor for his daughter. She is attending Kyunggi Girls Middle School. I called and discussed it with

---

16 This may have been done to document, in their opinion, who are rightists or leftists.

Moon Jusuk *koon* who said his friends might find one. I suggested to him that a female university student in natural sciences would be preferable.

Today, there were two extra-edition flyers, and newspapers also announced in large letters: 'Puppet military's illegal invasion all over the 38th parallel'. Facing the pages full of slander and curses against the puppet military, with the dull cannon sounds in the background, I cannot but wonder if these same papers will change their tune by tomorrow or the day after, into praise and flattery towards this puppet military. Contrary to the confusion and excitement around, the paper relays optimistic news of the 'Enemy's total defeat', 'South Korean soldiers entering Haejoo[17]' and 'A surrender of two enemy companies at the Eastern front'.

Upon reading these articles, Kang *koon*, who is just around twenty years old, with his childlike face, commented wryly, "Who knows if the enemy surrendered, or our soldiers surrendered?" These words shook me a bit. This was not a simple disdain of the newspaper articles, nor a distrust regarding the announcement of the Defense Department. I was taken because I could read the prevailing national nihilism in the face of young Kang *koon*. After going through what challenges it met and what struggles it went through, the national spirit has lost the purity in the minds of the youth and allowed twisted views to flourish in everything. I remembered a sad old song by a Polish poet, "We could

---

17 A North Korean city very close to the 38th Parallel which was the dividing line between the two Koreas before the war. This story implies that the South ROK troops pushed back the North DPRK troops beyond the 38th Parallel.

not but foster so many thoughts we shouldn't have harbored at such a young age."

On the way home, the streets were abuzz beyond the level I felt at the school. On big streets, there was an unending number of military trucks racing north toward Doenumee Hill, and schoolchildren all over the streets cheering. I do not know when the children were brought out from their schools; but the children were excitedly clapping their tiny hands.

My mind was consumed with thoughts… "The war is really taking place", followed by "The nightmare of an internecine war that has been weighing down on the national soul for the last five years is finally becoming the reality". My mind was in such a state that everything became dark. I felt a momentary dizziness.

June 27, 1950.

On a predawn radio program, the acting Prime Minister, Sin Sungmo, announced that the government would move to Suwon[18]. Although we could hear cannons a lot closer than before, we thought Seoul would still be safe and had decided to ride out the unavoidable hardship. But now, my once-resolute spirit is flagging.

I checked the chickens and ducks as usual in the morning, but my mind was elsewhere.

---

18 Suwon is a city about 20 miles south of Seoul.

I told Mansoo and Soonkyoo[19], who had been staying in our gate room, to go home; but they did not seem to understand the gravity of the situation. Mansoo is a student from my hometown, and Soonkyoo is his close friend from Choongchung Province. Although both found it difficult to disobey my command, they still could not understand why they had to pack and leave Seoul so urgently.

Both are students, each about twenty years of age. Both depend on me. I like them, too. Under normal circumstances I would have explained to them, so they could understand that the current military situation is unusually tense. If they cannot catch a ride today, there may not be a ride for them again. It may come to a point where they may not escape Seoul, even if they wanted to. I would feel much better knowing that they were with their parents. I cannot keep the children of other people through whatever situation that might develop during and after the war. Perhaps I should have explained the situation more carefully, but I just could not bring myself to it—so I just pushed them out.

"Please don't pack too much. You do not know what could happen on the road. Cars could be crowded. Just bring a schoolbag as if you are going to school, and leave", I urged them.

I even interrupted their breakfast, "Stop eating rice. Pack it into a ball and carry it. Hurry. The morning car may be the last one. It will be terribly crowded, so get on it as quickly as you can. If you can't catch it, don't come back; find ways to walk to your homes." I pushed them out.

---

19 Prof. Kim had taken in a couple of students from near his hometown to stay in his house while they studied.

As I watched them go, my mind felt anxious. What kind of turmoil would envelop Seoul in the future? Where would I stand if the world is turned upside-down? If I must evacuate, where would I find a haven in this small, palm-sized country, south of the 38th parallel? During the summer, where can I find a livable place for my young ones outside our safe abode?

I suddenly remembered Park Yunam, who said in Yulha Ilgee[20], "Chosun[21] people like to go seek some other places when troubles come along, but Seoul is the best place. Going to the mountains is the stupidest thing to do because it is easy to get sick. There is no place to go to when one is sick; food would be gone in a few days, and robbers would take it if it does not run out. Separated from the outside world, they would not know what is happening out there, and it is easy to die in the mountains. There wouldn't be a more stupid thing than that."

After breakfast, I called Jungyong (*a nephew*[22]) to bury some food, clothes, and blankets in the ground. We went

---

20 A China (Qing Dynasty) travel log/diary of Park Yunam, 1780. Park Yunam was a writer and critic from the 18th century. Prof. Kim had translated the travel log from Chinese into Korean, and he quoted the book often in the diary.
21 Chosun is the name of Korean Lee Dynasty from the 14th century through the twentieth century. Sometimes in this book, the names of Chosun and Korea are used synonymously by Prof. Kim. The name Chosun is preferred by North Koreans and the name Korea, by South Koreans.
22 Prof. Kim was the youngest boy in the family with four much older sisters, so he had many nephews only a half-generation younger than him. Some of them were very close to him.

through the drawers and burned a few documents, like national bonds. I sent a note telling Kyunghee (*a second cousin*), Daekyoo (*a nephew*) brothers and Janghee to come, but they did not come. Perhaps the messenger could not reach them? Even if they had come, what could I do for them? Even without my advice, I trust they could wade through this violent current with their agile susceptivity of the tumultuous times.

In the village, people everywhere are unsettled and upset. All the faces are strained. I stopped by the store of Kang *koon*, paid him what I owed and bought eggs, noodles, wine, cigarettes and cookies. I would have liked to buy as much food in the store as possible, but I refrained, not wanting to make a scene in front of others. Kang *koon* suggested that I buy more eggs, which I did. I must go into siege mode.

The situation is changing hour by hour. People who were crowding the streets an hour ago are now leaving the town with bundles in their hands and children on their backs. On the front hill, without enough time to build a position, hastily set-up cannons are firing. One or two soldiers with grass on their helmets can be seen coming down the hill slopes. They must be retreating from the frontline. Their crestfallen looks tell us what is happening; but when they say that their cannon balls cannot do anything against the enemies' tanks, even when they hit them—it still adds to the grim mood. We finally asked Jungyong to take the older children, with Wife[23] following them with little Kihyub (*the third son,*

---

23 In Korea, when a husband talks about his wife to others, he uses the word: 'wife', not 'my wife'. Here, the translator took the liberty of using a capital letter when he talks about his

sometimes called Hyub-a) on her back. She smiled courageously while suppressing her own feelings. I smiled also as I was telling the children to be careful.

After they left, I was left alone in the empty house and could finally relax with my mind and body feeling totally empty. I went into my room, lay on the bed, and thought about international conditions, the fate of the nation and the people, my home, and my personal situation. These thoughts passed through my head like a panorama, but none of them led to any tractable conclusions. Nearby, the cannons' roar is intermittent. How can we survive this turmoil? No satisfactory answer comes to mind. If I died tonight, I resolved to die a decent death.

The radio said that, according to the Information Service Directorate of the Republic of Korea (ROK), this morning's announcement of the government moving to Suwon was a mistake. The entire government, including the president and the cabinet members, were working in their offices as usual. The National Assembly made a resolution to stay in Seoul to the end and our courageous soldiers were fighting well. They have recovered Euijungboo and are chasing the fleeing enemy. Therefore, people were urged to trust the military and the government and stay at work without losing confidence.

But what about those gun fires, the sounds of which were getting closer every hour?

---

wife, as if it is her given name. Likewise, talking to others, a wife calls her husband: 'husband'. When they talk to each other, they call each other 'yubo (dear)' and do not call their given names.

Around two or three o'clock in the afternoon, there was an ever-growing mumbling in the streets. It went on for almost half an hour. I went out to see what was going on. All the village people, both young and old, were climbing into the hills. Our neighbor, Choonja's grandfather and mother asked me what I was doing here. I asked if there was an order of a sort to evacuate the village and they said they were not certain about that, but a soldier came by earlier telling them that this village would become the location of intense fighting by nightfall.

I recited Park Yunam's words once again in my mind as I came back to my room and put up a thick blanket on the wall where bullets might come through and stretched out my body on the bed. The radio repeatedly broadcasted a recorded message in the words of Mr. Kim Hyunsoo, Head of Announcement Division, Intelligence Directorate at the Defense Department, that a combat branch under General MacArthur would be immediately established in Seoul today and American war planes would take part in the fights starting tomorrow. It instructed frontline soldiers and the public to keep to their lines and workplaces under any circumstances.

I could not bring myself to believe this announcement. I was saddened that I could not rely on the credibility of these formal national government announcements in this critical situation. Whether as a nation or as a person, we always have to say the truth. I felt strongly that promoting falsehoods for temporary gain would eventually lead to self-destruction. Around five o'clock, Wife's family members came by and reprimanded me for staying alone in the house while the entire village was empty. I told them that covering myself with a blanket and remaining alone seemed better to me than going into the hills and taking all the troubles. They still insisted that I go with them, so I followed them out, thinking there is no real counter-argument on that point either.

But when I got there, every gully was filled with people and there was no space to squeeze into even on the corner of a rock. After peeking into this and that ditch for a better place to sit, we got tired and settled down under a pine tree in a corner.

Drenched in sweat, we cooled ourselves under that tree. Thinking about the situation, I questioned myself—what was I doing there while my family was elsewhere? If the people in Donam-dong[24] are also forced to evacuate to the hills, what would Wife do with the three children? As I dwelled on this thought, I got impatient and agitated and felt a powerful pull to get to my family as soon as possible.

By now, every ridge of the mountain was positioned with soldiers who began firing cannons, into which direction I could not fathom. I told my mother-in-law that I had to go to my children, and before she said anything, I almost slid down the slope in the general direction of Sungbook-dong. I walked along the slopes and crawled along the ridges between regularly positioned guns and finally reached the Sungbook-dong Valley. It was already getting dark. I ran in the drizzle all the way down to the Samsun streetcar tracks. Along the tracks, there were military vehicles zipping through masses of people swarming alongside them.

There was a pause in the car traffic and people began to move, so I ran forward to cross the tracks. A soldier shoved

---

24 The area where Jungyong's house was located and where his wife and the children were at the moment.

hard the butt of his gun into my side and swore at me in a Northwestern accent. It was so painful that I could not utter a sound. I almost collapsed there; but I collected myself and turned around. However, by that time, the mass of people had already been broken and they began crossing the street. I joined them again and ran across the street. I twisted my body to ease the pain on my side and ran to Jungyong's house completely exhausted. Upon seeing the faces of my family, I was relieved.

When I looked up toward south, I saw cannons positioned at the foot of the Naksan (*a small hill*) Rampart[25]. There were a lot of soldiers on the ground on their bellies. The enemy would target them. Jungyong's house was located right in front of these cannons and soldiers as if directly inviting the cannonballs. As I talked about this with Wife and discussed whether we should move to Mr. Lee Keunwon's house in front of the Kyungdong Middle School, a cannonball flew in and landed with a cloud of dust. Traffic in the street disappeared in an instant. We ended up spending the night in the middle of *the* danger zone.

Rain had started coming down hard since dusk and cannonballs were flying continually above our heads. Whizzing sounds of cannonballs flying through the air followed by the rumbling sounds of their explosions. With the fear that one of those, erroneously aimed might kill us all, these were not very pleasant sounds to listen to. The women folk went into the dugout under the floor with the children while

---

25 A remnant of old Seoul castle wall, facing north directly toward Miari Hill with a Donam-dong valley in between. Please see 'Diary Map of Seoul' at the beginning of the book.

my brother-in-law, Jungyong, and I lay down on the dirt kitchen floor on a mat. It was some challenge to deal with scared Meru (*a pet dog*) who kept trying to burrow himself in our midst.

June 28, 1950.

The rain fell on and off throughout the night, but the sound of cannons never stopped. Some worried about making smoke, but as we were all starving, we cooked some rice and ate it. With our senses becoming dull, we fell to short naps now and then throughout the night. Various thoughts occupied my mind: the irony of dying here after coming here to avoid death; a wish that at least my children could survive the danger; that perhaps it would be better for them to die here instead of becoming orphans; that if Wife survives, she may manage things in some way; how worried my old parents must be back at home, etc. Then I came to a point where nothing bothered me much anymore and my thoughts ended up with leaving everything to its fate.

Fate! I had never taken fate so seriously and to an extent, I had thought fate is somewhat dictated by one's own efforts. Now, faced with such an enormous obstacle in which I have no power at all as life and death hang on happenstance, with the realization that life may end very soon in a most unhappy way, fate does not seem to be trivial anymore. If I were a believing person of a supreme being, perhaps I could have gained my peace of mind sooner?

Near dawn, the fighting seemed to get fiercer as sounds of cannons and gunfire are mixed, sounding like popping corns. After such a tortured night, I seemed to have gained some measure of calm and I was able to tell which cannons were flying which way. But now, with such a heavy barrage, my head is just a blur, and I cannot tell which is which anymore. Occasionally, there are human screams from not so far away. It appears there already are street fights down in the lower flat area.

My brother-in-law, who is already in his sixties, said, "If they recognize their own weakness, they should retreat now lest more civilians get hurt." My twenty-year-old nephew said, "It may not be easy for them to spit out the cake when it's already in the mouth. Knowing that fights do not end in a day or two, they will continue fighting until they cannot anymore. Loss of civilian lives is important to us, but it wouldn't matter much to them." This could be a generational difference.

When daylight broke, I looked out the window. The cannon positions at Naksan (*in the south*) were nowhere to be seen. Far away over Miari Hill (*in the north*), something larger and heavier than cars are slowly rolling down. These must be the North's tanks that are not affected by cannon balls. On the streets below, I could see there are already people moving about on the streets while soldiers in strange military uniforms are marching.

As the wearisome cannon sounds ceased, one could see a feeling of relief on people's faces; but there is no denying that our world has been turned upside-down overnight.

Like it or not, we became citizens of a different country overnight and it is no longer the Republic of Korea.

Around noon, with the children in front, we headed back home leaving Donam-dong. On the streets, some people were already waving red flags shouting hoorays. At schools, the flags of the Democratic People's Republic of

Korea (DPRK) were raised which I had heard about but had never seen.

Tanks, cars, horse carts and walking soldiers were pouring down Miari Hill toward Dongsomoon. Even with heavy northwestern accents, they shared our language, custom, and bloodlines. I could not think of them as enemy soldiers. It was almost like my brothers who had left home were now coming back after a lengthy absence. When I saw them smile and talk, it was hard to harbor any hatred for them.

This does not mean that I lacked loyalty to the Republic of Korea (ROK). What was the difference between the South soldiers I saw yesterday and these soldiers? A small difference was in their clothing. Why was one soldier our friend and the other an enemy? When did we become such mortal enemies that we are willing to face each other on the fields of death? They should have embraced and called each other, "My brother". Why were they fighting each other, and for whom? I felt like dropping on the ground and crying until my tears ran dry. But I have become a citizen of the Democratic People's Republic of Korea overnight, and I am not allowed to dispense with these kinds of feelings.

On Arirang Hill, cannons discarded by the ROK soldiers stood forlorn, still pointing at Miari Hill. When we got home, Beeru (*a house dog*) came running out to greet us, and nothing much had changed. On the streets, there were occasional broken windows, but considering the fierce fight of the night, it was fortunate that there wasn't more damage to houses or to people. People who had evacuated were also coming back. Everybody greeted each other as if the dead had come back, but nobody mentioned any politics. Toward evening, there were already youths wearing red armbands on the street. I remember having seen one of them donning an ROK arm band on a bicycle only yesterday.

June 29, 1950.

They released Hong *koon*[26] from jail. He stopped by his family yesterday and then came to visit me today. He was one of my closest friends from college and one of the most intelligent and highly conscientious students of law. I liked him all the more for keeping coolheaded and honorable even in the unhappy years after the liberation, in which his talent and capability were not sufficiently utilized.

He visited me once and blasted both the Korea Democratic Party (Hanmindang *of ROK*) and the Communist Party (*of DPRK*). I couldn't believe my ears when I heard a few days later that they arrested him as a Communist Party underground cell member (*planted*) inside a law court. If it had been somebody else, I might have believed that he had said those things to me while being secretly involved with the Party; but considering his character, I just could not bring myself to doubt his integrity.

Following his release on a suspended sentence, he wandered about without a job or a house. I took pity on him and let him stay in the empty house at my orchard[27]. He ended

---

26 Hong Seunggee was one of the three best friends of Prof. Kim. The other two were Lee Chul and Kang Kyungsuk.

27 It was a peach orchard of perhaps 4-5 acres. It had a small house in it, normally empty. The translator has a fond memory of picking cherry-like berries from the bushes that

up opening a small law office in Choongmooro. Even then, he was the man of justice I had always known. He was not the kind of a hot-blooded man who would join a certain political party giving up the basic sense of right and wrong.

In those days, I saw him day and night, but didn't ask him whether he was indeed involved in the Party cell incident. It had been a big question for me. But when I saw him, he did not seem changed from his old self at all, so all my suspicions melted away.

For a while, there was a rumor that he had openly shouted to the judge on his case that there would be a day when their positions would be reversed, but I rejected the rumor as rubbish. Regarding his character, I knew him better than anybody else; he was not such a person. On the contrary, several times he had emphatically quoted to me the words of his presiding judge, Mr. Lim Hangyung, "No conscientious, intelligent person should be involved in an underground movement. He will eventually betray himself and his closest friends. The reality is such a hard thing."

In those days, he was brought into the Chongro Police Station a few times for questioning and was pressured to join the (*ROK*) Protection and Guidance Alliance (Bodoyunmaeng)[28]. Once he told me, in passing, that a person at the Alliance named Suh Bumsuk was being unreasonably mean to him. He was soon jailed once again in the Sudaemoon jail. This was just two or three months ago. Afterwards, his brothers-in-law were worriedly looking for any information about him. They heard that it was not a very

---

defined the boundary of the orchard.
28 An organization that was established by ROK in 1948 to try to convert and keep eyes on leftists.

serious matter. The North Korean tanks arrived at Sudaemoon yesterday. Jail guards fled leaving the jail doors open. He simply walked out along with all the other prisoners.

During his school years, he was called a stick; but in jail he lost more weight, and his face was pale as he hadn't seen the sun for a while. As he was burying a dead dog killed by a stray bullet two days ago, he said, "They say people released from jail grab things to do immediately and work feverishly, but I would like to rest for a while and observe what is going on. I can recover my physical strength in that way, and I was never a true Bolshevik, anyway." He told me, as if he was trying to persuade himself. I thought that these words were the true expressions of the person Hong Seunggi I knew.

There already were rough-looking youths wearing red armbands that read, 'Self-Governing Corps[29]'. Carrying unfamiliar guns, they visited every house, checking how much food was stored. Soon afterwards, they took away most of the recorded food leaving only a paltry amount.

"Because of the unparalleled tyranny of criminal Rhee Syngman, countless citizens are on the verge of starvation. Let us share food first. Then, in a week, DPRK will distribute enough food back to you.

"An unfathomable amount of food is being shipped through the Port of Inchon[30]. We will distribute food in a

---

[29] Readers may notice in this diary that many different self-governing offices appear at various organizations. They were stop-gap organizations before formal North Korean government offices were to be set up.

[30] Inchon is a port city near Seoul. Nowadays, it houses the

week. We could have come down to the South last year, but we didn't because we had not saved enough food. Now, in the North, we have three years' supply of food."

The propaganda was too beaming to be true. In the face of these statements, I realized I had done well to have the foresight to have hidden some food for the children. The argument about which side initiated the war also became clear from what they were saying themselves.

June 30, 1950.

I went to the school because I wanted to see what was happening there. I also needed to clean up what I was doing in the study. There were no streetcars running yet. On several electricity poles were leaflets posted saying, "Professors and students of the Liberal Arts and Science College, gather at 1:00 pm on June 30th." I stopped by Prof. Kim Sanggee[31]'s house on my way to the school.

Students with unfamiliar faces were guarding the gate, keeping strict watch. Many students, graduates, and expelled students who had been identified as North sympathizers were now actively moving about in the campus. There were a few I knew well who came running and said, "I am so glad to see you safe, sir." Most of the others, I did not recognize. Some students displayed bravado by driving a

---

Inchon Airport as a gateway to Seoul.
31 A respected senior professor at the History Department. He had helped Prof. Kim in preparing his thesis and they also co-wrote a couple of history books.

school car on city streets with a banner: "Liberal Arts and Science College Students Self-Governing Committee." It surprised me to see Lee Jongak *koon* of the History Department among them.

Students had taken over the office. One of them guided me to the School Affairs office. I saw the faces of fellow professors - Lee Byunggee, Lee Byungdo, Choi Yoonsik, Kim Kookyung, Sung Baeksun, and Kim Ilchool who had left the school last year, Lee Myungsun who had left the school several years ago, and Yoo Eungho who had run for office in Gongjoo in the May 30th election and been arrested.

They said that the meeting to be held at 1:00 pm today was only for students. There would be only a preliminary meeting of professors today for the main meeting tomorrow. Some showed hints of not wanting too many people around, as if there were some secretive discussions to be had. I returned to my study, cleaned up the drawers of my desk, took a few books I had been reading recently, and returned home right away.

On the streets, propaganda posters that had been quiet for some time were resurrected in force. A while ago, I had teased my Communist friend Lee Chul[32], "It's good not to see leftists' posters with their vulgar language anymore. Electricity poles and walls look so clean." I thought these posters would make Chul *koon* and his friends feel very good.

There are signs such as 'Total Annihilation of the Gang of Puppets of the Traitor of All Ages, Rhee Syngman',

---

32 Lee Chul was another one of Prof. Kim's best friends.

'Overthrow the Spiritual Offspring of Lee Wan Yong[33]', Traitor Rhee Syngman', or 'Capture of Rhee Syngman, Traitors' Ringleader'. And then there are signs such as 'Hooray for the highly respected leader, General Kim Ilsung', 'Hooray for the Chosun Democratic People's Republic', 'Hooray for the incomparably courageous People's Army, Chosun's superb sons and daughters', painted over and over as if they desired to pass on these messages to thousands of future generations.

There are signs taking things one step further: 'Hooray for Generalissimo Stalin', 'Hooray for the Rampart of the World's Democratic Encampment, the Soviet Union', 'Hooray for Generalissimo Stalin, a Loving Friend of Chosun People and the Liberator of the World's Weaker Nations'. I could not resist a wry smile at myself for getting angry, realizing that the rumors of past several years from the North about the Soviet Union and Stalin had been confirmed.

One thing I had acutely felt while walking down the road was that I was too conspicuously well dressed. Normally I am not keen on dressing up and have often been told by others that I should wear some better clothes. Today I am the only one wearing a suit and a felt hat. Everybody else is wearing laborers' pants with a shirt and straw hats or no hats at all. Only my sneakers seem passable as I haven't been wearing leather shoes for the last four or five years. Everybody except me seemed to have agreed upon what to wear, making me uneasy.

---

33 The last prime minister of the Chosun Kingdom accused of selling the sovereignty to the Japanese in 1910.

Upon leaving the school, I wanted to see how the streets had changed. As I passed a Myungryoon-dong road, I happened to pick up an unfamiliar piece of paper on the street. It was a military ID card for a person named Kim Ik Ro issued by the Chinese military. It was issued only a few months ago. I pocketed this unexpected and historically meaningful piece of paper. After the North Korean soldiers had come into the city, there were rumors that Soviet soldiers were driving tanks in the streets; but as I had not seen them myself, I did not believe it. There were also rumors that the Chinese military was involved. This piece of paper proved that, at the very least, a Korean soldier in the service of the Chinese Red Army has taken part in the war.

Circling around the Changkyung Palace Park and passing near the Youngan Morgue, I saw a group of people murmuring, looking over a barbed-wire fence. Out of curiosity I walked over there and saw corpses covered roughly with straw mats. There were quite a few of them. According to the bystanders, North Korean soldiers came into the hospital, took injured South Korean soldiers out and shot them. I could not believe it. How could it ever be possible? This made no sense. For the honor of the Korean people, I hope it was not true.

July 1950

July 1, 1950.

Early in the morning, Lee *koon* of the Korean Language Department came over. On the 27th, he wanted to go to his home in the countryside but did not have enough money to pay the fare. I gave him the money, but he now said he could not go home after all as there were no longer cars at the train station. Lee *koon* told me since soldiers would occupy the school, we had to evacuate all offices. I did not want to attend today's school meeting considering yesterday's events. But I had to go in order to pick up the books I had been reading and notes I'd been preparing. It may pull me into the meeting involuntarily after all.

I do not want to be stubbornly loyal to the Republic of Korea which deceived its own innocent people and fled; but the world has been suddenly turned upside-down and people like us who are slow to respond have a tough time coming to terms with a new country to which we now appear to belong. Whether or not to attend a meeting might be a trivial issue in normal times, but it may be a sensitive matter now. I feel helpless for not being able to transform myself quickly as cicadas can cast off their old skins.

I went to the school with Lee *koon* at around ten o'clock. I was wearing a short sleeve shirt with no tie and a modest pair of pants. I bought a straw hat on the street for 200 won. An old saying says, "A nation is broken into pieces, but its mountains and rivers remain nonchalantly unchanged." When a nation is taken over by another of disparate character, is the first change supposed to appear in people's clothing? I could feel how the Ming Chinese were heartbroken when they were forced to don their hair and clothing strictly in the style of Qing Dynasty.[34]

North Korean soldiers were already using parts of the school. Even though offices had not been taken over yet, they forbade us to take books outside. When I got close to the North Korean soldiers, I saw many of them were youthful soldiers. I was also somewhat surprised to notice that their faces belied malnutrition. They seemed to be well-trained and followed rules rigorously. My first impression of the People's Army soldiers was very favorable. Then, an hour later, an event broke out that shattered this impression.

The meeting was held at the same place with the same people as yesterday, but with a few new professors. They were discussing things in a subdued atmosphere when two soldiers appeared and, aiming Russian submachine guns at our chests, ordered us to raise our hands. This was the first time that anything like this happened in my life. My heart fell as if it was being crushed. I followed their order and raised my hands high. My hands were shaking. It was -- not out of fear, but from indignation. The soldiers looked at our faces deliberately, one by one, and asked, "Aren't there treasonous agents among you?"

We answered, "We are all professors at this university," but that was met with vulgar smirks. "Is there a law that

---

34 The people of Han Chinese of Ming Dynasty had regarded their conqueror who established the Qing Dynasty as barbarians from Manchuria.

guarantees there are no treasonous agents among professors?" The tall one who appeared to be the leader between them yelled, "Weren't universities of the South a haven for traitors?"

"No, no, not at all. Actually, we had been targeted by the (*ROK*) puppet government as the hotbed of leftist ideologies," said a professor who was a supporter of an earlier discussion about 'teacher cleansing.' I took his comment as an attempt to protect our lives and was grateful; but at the same time, I felt pity for myself—trying to save my life in such a way.

Finally, we could lower our hands; but one soldier still aimed his gun at our chests. The other left the room, came back an hour later and called out, "If there is one with the name Kim Kookyung, step out." Suddenly, all eyes went to Mr. Kim. He paled as if he had been stricken by something, but followed the soldiers. A stillness fell upon the room into which no one dared to speak.

After this, the staff meeting turned into a spiritless one. Lee Myungsun and a few others, based on a prepared plan, directed us as we elected Mr. Lee Byunggi as the chair and finished other items quickly. Near the end of the meeting, the two soldiers brought Mr. Kim Kookyung back. A greenhorn North Korean soldier with his shoulders raised in a swagger addressed the white-haired, old professors among us, "Fellow comrades, I want to hear your opinion on whether he deserves death. Our People's Republic listens to the people when punishing criminals."

Nobody wanted to say a word. The soldier must have thought we did not want to speak in front of the guilty person. He sent Mr. Kim Kookyung to the next room and urged us, "A student said earlier that he is a traitor. You all work in the same school and know him well. Why are you not saying anything?"

Under duress, one professor said, "He teaches about China and Chinese literature at this university. Other than that, I know little about him." The soldier said, "Aha, he is one of those who says, "Confucius said this, Mencius said that," right? Therefore, his brain must be full of all the old, un-democratic ideologies. It is probably not a baseless accusation that he is a traitor who strikes students without regard." He seemed to be looking for some kind of agreement from us. He must have been a political member attached to the military, close to a complete ignoramus believing that Confucius and Mencius are all there is to China and Chinese literature.

One professor defended Mr. Kim, "At this university, nobody, including Mr. Kim Kookyung, strikes students. Ours is not such a school." But the soldier growled, "You mean then that the student lied?" He seemed to be at a loss at how to proceed, and hesitated for quite a while before saying, "I, myself, don't want to kill this man, provided you all guarantee his future actions." Nobody stepped up to guarantee him, but then the soldier went away, releasing Mr. Kim without a word.

In this way, a scholar passed through the valley of death. Whether he died or not depended solely on the whim of a seemingly intoxicated soldier.

July 2, 1950.

According to the villagers, our *banjang*[35] had been a devoted follower of the People's Republic, and hence he'd been elevated from a twenty-household *banjang* to the leader of two-hundred-household *dongjang*[36]. That must be why I no longer see Mr. Sung Yoonkil, the old *dongjang*, at the village office, and instead see Mr. Lee Yoonki's face all the time. The affairs of our *ban* are now taken over by a perpetually intoxicated person from Jinjoo who was renting a gate-space in a house opposite ours. I didn't know his name, but he is dirt poor. He is always drunk, hanging out at Kwanggee's grandmother's grogshop. We used to call him a "forever drunkard."

The ROK military and the police, who appeared so menacing until only a few days ago, have now disappeared with their families. Or they tremble with fear as they are pushed out of their houses having been labeled as traitors. On the other hand, communists and their sympathizers who were hiding now came out and welcomed the new world, swinging their arms and legs with glee.

The world has been completely turned upside down. A young person, who had been working hard as a leading member of the Korea Youth Organization (*of ROK*) and who had once made me uncomfortable by asking that I give him a cultural lecture series, had a full turnabout and now reached for my hands, shaking them vigorously and said, "A

---

35 Leader of a ban, a small group of neighborhood houses. Every house in the country belongs to one of them.
36 Leader of a dong, a larger group that is a collection of many bans.

really good time has come," as if I brought the communists to our city.

We are placed in a very tough situation regarding when answering such comments as we no longer really know who is asking. Was he a member of the Korea Youth Organization who could not run away and is now acting out? Or has he really been a member of the Communist Party? I have no way of judging. I cannot really tell whether his words were from his heart, if he is lying to save his life, or if he is trying to figure out where I stand.

There are many who wear red armbands on the streets. Some have letters on them, and others are just plain. I cannot tell whether they wear the letter-less armbands just for the sake of it or whether they actually mean something. Among them are those who used to be ardent members of some anti-communist groups and were threatening us for not helping them. I hurried home avoiding their eyes, lest they catch and yell at me for not stepping out into this red world with rolled sleeves.

July 3, 1950.

People's Republic flags are now flying at every house. How had this flag, with a red star on the red-and-blue background that symbolized revolution and liberation, been such an object of yearning by the youth of this country or a target of hatred?

A few months ago, when a moonlight was striking a crumbling rampart at Naksan at dawn, there was a clash between a group of youths trying to raise a People's Republic flag and another group trying to stop them. They fought tooth and nail to win for their ideologies.

It could be a poetic story in a sense, but considering that they are all really one people, it was a heartbreaking one. This dream-like story is now a solemn reality while the roaring cannon shots are still ringing in our ears.

I brought out red and blue ink and started drawing a Republic flag intending to fly it at our gate. Just in case the next-door house's flag was not drawn properly, I made a trip to the village office to confirm the correct layout. As we made the flag, Wife and I laughed dryly. We were lamenting our situation which forced us to draw and redraw our national flags every other day.

I had often seen village elders getting slapped on the face and kicked by Japanese policemen for not hoisting Japanese flags on their national holidays. I must have been about ten years old. I don't remember who taught me, but I once stuck a hand-drawn Korean national flag inside the men's quarter of our house with a trembling heart. Looking back at it now, I think I must have been influenced by the March 1st Independence Movement [37].

Tears were flowing on my mother's cheeks as she quietly tore down and burned the flag. That night I dreamed I was caught by a Japanese policeman and woke up crying.

It seemed like only yesterday when we could draw our flag without fear after the August 15th Liberation (*1945*).

---

37 A peaceful national demonstration against the Japanese occupation of Korea in 1919. Many Koreans were persecuted afterwards. March 1 is one of the national holidays in Korea now.

Today we must draw another flag under screaming cannon fires.

I thought raising the people's flag would be enough to show that we are now citizens of the People's Republic, but it doesn't look like that's enough. Slogans are also posted on every house gate: "Hooray to Chosun Democratic People's Republic," "Hooray to our Distinguished Leader General Kim Ilsung," or "The Friend of the World's Weak and Small Countries, the Generalissimo Stalin." They all look so fake that I cannot bring myself to copy them. If I had to, what would be the right phrase?

These phrases seem more appropriate: "We are Happy We Accomplished a North-South Unification with Our Own Hands" or "We Welcome the World Where Hard-Working People Would Not Go Hungry."

I thought about posting a slogan that I believe in more, but I had second thoughts because it felt as if it was like posting a dog tag on the house. Even if I did, there would be people who would put me on a list: "This guy is so lukewarm. He needs to be re-educated." Others may spit at me, "His head follows the sun (*the power*) all the time. Even sunflowers would envy him."

July 4, 1950.

Today is my father's birthday. This must be the first time I haven't visited him on his birthday. Furthermore, he and I are now people of different countries. Some say that the People's Army made it to Chungjoo[38], but others say they

---

38 A city about 70 miles south of Seoul.

are still fighting just on the opposite side of the Han River[39]. A person said he saw a poster in the streets claiming, "A Complete Liberation of Suwon[40]." Did they really get down there now? I can still hear cannons around here. Regardless, it appears that Seoul and Kyungsang Province[41] already are in two different countries now. How much would Father be worried from the war news? Would he now be wetting his white beard with tears at the dinner table?

Around noon, brothers Shin Hyunwoo and Hyunsoo and Chang Sejin came to visit me. Hyunsoo and Sejin were government officials but they betrayed ROK. They were expelled and escaped to Seoul to hide. Hyunsoo is my bosom friend from childhood. During the time of the Republic of Korea they never came to see me. All three of them now visit me causing me some bewilderment. While they laughed and talked, I got very cautious about what I said to them. Why is talking to them now so awkward? We were such good friends. We would have shared wine together and laughed heartily under normal circumstances.

When they said, "Why are you at home doing nothing at such a time?" I couldn't tell whether these remarks were just passing words, or if they implied a hidden meaning.

I laughed them away by saying, "Well, there are people whiling their time away in the middle of the day just visiting an old friend, aren't there?" I did not know for certain whether my friends were whiling away their time now or if they were on a mission.

---

39 A River that runs through Seoul in the south side.
40 A city about twenty miles South of Seoul.
41 A Southeastern province where his hometown, Yungchun, is located. Cities of Daegu and Busan are also located there.

They said, "Put this musty-smelling research into your pocket for a while and let's work on supporting our people and our nation. You can always go back to your research afterwards, can't you?" In earlier times, I would have taken this as a joke and responded with abusive language, but today I couldn't do that.

After the guests departed, I put my affairs in order. I do not want to be taken by surprise should something happen unexpectedly. Even Wife, who always rebukes me for being too cautious and too worried about the world, has become timid these days. I wish the children, Bong-a, Mok-a and Hyub-a, do not have to live a life while being worried to death day and night as it is now. Could that indeed be possible?

July 5, 1950.

Daekyoo came along and said he was concerned that I continue to stay home and do not go out. He said that this person goes to this place and works on this work, that person has an active life, and everybody is busy or is pretending to be busy. If I sit at home quietly, I may be accused of being a counter-revolutionary[42]. What he said made sense. Among the people Daekyoo mentioned are some old leftists, or those who sympathized with such ideologies, but at the same time there are also people who were not leftists at all.

---

42 The words 'counter-revolutionary elements' or 'reactionary elements' mean people who oppose communist doctrines.

I said, "People who were communists would of course be jumping with joy because they like recent developments. Those who were on the opposite side may be pretending to be so in the fear of being singled out. But what could a person like me do? Isn't reading books diligently good enough?" However, I suspect that this may not work in this world. Daekyoo also laughed, unconvinced.

When he said, "Such a person as Mr. Choi - - (*sic*) who is in a similar situation as you, Uncle, has come out to Hyehwa Police Station since the 28th, directing things on the forefront," I told him he must be mistaken. But Jungyong happened to come by and said he also witnessed this.

This is inconceivable to me. Although Choi had been somewhat sympathetic to the leftist ideology and was close to Mr. Baek Namwoon in the North, he had always called himself a rational scholar.

I asked, "How can a scholar become like that?" Daekyoo responded and said, "This may be a world where even scholars must do such things."

He then relayed a story of a people's court in Myungryoon-dong. When a notice came through the *ban* system, calling one person per each household to the front of Sungkyoonkwan University, he went. Some People's Republic soldiers with machine guns brought out a few young men. Pointing to one of them, the soldiers asked the crowd, "Is this man a counter-revolutionary or not?" Everybody was too scared to say anything.

One or two among the crowd – they were probably pre-planted accusers – yelled, "Yes, he is the worst counter-revolutionaries." Without any further ado, they shot the man right there. The sight of a man spurting blood writhing and dying was so grotesque that Daekyoo slid away, almost running. All this happened without the crowd knowing what kind of counter-revolutionary things those young men had ever done.

"But now, people's courts are forbidden by a military order." Daekyoo added as we became horrified.

July 6, 1950.

I went to the University. While I was away, a University Self-Governing Committee was organized with Mr. Yoo Eungho as the chairman, Mr. Kim Ilchool as the deputy chairman, a few people including Mr. Sung Baeksun as committee members and an unfamiliar person as the secretary. I was told he used to be an assistant at a psychology laboratory.

Everything seemed to be under the control of Mr. Lee Myungsun. It was almost pitiful to see that everything Mr. Yoo did and said followed Mr. Lee's implicit directions. It could have been ascribed to Mr. Yoo's nature. But it was amusing to see a real example of so-called puppets or marionettes. Why didn't Mr. Lee just become the chairman himself? It was the result of an election, to be sure, but such so-called elections could have been easily rigged...

During the few days I was away, the People's Republic Army moved into the University. The Self-Governing Committee now occupies the second floor of the University president's residence. The first floor became the office of the University.

My main reason for going to the University today was to get an identification card as a member of the Self-Governing Committee. This secretary, a Mr. Kim - - (*sic*), refused to issue me one, saying that my attendance had not been good. I countered, "This is summer vacation time. Why should professors come to the University every day?"

He said he himself didn't know why, but everybody had to come and stamp the attendance list every day. And Sundays would be the same from now on.

Looking around, I saw a few professors simply chatting. Indeed, it must be because of the mandatory attendance rule even though there is no work to be done. Street cars to and from Donam-dong are not operating these days and walking three miles each way in this heat just to have purposeless chats would be a pathetic waste of time and energy.

I called upon the chairman who was in discussion with executive committee members and asked him for his help on my ID card. I explained why coming to the school every day was unreasonable. His response was, "It is not that there is nothing to do. It is that you do not want to do anything. They told us to go out to the streets with students and demonstrate until August 15th. Today, students went out to the streets, marching in rows. I don't know how many professors went with them."

On the way in I saw a bulletin to that effect, but had thought to myself, "This can't be true. Somebody must have made a mistake. Who would demonstrate every day for two months?" Either I don't have common sense, or this world is not making sense. I really can't tell any more.

On the streets, wall posters were everywhere. I wondered if this over-profusion of repeated propaganda was possibly undermining the effectiveness of their own messages.

There are lots of rumors that this person works at this Literary Union, that person at that Education Federation, this person at the Chosun Scientists Union (Kwamaeng), that person at the Unified Labor Union (Junpyung), one at the Chosun Youth Alliance (Minchung), another at the Women's League (Yumaeng), etc. I wonder if everybody's work involves demonstrations in the streets until Aug 15th. Do all these works also include making and posting the posters everywhere? They must be extraordinarily diligent people. It seemed that same words were being copied and posted by each organization as if they are in a competition to do better than others.

The leaflets uniformly praise the Chosun Democratic People's Republic, General Kim Ilsung, the People's Republic Army, or Stalin. Others criticize the Rhee Syngman traitor group. Many posters are notices urging workers to present themselves by a certain time while others tell teachers and students to come to school by a certain date, otherwise they will be eliminated from their rosters. During the last few days, there have been no posters talking about the live capture of the so-called traitor of all time, Rhee Syngman. *Did they capture him?*

One headline with big, special letters said, "The American President Truman declared that America would keep its hands off Korea." Other headlines stated that the UN members and American military envoys ran away to Tokyo. Exaggerated stories with interesting twists included their swimming across the Han River, barely escaping. The stories were sprinkled with curses.

"America will keep its hands off Korea." Recalling what they did in China, I can see it is entirely possible. If so, was the repeated radio broadcast a manufactured lie when the

Defense Department, in the name of its information officer, Kim Hyunsoo, announced in the afternoon of the 27th that a branch of McArthur's war command was formed in Seoul that day and that America would join the war starting on the next day? Or, even if it was not a lie, America probably did not have enough time to do anything to prevent the defeat of the Republic of Korea?

On the other hand, the newspapers reported on the 27th about a UN Security Council meeting that urged pullback of the North Korean military. Would they do anything when the North did not listen to them? As a matter of fact, in the past, such international alliances had allowed Ethiopia to be sacrificed, and also allowed Japan to take Manchuria and to salivate over China simply by not acting decisively.

Still there is one thing I do not understand: the 38th parallel is a line that separates the powers of America and the Soviet Union. Being pushed back involuntarily from this line is tantamount to giving up the spoils of World War II by one side. Could that really happen?

July 7, 1950.

Expecting to get the ID I asked for yesterday, I went to the school again early in the morning.

The school asked us to write a resume and a biography. If the forms are well prepared, they say the Department of Education of the People's Republic would accept us. To me, nobody looked qualified enough to pass, but everybody is hard at work just in case. When I commented that I felt embarrassed about writing a 'biography', they told me to spell out everything about myself since I was 8 years old.

Required items included all activities, especially ideological activities, my ideological disposition, association with political organizations, and people who influenced me or whom I worshipped. Everybody was writing in tiny letters, and one even prepared a book (Kim *koon* at the Philosophy Department), but I was unable to write more than five lines. It was especially wearisome to have to write my own ideological disposition:

- Personal history: Same as the separately prepared resume.

- Strike (*against 'unjust' establishments*) history: None.

- Association with political and/or social organizations: None.

- Figures whom I worship or who influenced me: None.

Reading it over, it was too dull, even to me. I added, under the heading of Ideological Disposition: "Although I have believed in the inevitability of history, I am not an aggressive person and hence I have spent my life in moderate studies." I blushed when I read it again thinking I was trying too much to please the reviewers. At the same time, I felt as if a cold sweat was flowing down on my back while imagining that they would snicker at this woefully short report, "What's his problem with this crap?" I thought that answering 'none' to all five questions might look as if I am rebelling deliberately. But I couldn't find any other way of answering. I submitted it as it was.

In the resume, there is an item called 'Social Composition'. I wondered what I was supposed to write; but everybody was filling in the blanks with words like intellectual, lower, middle class, etc. They said the best words were 'poor peasant' or 'laborer.' There must have been many people who suddenly turned into sons of poor peasants and brothers of laborers.

The resume asked that I carefully write down any and all activities since I was 8 even if they lasted only a few days. These included any incarcerations or hospitalizations with their reasons, durations, and locations. Mine looked too simple when I finished it. If only those with carefully recorded resumes and biographies could pass the test, I was sure I would fail. Still, in the corner of my mind, there lurked a thought, "They would not fail me, would they?" A man really must be a well-put-together animal to be able to think both sides of thoughts, like me now.

However, when thinking realistically, I would most likely not make the cut. I worried about what would happen if I didn't. *Luckily, I still have a piece of farmland, and can subside on its produce. But would they let me do that? If they expel me from the school as a counter-revolutionary, I would probably be punished in some additional ways.*

More thinking induced more worries. On the other hand, these thoughts also circled around in my head: *Whatever will be, will be. What talents do I possess to navigate through all these challenges? It's an avaricious life, anyway. When I must clear out of this life, there is nothing more than simply clearing out, right?*

At the school, I read the newspapers; Chosun People's Daily and Liberation Daily. It feels marvelous to see newspapers after such a long time. The advancing speed of the People's Republic Army appears very fast as it already reached Wonjoo and Jechun in the east and is going down to Pyungtaek and Chunan[43] through Suwon in the South. But as the participation of the U.S. troops appears to be real, I wonder what our nation's future holds.

July 8, 1950.

I saw student demonstrations on the street. When I asked a bystander about them, he said it happens every day. Does this mean it will continue until August 15th? While everybody is hungry and goes about with tightened belts, I was curious to know what they ate to maintain such energy. Their steps were firm, and their attitudes were gallant. Despite their flustered faces, they were beaming with hope. At the front were young middle school students. I didn't care much for the lyrics, "Glory to our death, having fought against the enemy, Cover me with a flag, the red flag." They seemed to reek with the smell of blood. Still, the tune was pleasant, and the singers looked dashing. I wondered, "While life also encompasses love and peace, why do they stress the enemy, fighting, and death only?" If it were sung by fighters who had gone through social hardships, it might have been appropriate. But seeing the middle schoolers who should be wide-eyed and innocent singing loudly, "…death, having fought against the enemy…", my heart ached.

---

43 All these four cities are about 40 to 50 miles south or east of Seoul, spread out in a fan shape. There is no west side of Seoul and, of course, north is where DPRK came down from. This sentence implies that the North Korean Army is spreading out like a fan to the rest of the country from Seoul.

Following them were girl students, and they also looked gallant and energetic. They were from many schools, but each school was represented by only a few students. I heard that students who had been expelled from schools before as leftists were now leading these demonstrations which may explain their energy and enthusiasm.

Next followed university students. Dozens of students from our school were leading the parade. I saw many students who were formerly expelled. Placards such as, 'Overthrow Rhee Syngman's Puppet Regime', or 'Hooray for Chosun Democratic People's Republic', seemed understandable; but carrying portraits of General Kim Ilsung or General Stalin didn't look good. I felt my inadequacy in the education of young people when I saw these college-educated students who called themselves bright, behaving this way.

July 9, 1950.

I thought of weeding the orchard and having a chat with Hong *koon* today, but Mrs. Hong said that when he was paying a visit to my house on the morning of the 29th last month, a person called Suh Bumsuk came by and took him away. She had agonized for a while as there was no news from him since. He came home only a few adays ago and told her he had been taken to his friend's workplace and started working for the Court Self-Governing Committee. They ate and slept together at the courthouse as things were so busy. He would not come home too often, either. I felt as though I had been hit with a hammer on the top of my head.

That morning, Hong *koon* said to me, "Although they say people released from prison should get work immediately, I plan to lie low and get some rest. I believe only then could I recover my strength properly. I had never been a true Bolshevik anyway." Then a youthful man came by and after dispensing a few words in an overbearing tone, took Hong *koon* away with him without saying a word to me.

He must have been this Suh Bumsuk. Some time ago Hong *koon* had mentioned that there was a (*ROK*) Protection and Guidance Alliance person, called Suh. Wasn't this person the one who had been urging and bothering him continually to make speeches or to do this-and-that to the point that Hong *koon* thought he would have to join the alliance?

Should I now regard Hong koon as untrustworthy from now on? How did the world come this far?

When everybody else is seen busy working on something or other, I did not want to be seen as idle by working alone in the orchard, so I therefore hid myself under the trees, weeding. It became so hot at midday that I was wiping off sweat under a platanus tree when I overheard two young men passing by.

"Hey, it is nice."

"What do you mean?"

"This orchard. They planted peach trees."

"Why, you... Does it tempt you?"

"Indeed, it is tempting. Who owns it?"

I hid myself under the shade of the tree and listened intently.

"Gee, I don't know. But what does it matter who owns it? We could label him as a counter-revolutionary and expel him."

I watched their gradually fading backs through an acacia fence. Swaggering with red bands on their arms and carrying a bundle of papers in their hands, they looked energetic. They must be members of the Chosun Youth Alliance, I thought, wiping the sweat off from my forehead.

July 10, 1950.

I went to the school upon being given notice of a meeting. The Department of Education announced the heads of each school:

The overall University Head is Mr. Lee Myungsun.

For the Graduate School, Mr. Kim Ilchool.

For the College of Arts and Sciences, Mr. Yu Eungho.

For the Central Library, Mr. Sung Baeksun.

Also, I heard that Mr. Kim Sukgyoo was nominated for the College of Business and Mr. Lee Wonhak for the College of Education. Mr. Lee Bonnrung for Dankook College and Mr. Cha Nakhoon for Hankook College were also nominated.

Mr. Lee Myungsun used to be in the Chinese Literature Department when I was attending the school. He acted more like the houseboy of, rather than an assistant to, the evilest Japanese professor named Sindo. At research presentations he looked so pitiful with his mouth open all the time. Still, he is preferable to Mr. Choi Kyoodong who, during the time of the Republic of Korea, led the school to near self-destruction. At the least, his youthfulness is an asset.

His inauguration speech went in essence as follows: "We first of all need to realize that we are now fighting against the traitor gang of Rhee Syngman and the American imperialists who incite and control them. Therefore, we need to direct all our energy to protecting our Mother Country and leading it to a victory. In doing so, we ourselves need to pick up guns first and let the students and society follow us. We must know there is no other way for us to choose. If there is anybody who has any inkling of doubt on this, he should be removed from our people's march."

I was staring at his face entranced because his half-closed mouth could still roll out such forceful words. If these words were a declaration of war, they would have been excellent, but as an inauguration speech at a university, I could recall nothing like this - even during the time of the Japanese harassment during the Pacific War (*World War II*).

Now the world has changed, I should accept that one would not necessarily follow the expected formalities of the old society; but there were many professors sitting there who were senior to Mr. Lee. Perhaps my thinking like this proves that I have not fully grasped the reality yet.

July 11, 1950.

These days, the three most pressing issues in Seoul are 1) shortage of food, 2) coercive recruitment of volunteer soldiers, and 3) 'transfer' - a new word that is most widely used these days.

As they say, "For people, eating is most important," food is the biggest issue. The People's Army came in, investigated how much food each household had, and then took it to feed hungry people in town and themselves. Their grand promise was that they would return the food within a week. After two weeks, I still haven't heard of any food distribution, and nobody even harbors hope anymore that this would happen. Some who came down from the north now admonish us who had been paying only casual attention to their propaganda. They say, "See, I told you not to trust their words".

It seems like only yesterday when, during the time of the Republic of Korea, people raised an uproar about the price of rice going over 2,000 *won*. When the People's Army moved down, the price passed the 5,000 *won* mark and now it is close to 10,000 *won*. However, I have seen nobody openly complaining about it. There is a rumor that our neighbors who live in the front and back of our house go without food, and the entire village seems not much different. Affluent villages would have had some stored grains and, if not, selling old clothes for rice even at 10,000 *won* might have been a possibility, but poor villages like ours are truly suffering. It was a saving grace that there were a few households that had harvested some barley. Otherwise, I can't imagine what would have happened.

The faces of women who appear at water lines look quite swollen. Children playing in the alleys seem feeble and yellowish. Fortunately, there are a lot of green vegetables available as we are in the summer season. When that runs out, one could eat grass. Deaths from famine are still rare. One thing I heard from village people is that we can mix most of the grass with oil to prevent food poisoning. As a result, the price of oil has skyrocketed. The price of clothing gets lower and lower because everybody wants to exchange their clothing for food.

At home, we shared the food we had buried earlier with a few close friends and relatives, with about half a bushel for each. With the rest of our rations, we planned to eat rice in the morning, then skip lunch and eat porridge in the evening for the next few months. Still, I feel sorry for other people because we are eating at least one rice meal a day while others are not. Lest the neighbors hear us, I cautioned the children not to speak out loud while eating. Wife and I keep tightening our belts every day.

The next is the problem of the forceful recruitment of volunteer soldiers. The authorities mobilize all their organizations to clamor that all young patriotic men and women must join as volunteer soldiers. Villages round people up, schools send students out, and businesses force their workers to enlist. However, that still may not be enough. There is panic everywhere as young people are randomly rounded up on the streets. That may be the reason why not too many young people linger on the streets these days.

Another problem is what is called a 'transfer'. Earlier, Lee Heeseung *sunsaengnim*[44] said that there was a directive

---

44 The title, sunsaengnim means a respected elder or a

from the top, in one *banjang* meeting, to reduce the number of people in Seoul from one and a half million to one million by move half a million people out to elsewhere. During the last few days, transfer orders came down from everywhere making the city buzz like a stoked hornet's nest.

What they say is that people who do not have to be in Seoul are sent to farms, factories, and mining towns elsewhere. Once the order comes in, they must leave within a couple of days. If they pack things, they promise, the People's Committee will keep them for a while before delivering those things to their owners. Once they arrive at their designated locations, they are told that all things (housing, clothing, and food) would already have been prepared for them. The people who are ordered to leave their own house within two days and sent to go to a totally unknown place cannot possibly cry louder and shed more bitter tears.

July 12, 1950.

Newspapers reported that dozens of people from this university, hundreds of students from that high school, and all two hundred of the 5th and the 6th year students from Dongduk Girl's High School volunteered as soldiers, united in their hatred of the American enemy and the Rhee Syngman gang. Such stories of courage keep coming. Once having volunteered, in line with this country's modus operandi,

---

respected teacher. Sunsaeng, without nim, is a familiar expression of sunsaengnim.

they would go out to the war fronts right away. Village parents are abuzz with worry about their children who do not come home from school. Unaware of what is happening, they go to the schools and learn that everybody 'gloriously' passed their examinations and joined the army already.

Foolish mothers cry out, "Such a terrible child. Why didn't he come home and see Mom and Dad just once before going? With inadequate clothes and worn-out shoes, where on earth are you? How can I visit you when I don't even know where you are? Oh, I am paralyzed with a heavy heart!" They complain because they don't properly understand the gravity of the current state of affairs. How can they be so unaware of these urgent times to make such trivial personal complaints?

The gossip mill claims that there are reasons why university students volunteer although their numbers are small. First, they don't have anything to eat. Country students who were staying at boarding houses in Seoul are going hungry. Roads that lead them home to their countryside are blocked and they don't have money to buy expensive rice. Succumbing to hunger, they have no alternative but to volunteer.

Some students do intentionally volunteer. But the Party needs some of those who have connections to the Party to remain behind as recruiters. So, it intentionally disqualifies them so that they won't be sent to the war fronts. Those students call themselves, 'cell members'.

Another group of students volunteer for the following reason. Incessant propaganda by cell members says: "University students need to go out at least once as a volunteer to become productive members of the People's Republic. Otherwise, as they were members of ROK before, how else can they atone for that and prove that they are not counter-revolutionaries anymore? In order to shed their old skins and become a member, or a leader, in the new country, it is an absolute necessity that they volunteer. And the faster, the better." This kind of persistent propaganda stirs their minds and stokes their desire for fame.

However, the situation with high school boys and girls seems different. Leftist teachers and students step up and urge the students to come to school without giving any reason. "Students at this school come to the school by a certain time… There will be a 'culture lecture.' Those who do not come will be expelled from the school." There is also a lot of propaganda on wall posters. "Those who do not come will be treated as counter-revolutionaries and handed over to the political security office." Once they have them all, under the guise of a 'culture lecture', students are inundated with feverish propaganda campaigns using material from The Haebang Daily or The Chosun People Daily[45]. When they get disoriented, a rally takes form.

Several cell members come up to the podium and exhort: "For the mother country and for our people, we should vanquish this virulent American imperialism and their cat's paw, the Rhee Syngman traitor gang. There should be no one who would cowardly fall away from this sacred rank to fight for the country's complete self-independence. At least not from this school. If there is one, he should be tried under the name of our people." There would be shouts among the students, "Correct! Absolutely!" Some would shout, "We should fight mercilessly against these counter-revolutionary elements first." They would then shake their fists at the sky.

---

45 DPRK newspapers

Incited by these words, the whole crowd goes into a state of excitement. Urging them further on, the chairman says, "Then, let us all apply for the Volunteer Army!" There would then be shouts of "We agree!" and "Yes!" Perhaps overwhelmed, some would yell twice or thrice. However, before long, as if cold water has been splashed upon them, the atmosphere turns chilly as reality sets in their minds.

The chairman, trying not to lose the momentum, confirms, "It looks like everybody is in agreement, but if there is anybody who opposes, do let us know." Mean-looking men would bore their eyes into the crowd and spit out, "Oppose! If you oppose, say it!" After thirty to sixty seconds, the chairman declares, "As there is no opposition, it is unanimous." Signatures are then obtained from each of the new volunteers before they are marched into an examination hall.

In some girls' schools, the students held onto each other, wailing after these rallies. These outbursts were dismissed as the result of students being emotionally overwhelmed.

July 13, 1950.

Kim Sangsool *koon* came over. He is a son of a cousin of mine. His family was poor, but he was bright. He finished teacher's school early and became a teacher at a country high school. He came to Seoul last summer unexpectedly saying that he was expelled from the school because of a suspicion that he was a leftist. He got a job at a girl's high school here. As he is now close to some members of the Education Committee, he must be doing well.

He said that he never lost touch with the Party all this time, even before the war, and he is now working in the area of 'culture' for the party. His duties mainly involve monitoring counter-revolutionary men of culture. He had already visited such people as Mr. Chung Inbo[46] and Choi Hyunbae[47]. He is busy because there are still so many university professors to visit. Then he asked me to loan him 80,000 *won,* not just for his own necessities, but also for work.

Even when I said, "How could I have that kind of money now?", he insisted, "Uncle, you could still do something about it if you try, couldn't you?" I could have accepted his unreasonable demand under normal circumstances, but I was not pleased by the general tone of our conversation.

I did not have the money anyway, so I could refuse his request with a clear conscience. In his honor, Wife prepared a lunch although we normally skip it ourselves. The tone of his compliments did not please me however, "Here at Uncle's house, I could even eat lunch. This is a wonderland."

I didn't like it either when he implored me, perhaps it could be a gesture of goodwill on his part, "Why don't you go to the school every day? Every organization continually reports their member's attendance records to the Party. At the Party, that becomes the most important reference data. And the Party doesn't care about one's old inclinations and whatnots but looks at his current attitude and the degree of his cooperation. Do not skip any day. You can work in oratorical campaigns, or in restoration campaigns. Of course, you will not be selected, but it may be construed good to apply to the Volunteer Army."

---

46 A respected historian, newspaperman and writer.
47 A respected linguist and educator.

I was so flabbergasted listening to him that I could not find words to respond. My nephew continued, "Mr. Chung at Hongik University works really hard. His wife is suffering from tuberculosis while his six children are hungry; but he ignores all that and walks miles in this hot weather as a member of an oratorical campaign member. And then he comes to the Party asking for any more work he can do. He impressed everybody at the Party. Many said they would pick him up as a candidate for a member of the Party soon."

When I asked, "You mean he does all that without being a member?" he said, "Of course. His line had been severed for a while. Nowadays, it is extremely hard to become a new Party member."

The words being used, 'lines being connected or severed', are new ones to me, but they represent a certain harsh reality. I believe they mean that a line of an active Party member to his cell member is severed if the latter cannot be contacted if he died, captured, or left the Party. It is easily plausible that such things could happen in underground activities, but the affected person would become nervous about his future as he now does not know where he stands in the eyes of the Party. Before, he fought with his life to bring out this new world; now, nobody recognizes him when that world finally arrived.

Kim *koon* also showed me a list of professors at our school and asked me to investigate, in as much detail as possible, each person's ideological inclination; their past attitudes toward leftist and rightist students at the school; their personal activities after June 25th; their current thoughts if possible; their family situation, relationships, contacts with community or political organizations, and major publications or papers.

I told him that, "Beyond scholastic interactions, I have maintained no contact with them and therefore I did not know of any such information. As I live in a suburb, I go to school only in the daytime. I therefore know very little about them. Even when I am at the school, I devote my time fully to my studies and therefore I did not have as much contact with other university professors, unlike a worker elsewhere such as in government or company offices. It would not be an overstatement if I said that I am totally disconnected from them. Furthermore, I could not be of any help because I could not come to the school often as I suffer from hemorrhoids." I gracefully refused, saying that even if I was keen to help, I am not able to do so.

He said that perhaps I could at least let him know of their addresses or draw maps of their houses. I told him, "How can I remember all those addresses? As I have not visited their houses, drawing a map is still more impossible. If you want to know their addresses, go to the self-governing office of the school." He said, "Oh yes, I know that." And he went back home with a dissatisfied expression.

After sending him back, I didn't feel quite right.

July 14, 1950.

Kim Ikhyun *koon* came visiting. He is a distant junior family member from back home. He is now working as *banjang* in Waryong-dong. Volunteer Armies and transfers are constant headaches for him, and there are directives every day from the top about mobilizing people for work or demonstrations. When he attempts to bring people in, he finds that everybody is in bed suffering from hunger. So he just cannot possibly order them to come out. Perhaps he should resign from *banjang* duty, but then he may be called upon to join the Volunteer Army. Then, through some connections, he had opportunity to work in a Dong People's Committee. If he took the position, his status would be guaranteed, which may help a bit with his living conditions; but, on the other hand, it also meant actively helping the People's Republic which makes him worried about the future.

He was asking me about what he should do, without having a firm answer of his own on the question, "Is the Republic of Korea right, or is the People's Republic, right?" Essentially, he wants to know which side, ROK or DPRK, will eventually win so that he knows who to work for now.

He didn't say all these himself but wanted to hear what I had to say. Therefore, my answers cannot be straightforward either.

"Really, it must be hard to be a *banjang*.

"Whether you work for the Dong People's Committee or not is your decision--what can I say? As you know well, novice academics like myself are struggling to figure out which path to follow in these confused times, so how can I advise other's affairs?"

"Please don't consider it as somebody else's affairs. You just let me know what you would do if you were facing the same situation," he implored.

"Well, I don't even know what this People's Committee is, or what it does; I know nothing about it. As I have never thought about it before, how could I make any decision as if it were my own affairs? Don't you agree?"

"Please do not be modest. Wouldn't it be proper to give clear guidance to the younger generation? I came to see you, Uncle, in the early morning, hoping you would give me some answers."

Using *Andong* dialect[48] freely, he intimated a highly sincere demeanor. But it would certainly be imprudent for me to talk about these things carelessly. I decided not to show my true mind.

"In this fast-paced world, people like me become obsolete quickly. To understand this time and period accurately, I believe that the sharp sensitivity of the youth is necessary. Thus, it is rather I who should be asking for guidance," I countered.

"Then, how is this war going to end?"

"How would I know that when the war participants themselves don't know?", I sighed.

"I am not asking you to make a prediction... perhaps a guess?", he persisted.

"What kind of guesses can I make sitting at this remote place? If I know something, and if it's the right thing to do, of course I would make a recommendation to you. I would appreciate it if you could understand that I cannot give you irresponsible words without knowing what is happening."

"I understand very well," he conceded. Time would tell

---

48 Andong is a place near Yungchun where Prof. Kim came from. By reminding him that they are from hometowns close to each other, Kim Ikhyun wants to reconfirm his closeness to Prof. Kim.

whether he really understood me.

July 15, 1950.

Wife went to the inauguration meeting of the Farmer's Union at the Kyungsin School grounds. These days, if there is any kind of meeting, womenfolk go. Some meetings quickly turn into rallies where people are plucked out for the Volunteer Army. People got the message and nowadays only women and elders cover these meetings. A few young men come to those meetings, but they all are obviously either meeting organizers or their henchmen. As no other men come to the meetings, they stand out. Also, because their intentions are obvious, even children can see through them, I am told. Quite an interesting phenomenon.

But these meetings occur so frequently that housewives are suffering. In the days past, people from the North used to say, "We spend days attending meetings." I thought at that time they were exaggerating, but now I see it was not idle talk. As housewives must attend every one of these meetings, they get exhausted. In households without food, worries are double-fold. The only way for men to help make a living is to work for the Communist Party or to go out into the streets, exchanging old clothes or personal belongings for food. Even this is dangerous as young men are snatched in big downtown streets like Chongro[49] and become a *hamheungchasa*[50]. Households without old men do not have any

---

49 The most well-known street of downtown Seoul.
50 A term based on an old historical event in which a series of

choice but to send women out into the streets.

Thus, men of many households stay home, watch kids, and take lazy naps in back rooms. It is not a physically harmful condition, but their minds are worried sick with fear of the unknown every minute.

At the Farmer's Union, women and old men of the town gathered for the meeting. An outsider ran the meeting. First, he gave a long speech saying, "People who have had a position in town, who have worked for the government, or who have a piece of land cannot work here. The Farmer's Union is for poor farmers or hired hands only." Then they had to select the committee chairman and members, but a search among mostly ignorant people did not yield any viable candidates. In the end, it was agreed that a committee nominated by the leader would select committee members. The resulting picks must surely be the Workers' Party of South Korea[51] (Namrodang, *a communist party*) members or their followers only… I was told they were definitely not poor farmers or hired hands.

July 16, 1950.

On the streets, posters depicting opposition against the American military takes up as much wall space as those

---

messengers were all killed by the message recipient and thus never returned home.

51 The Workers Party of South Korea (Namrodang) was a communist party established in the Republic of Korea (South Korea) in 1946.

against the Rhee Syngman puppet regime. Nowadays, in official meetings, they do not say 'America', but use words such as 'Robber American Imperialists'. Newspapers also use words like, 'Aggression of American Imperialism,' in large gothic letters. In portraying the puppet government, they always use phrases like 'a cat's paw of Robber American Imperialists' and 'instigated by Vampire American Imperialists'.

Some of them use Chinese characters. The change in Chinese characters for the sound mi[52] (*in Mi-kook, America*) from beautiful to rice reminds me of the times when the Japanese used to call America and England the 'demons/beasts of Mi-Yung,' using the word *mi* meaning rice.

It seems only yesterday that we had welcomed Americans with heartfelt happiness as 'the benefactor of our liberation'. Now, the people use all the words they can conjure up to swear and curse them. I am not saying this to take sides with the American military. It is just sad to see such repeating reversals in human affairs.

During the last few days there were some sporadic bombings by American planes and machine gun fire followed by anti-air responses from the ground. These events have given

---

52 America is called Mikook in Korean. It is a combination word of two syllables, 'mi' and 'kook'. The first syllable 'mi' is coming from the sound, '(A) me (rica)'. The second syllable, 'kook', means country. The transliteration of this word America is 'beautiful country', as 'mi' means beauty. However, the sound 'mi' can also mean other things, including rice. Japanese called America as the 'rice country'. England is called, similarly, 'Yung(Eng)kook(land, country)'. America and England together were called 'Mi-Yung'.

bored citizens something to talk about. Today, there was an all-out bombing in the Yongsan[53] area.

Several formations of airplanes, perhaps B-29's, pierced through clouds this afternoon, dropped bombs and disappeared. They then came again to drop more bombs and disappeared. This continued for a couple of hours as the sound from these bombings shook our house ten miles away. It felt as if magazines were exploding everywhere. The sky in the Yongsan area was as black as Chinese ink, with shooting flames appearing in between. It was a horrible sight.

It is strange that the citizens do not seem to bear much hostile feelings toward the American Imperialists, despite these fierce bombings. Some even seem to see some kind of hope in the bombings. It is even more surprising to note that these sentiments are not necessarily limited to persecuted people who were so-called counter-revolutionaries on watch lists or families of soldiers and policemen of the old Republic of Korea.

The news was that today's bombings destroyed some military installations and transportation facilities. However, severe bombings also occurred at Haebang-chon which incurred several thousand innocent casualties. I was also told that there was a woman who climbed up to a high place to wave a white handkerchief at these planes while her town turned into a sea of fire and bombs were falling onto her

---

53 A southern district of Seoul, about 2-3 miles from the center of Seoul, north of Han River.

head. She was not crazy. She was from a family that received a transfer order that morning.

July 17, 1950.

I went to the school today after a lengthy absence. They mobilized all professors to the bombed Yongsan region to help sort things out. Mr. Kim Ilchool was the only one remaining at the school. I had a chance to talk to him in a quiet room.

As Mr. Kim is in the same department as I, his study is next to mine. He also came from my home province, Kyungsang Province, and he is one or two years older. He is not only regarded as a competent scholar but also a sincere and calm person. I have always respected and cared for him, and we have become close over the years.

But he is not just a scholar. He also has a very keen interest in politics. He seems to have been close to the late Mr. Yeo Woonhyung [54] and, as a brother of Ms Lee Yusung [55], he was active from the beginning as a leading member of the People's Party. However, he never slacked

---

54 Yeo Woonhyung (1885) was a liberation fighter and writer. Right after the liberation in 1945, he became a Deputy Chief of the Democratic People's Republic of Korea until 1946. He was known to have more neutral views between the leftists and rightists. He was assassinated later.

55 Ms Lee Yusung was a politician and artist in the North who worked closely with Mr. Yeo. It is not clear how Ms Lee and Mr. Kim Ilchool are related as brother and sister.

in his pursuit of academic research and actively guided students. His lectures were very popular as well. He had also opened a New Culture Research Institute on the Ulchiro Street to publish a monthly magazine, called New Culture. He had organized a historical research society to foster an atmosphere for research.

After the two events, – the merging of the Chosun People's Party[56] (Chosun Inmindang) into the Communist Party which he had objected to and Mr. Yeo's so-called fatal accident –, he spent his time in his study. Although his understanding of historical materialism[57] was thorough and he resonated with it, he never flaunted his knowledge to instigate any problems.

He caught the watchful eye of Mr. Ahn Hosang who labeled him as a leftist professor together with Mr. Lee Myungsun and Mr. Lee Bonryung. He the Army prison thanks to an 'incident with Lee Yungmoo', who was his brother-in-law. He was released soon afterwards as there had been no particular crime. However, because his painter brother-in-law, Mr. Chungjung Hwabaek, was in the North and his younger brother, Mr. Kim Taehong, made frequent

---

56 The Chosun People's party was established by Yeo Woonhyung. It was leaning toward the left but tried to work with the right at the same time.
57 Historical materialism, also known as the materialist conception of history, is a methodology used by some communist and Marxist historiographers that focuses on human societies and their development through history, arguing that history is the result of material conditions rather than ideals. - From Wikipedia

runs to the South as a messenger for the North Korean government, I could hear news about the North regularly. He trusted me enough to relay this news to me.

He always said with a desolate smile, "There is no place for us to go because the North doesn't seem to allow a liberalism that honors individuals' rights." Then he had said in the spring, "As we don't know what will happen in the future, let a few of us get together and prepare ourselves by reading books on that subject." I rejected the offer then, telling him I didn't like two people who already committed to joining the group. Even after this happened, he and I trusted and cared for each other more.

I saw him at the school twice after June 25th, but now as we could no longer study and he seemed extremely busy, I never had a chance for a quiet moment to talk with him.

He first told me that Mr. Lee Myungsun had singled me out, saying, "I had trusted Kim Sungchil to help us, but he disappointed me." He cautioned me not to arouse any more unwanted notice from him.

Mr. Kim then told me that the Chosun Labor Party (Chosun Nodongdang) [58] was treating the Working People's Party (Keunmindang)[59] too harshly. The all-powerful City People's Committee or a military organization expropriated all buildings that bore signs of the Working People's Party.

---

58 The Chosun Labor Party was the only political party in DPRK.
59 The Working People's Party (Keunmindang) was the leftist/middle political party in ROK. It was not very well accepted by the Chosun Labor Party when the North came down, even though it had philosophically aligned itself with the Chosun Labor Party before the war.

As a consequence, the Working People's Party headquarters and local chapters need to move around with party signs on the backs of their members. He hadn't known that Mr. Lee Seungyup[60] was so narrow-minded. Members of the Labor Party openly said that the Working People's Party needs either to go through a process of self-criticism, or the members need to transform themselves. He lamented saying, "How can this be possibly happening...."

He smiled desolately again and said, "But I learned this time that when a person is assigned a certain label, it is extremely hard for him to shake that label. I am so tired of politics now that I want to do something about it, but as long as I breathe in this world, I suppose I could never wipe off my Working People's Party label."

Even though he became a citizen of the People's Republic, I thought he could not shed the liberalism clothing now. He could never do so in the future either.

July 18, 1950.

On the way to school in the morning, I indeed noticed that an old Working Peoples' Party sign that I saw only a few days ago in front of a bank branch office in Donamdong had disappeared. A new sign that said 'People's Committee of Seoul City, Sungbook Transfer Guidance Office' replaced it. On the opposite side of the street, a luxurious

---

60 A pro-Japanese communist under Japan and politician in DPRK.

house on the hill at an old abbey site displayed a shiny sign, "Chosun Labor Party Sungbook Branch."

At the school, I found a piece of paper on my desk that read, "Construction Corp Volunteer Application Form." It already contained the signatures of several professors. When I pretended not to have seen it, Kim Sambool *koon* called me to him discreetly and urged me saying, "Sir, it may be better to sign this form. Everybody does so. We are signing up to join the work of the restoration of war-damaged areas. Even if you sign it, they may not call you every day like day laborers. The authority just wants to gauge your sincerity. For many professors, signing it would show their eagerness to clean up their past and help our People's Republic. See, everybody signed up including the old professors."

I managed to suppress a burst of anger: What kind of past do I need to clear up? I managed to say, "I am not healthy these days and as you see I am not coming to school as much as I would like. I would rather wait to get healthy than to sign this form now and not be able to carry out my promise." I left the place lest there would be more discussion on the matter.

As Kim *koon* said, I am sure they would not call us every day to report to the work sites, but when I heard words such as 'cleaning up the past', I felt enraged. I could not bring myself to put my name there after hearing such detestable words.

Kim Sambool *koon* is an intelligent student in the Korean Literature Department and his future is bright. I had known that he sympathized with the left but didn't know he could become this nonsensical. These days, graduated students like Kim Sambool *koon* and Lim Keunsang *koon* came back to the school and aggressively set up their own positions. Goons who used to write propaganda flyers and follow instigators are now showing up as professors of the Arts and Science College.

July 19, 1950.

A part of the People's Army at the school moved out and in its place a group of The City of Seoul People's Committee[61] moved in. They will now occupy the library and professors' laboratories as well. This must be a stop-gap solution to the bombings at Yongsan by the bewildered authorities. As we were told to clear up our offices after a long absence, I went inside the school building today.

I am told that the Seoul People's Committee has absolute power until the real North government moves in. Until then, it acts like a government and anybody who works here must be a member of the Party. This must be the reason why they now control entering and leaving the campus strictly. It is much more severe than with the earlier regular army.

Inside the laboratory, things looked deplorable. Doors that are easily accessible were left intact, but some hard-to-open doors with locks had been smashed open. The inside was in complete disarray. They turned research documents and old literature into dishcloths. English books stripped of

---

61 A self- organized, self-governing private committee that replaced the previous South Korean government offices, including the City of Seoul.

their covers were thrown to the floor. Chinese Tang Dynasty books were used as tissue paper. This disarray has left me frustrated. But what really pained me was to see that all my carefully prepared research cards are now mostly gone except for some bundles that were tossed away into the corners of the room.

I had given high points to the People's Army for its discipline and its character, but now, confronting this debacle, I wonder if soldiers everywhere are all the same in their barbarity.

The 50,000:1 scale map I wanted to use at the Places Name Research Committee was turned into a rag. Much of the valuable research data of the committee had been used as tissue paper. Thinking about all the work we had poured into this project and the data collection, I suddenly felt as if whatever strength I had managed to reserve in my body was deserting me. Is this what a war is like? It's people against one's own people, and not against different people. How could they fail to recognize our valuable cultural assets? Thinking about this and the lost cards, I feel like dropping to my knees and crying out loud.

One laboratory shows a poorly written sign on the bookshelf, "Kultur of the Sooth Half is beheind *(*the translator's attempt to simulate mis-spelled words)*." It must have meant, "Culture of the Southern Half lags behind."

"As there are no books in Russian language here, but only Chinese or English books, they might have thought that only a despotic and anti-communist sentiment exists here and concluded that we are behind," a renowned professor ruefully explained.

The words such as 'the South Half' and 'the North Half' are ones they use without fail. If one assumes that unification is a foregone conclusion, these words make sense. However, if these words only are used, it might make them more anxious for unification.

July 20, 1950.

I went to the school again today. As the City Committee had arrived there and Chul is working in the Cultural Public Affairs Office of the People's Committee, I wished to see and talk with him freely about the world's affairs. There must be people like me who had expected a certain amount of hope from the People's Republic but, instead, are extremely disappointed. I want to know how they would view these current affairs. As Chul differs from the other 'blind' communists and follows the dictates of reason, how would he see the current reality?

I think there are a lot of things we must talk about when we see each other. I could dump on him all the pent-up anxiety and anger about the various things in society that I had been angry about, and even if we do not reach any conclusions, at least my mind would become somewhat clearer. My steps this morning were a lot lighter in anticipation.

But getting past the school gate itself was a challenge this morning. Although Mr. Sung, who oversees the library, assured me yesterday that he would leave my name at the gate, my name was not on the list today. I wonder what witty Mr. Sung would say later, trying to explain this away somehow. Having waited outside for more than half an hour with no communication to the inside, I was thinking about giving up, but then a passing communist party member recognized me and talked the guards into letting me in. Thousands of emotions crowded my mind: *This is my school. I have been in and out of this gate mornings and evenings for the last several years!*

Luckily, I found Chul at the Cultural Public Affairs Office. I told him directly, "I came to find you. There are many things I want to hash out with you." Unexpectedly, he was very hesitant and said, "I am very busy right now. If you wait outside, I will come out around lunchtime." Now I could see that this may be a horrendously busy time for them, and that it was my mistake to leisurely drop by in the early morning. So I decided to wait two-and-a-half hours without complaint. I could not possibly go out and come back in through such a challenging gate again.

Chul is my closest friend since our college days. Even after school, we have been close friends for over ten years. After the August 15th[62] when he left his conservative family and started leftist activities, our paths went separate ways. I had said to him, "Give up the job of a political fanatic and continue studying French literature. That is really the way to help people and society. However much you guys try, do you really believe you can correct things to the way they should be? After all, you all will only end up becoming front men for one of those countries: America, the Soviet Union or China. Isn't that foolish enough?"

Then he would say, "How can people like you care to watch things from the narrow window of your study as if

---

62 'The August 15th' means liberation of Korea from Japan, 8-15-1945. Similarly, 'the June 25th' means the Korean War, sometimes called the 6.25 incident, or the 6.25 war.

they are someone else's problem and let the fate of the people and the country follow random direction? If you possess a youthful conscience that can decipher right from wrong, how can you sit around the study and not come out and work?" We were constantly in this mental tug of war whenever we had a chance to get together.

I challenged him sometimes directly by picking out wrong deeds of the Communist Party. He would then try to explain how they could not but do such things. When it seemed I pushed him too hard, he would say, "When our world comes, we will round up reactionaries and opportunists like you and behead them."

At the end of our discussion, he would say: "It all comes down to what people do. How can you expect them to be perfect and beautiful? If one understands that the fundamental path is the right one, we all should endeavor to correct wrong things together. How long are you going to watch things as a bystander?" We would then laugh together.

However, when we saw each other at other times, we would argue again, yelling at each other. He would say, "You bastard deserve to die. Do you still think staying in your study is all you do when our people's rise and fall is at a most critical point? You stupid bastard."

I would then counter. "Stop these crazy words of a maniac. As you guys say, this is not something to be settled in a day or two. If all our 30 million people get hung up on politics and leave education to its own haphazard device as a consequence, what can a future Chosun do with their empty heads? You are the dumbest guy with a viewpoint as narrow as a needle's eye."

During times when there was so much to discuss, like when there was a rampant rumor that the Soviet Union was tearing down and taking away industrial equipment in the North, when the decision of the Moscow-Three-Ministers Meeting[63] on our country's trusteeship was overturned overnight by the Communist Party, when the continuation of the United States-Soviet Union Joint Committee was in doubt, when the October 1st Incident[64] created a fratricidal tragedy, or when the North cut down electricity to the South paralyzing the South's production capability, he and I used to argue through the night when we saw each other.

Even when there was no particular disagreement to be had, as in the electricity issue, I would say, "Isn't South Korea not a part of Chosun? If the South's industry collapses[65] and its people become hungry in rags, what good does it bring to you guys? In the end, the entire country would fall further behind just to become the laughingstock of other countries."

He would then shoot back saying, "Did I cut the electricity myself, you silly bastard? If the cutters were not stupid idiots, you should know there must be reasons for doing

---

63 In December 1945, foreign ministers of the United States, the United Kingdom and the Soviet Union met in Moscow and decided that Korea would establish its own temporary government, but a trustee government (made of US, UK, Soviet Union and China) would take over actual governing for up to five years until Korea can stand on its own feet.
64 A riot that started in Daegu about rice distribution in 1946.
65 At this time, most of electricity in the Korean peninsula was generated in the North. Cutting its transmission to the South crippled ROK.

such a thing. Speaking of laughingstock, what would you idiots care to say regarding your obsequious behavior toward the Americans when they take raw materials such as tungsten out of Korea and perpetrate electrical torture on people while you obligingly look the other way?"

Arguments like these would branch out to other related issues and then drift into ideological realms preventing any reasonable conclusion to our discussions.

In the meantime, however, through these deep discussions, our friendship was deepened by the day. He would call me names such as a slippery eel with an oil coating while I would counter by calling him a lunatic with an air hole in the lung. He still trusted me enough to show me books signed by Ijung[66]. As for me, he was the only person with whom I did not need to refrain from talking freely against the Communist Party.

I am not such a fool who would talk negatively about the Communist Party even to a non-communist. Certainly, only a person without a modicum of sense would risk his life by talking negatively to a communist about the Communist Party. So, the only time I could unleash my complaints about the Communist Party was when I saw Chul.

When he finished his work at the Left-Wing Publishing Cultural Committee and was busy running around with no particularly visible pretext, he would stop by my house and stay for a few days. We greeted him happily, thinking he

---

66 A pseudonym of Park Hun-yung, the chairman of the Chosun Communist Party (North). Before the war, anybody who carried books with his personal signature would have been arrested on the spot by ROK.

wanted to take a rest from busy city life. When he said he was out of money, I would give him some money to buy food saying, "Don't spend it for the Party. I am saying this not because I may get arrested for this, but because I am still not sure whether what the Communist Party is doing is right or wrong." He would then answer, "Ah, an eternally wandering, pitiful wobbler, never white and never black." But I still could firmly trust that he would not betray my request.

Regarding his marriage, he told me that he would marry a daughter of an old revolutionary fighter in Inchon, and she was a fierce fighter as well. I aggressively recommended Miss Koh[67] to him instead. He appeared attracted to Miss Koh, but seeing him still hesitant, I argued, "A revolutionary with another revolutionary are best to remain as comrades. Once they get married, the household would become cold and dry. A household should not be an extension of revolutionary fighting, it should be a comfortable recharging place for a fighter. You, a so-called student of literature, should know that a marriage should not be swayed by obligation."

"Also, I offer my words for the benefit of the Communist Party: Wouldn't it be better if you marry Miss Koh and brainwash the conservative while the lady in Inchon marry another person to do the same?" It was not clear whether I was persuasive enough or Miss Koh's attractiveness was the

---

67 Ms Koh Oknam was his wife's classmate at the Kyungsung Imperial College and a very close lifetime friend. After the war, she would become an English professor at Ewha Womans (Women's) University while his wife was an Korean language professor at the same university. They also lived close to each other.

factor, but he and Miss Koh got engaged. However, the next big hurdle was the obstinacy of his big brother, Mr. Lee In, who would be his marriage sponsor.

Mr. Lee In was the Attorney General at the time who thus would not take his brother's activities kindly. He was angry at Chul's words and actions attempting to indoctrinate his nephews and nieces (*Mr. Lee's children*) in the leftist ideas. He would howl in the house, "Chul is the one who will destroy our family'. He invited newspaper reporters to declare, "A guy like Chul should be arrested and executed."

But the bride's marriage sponsor insisted that, without an agreement from the bridegroom's marriage sponsor, the marriage cannot be consummated -- which is a proper request. I recognized that it was a really tough challenge but couldn't give up the role of the matchmaker. Drumming up the courage one day, I visited Mr. Lee's official residence in Namsan, being accompanied by Mr. Ha Sangyong who was Chul's brother-in-law.

I first saw Chul's mother and stated the reason of my visit. She held my hand crying, "How gracious of you! I had him late and raised him as the darling baby child, but then he turned into this and is not accepted by his brother. He is not married even though he is past 30, and I can't sleep when I think he may end up immoral. I can't thank you enough." Although she was so moved, when I suggested to her that she talk to the eldest son to make it happen, she became deflated and only said, "If my words had any weight, things would not be this dire. Please try yourself. It will be a charity, a charity for sure."

I had no choice but to see Mr. Lee by myself. I had asked Mr. Ha beforehand to introduce me as a close friend of Chul's, but not a communist. As I opened my mouth, he interrupted me and said, "Because you came here with special kindness, let's spend some time chatting about a few things. But do not bring up Chul's name again. He is not human." He then poured out to me a long narrative about the Communist Party that it is a group of thugs with destruction in its trail, it organizes such groups like Sal-Boo-Hoe[68] and it constitutes a vile and evil group that cannot be tolerated under the sun, by citing examples from some recent criminal cases.

When I think about it, a man drenched with such a thorough abhorrence of the Communist Party is surrounded by a brother, a sister, a son, a daughter, and a nephew who all sympathize with Chul, I cannot but think it is a cruel twist of fate for this generation to be led to a national tragedy.

Mr. Lee came through the difficult Japanese era honorably and was a person we all admired. During the that time, as a lawyer, he volunteered to take on any ideological cases, spending his own money but receiving no payment. He did not care whether they were nationalist cases or communist cases. With his disabled body dragging one foot, he did not shy away from trekking long distances - he even took care of rural students' demonstration cases with utmost devotion. His presence at court looked almost holy. But this work ran him afoul with the Japanese authorities, and as a result he was incarcerated in the Hamhung Correctional Facilities based on a charge related to a case of the Korean Language Society[69].

---

68 The name literally means 'Kill-Father Association'. It was an extremist organization supporting communism. It was formed before the liberation from Japan.
69 In 1942, Japanese authorities arrested and tried members of

But then, is Chul a wicked deviant for not following his big brother's footsteps? As far as I can see, he is one of the most honest youths. This division between a big brother and a younger brother is another national tragedy.

I tried again to argue for Chul's case saying, "You said you disowned him, but does a bloodline get cut that easily? You also said you do not accept your younger brother; but you do not reject the person himself but reject his ideology only. An ideology, unlike a bloodline, can be changed, can't it? You may think your brother's ideology may never change, but I suggest you look at it from a different angle. It may be true that Chul's ideology has not changed in the face of his parents' and brother's persuasions, or through discussion with his friends; but then should we just give up saying that we have done all that we could? We know bloodlines and friendships cannot and should not be abandoned.

"Isn't it our duty to make one last attempt here? What I mean is that we should get him a spouse who is civilized with a warm and good heart, whose ideologies are moderate, and who is steeped in moderate thoughts? She may be able to influence him… It may sound strange, but husbands and wives do influence each other…. Even though one cannot say whether she would turn Chul's ideology around, wouldn't this be our filial duty to try this last hand? I myself don't think his ideology would be easily changed, but his sharp edges may be blunted. If we could bring him back to

---

the Chosun (Korean) Language Society and their friends. Many prominent Korean language scholars were incarcerated. It was the time when the use of Korean language was forbidden in Korea.

his studies, it would be a fantastic success. This is not to forcefully overpower Chul, but to bring out his fundamental nature that has been shrouded all along. As you know, deep inside he is not a communist."

Mr. Lee grunted but said nothing.

There followed a marriage ceremony between Chul and Ms Koh at the official residence of the Attorney General under his sponsorship. A year later, Chul also became a father of a daughter. He adored her very much.

Ms Koh was brought up as a moderate person at home and at school, with an innate bias against extreme ideologies. She studied English Literature in college and was plump and very calm. When talk of the marriage began, I happened to tell her, "The bridegroom cannot be better as a human, but his ideology is traditional Bolshevic." Interestingly, this intelligent twenty-eight-year-old lady answered, "Who marries ideology? Honesty is enough." On one hand, we thought it was promising. But on the other hand, we felt the danger and uncertainty of whether this marriage can transcend ideologies in the face of the current unstable reality.

When Chul got arrested in the spring and was incarcerated in the Seodaemoon Correctional Facilities, his family announced in the *Seoul Newspaper* his secession from his party. Mr. Lee In arranged it so that the prosecutor would release him if he acknowledged this announcement. When he was called into the prosecutor's office, he did not hesitate to say, "This announcement is against my true position," making Mr. Lee, who was in attendance, very uncomfortable. Some who heard this story said, "Thanks to his brother, this stupid moron does not know what torture is." Others said, "Chul is indeed Chul," impressed by his personality even though they disagreed with his ideology.

I waited for two-and-a-half hours and it was past noon, but Chul did not show up. Thinking he needed to finish what he was doing and was thus delaying lunch, I waited longer, but there was no sign of him. Half an hour passed and then another fretful half an hour. After one o'clock, I went back to the Cultural Public Affairs Office and found that Chul was still working in his seat with his back turned.

Thinking I should wait a little longer, I turned around. Another hour passed without any news. I went back and found Chul still in that position. As I couldn't wait any longer, I told a person near the door, "I came to see Comrade Lee Chul." He slammed the door shut behind him saying blatantly, "He is not here."

"But he is there, don't you see him?"

He answered, "Not so."

I said, "Well if he is busy, I don't have to see him today, but I need to make an appointment for a next time." "No, you can't." He was like a stone wall.

I turned around. I felt dizzy.

Chul was there ---

He should have heard me ---

My legs trembled not only because I skipped lunch. Wasn't lunch something that we all gave up when we became members of the People's Republic? Coming back home, I could sometimes see the road and other times I failed to see it. I did not cry, though.

July 21, 1950.

As soon as I came back from school yesterday, I took to bed. I don't feel inclined to do anything today either.

In the afternoon, Daekyoo came and said to me, "Chul said that he was truly sorry for yesterday and will drop by sometime soon."

I do not think Chul means it. I don't believe he will come, either. Even if he comes, I don't think there will be much to talk about.

July 22, 1950.

I went to the orchard and saw Hong *koon* who happened to be there. It had been only a month since I last saw him; but it felt more like several years.

He said, "I didn't have a chance to come to visit you as things have been so hectic." In contrast to his tense demeanor, I felt that I, by coming out to weed the orchard in the middle of the day, was excluded from the world. He said Mr. Kim Youngjae became the chairman of the Self-governing Committee of the Public Prosecutor's Office, and he sits next to Mr. Kim. He conveyed to me Mr. Kim's wishes to get together sometime to have a beer or something. He also said that things were getting interesting at the court.

I thought about Hong *koon* working at the court and Mr. Kim working at the prosecutor's office…. It made me feel safer even though I have done nothing wrong at all.

Hong *koon* told me about the two times the Self-governing Committee was forced to move. Each time, the military came to give them thirty to forty minutes to clear out. He said it was hard to move out in the scanty time given but added that he liked the way the military handled things decisively.

I was speechless, unable to make any coherent response, while looking at Hong *koon's* face, fascinated. I rather fancied that it should be a wonderful thing if he could rack his brain this much and this fast.

Frequent moving of the Self-Governing Committee is not limited to the court; it is the same with the school. Soon after the start of the war, I was told to move my office to the President's residence. Later they moved me to the Veterinary College as the President's residence would be occupied by the Department of Education. After being kicked out again, I now have my seat in Mr. Shin Dosung's house.

I had heard many stories of other organizations having to make countless moves. We are living in a time when a guy with a fist one ounce heavier than another's can push out the weaker one at any time. Thirty minutes, or at the most sixty minutes, is the time given to move. Nowadays, a guy, for no good reason, may have to vacate his house of several decades at a day's notice and end up wandering on the streets. But the real problem lies in the way countless people like Hong *koon* find beauty in this inhumane behavior and praise it.

July 23, 1950.

Visited Choi Bongrae *koon's* house. The wife of Mr. Nam of Kyungdong School was relaying her troubles to Choi *koon* in tears, "You know Mr. Nam has done nothing extreme in his life. He taught mathematics for several decades every day.... Then he became the deputy principal of the school. The position was a reward for his long years of service at the school and was not deemed a promotion, per se. Most people of his age are now principals anyway. He is taciturn and cannot be swayed by the blowing winds. I have come to think perhaps it may be a blessing to have those traits during these times. Some teachers hid themselves, but Mr. Nam never considered it as he has done nothing wrong.

"Still, rumors were flying.... Mr. Kim and Mr. Shin were held in a warehouse without food for several days being beaten by students. They were then taken away by them in a wretched condition to another place and never to be seen again by their families. The students took the principal also and handed him over to the Political Security Office. I was terrified upon hearing these rumors and told Mr. Nam that he should go someplace else and hide; but he only said, 'In my fifty years, I have committed no crime other than teaching students, so why should I go anywhere and hide?'

"About a week ago, two students came and took him to see the new person in charge of the school, and since then he never came back. He is such an inflexible person, so I can't go to sleep, afraid that something happened to him." She wept again.

As Choi *koon* had learned mathematics from Mr. Nam when he was attending the Kyungsin School and had worked for the leftist movement before going to the North last year, Mrs. Nam came to see if he could somehow help his old teacher.

July 24, 1950.

There was a notice given to me from Professor Son Woosung of the French Literature Department with the directions to come to the school. I went there early in the morning and saw the largest number of professors I had seen in a long while. They say there will be an examination/screening. In preparation, we are told to submit a resume and an autobiography, two copies each. This is the third time! Furthermore, they need to be more detailed. When asked why we should write resumes day and night, a person from the Department of Education stopped his instructions on how to write them and said chuckling, "We too wrote resumes over 50 times during the last five years. You professors may have to write resumes again and again." Everybody laughed, but I still wondered why we should write so many resumes? The fellow may not know the answer either.

Kravchenko's[70] book came to mind. I remember something to the effect of: "These elaborate resumes ... After one goes into the minute details of relationships with friends and relatives, over and over and in different formats every time, he loses much of the confidence in his own life history and

---

70 Victor Kravchenko was a defector from the Soviet Union to the United States who wrote a book, 'I Chose Freedom'.

his life surroundings. When he is interrogated by the authorities, the people of the secret service or political security have more complete and detailed records of him than he himself does. He doesn't have any room to wiggle."

July 25, 1950.

Hearing that they sell books from the North, I went downtown for the first time since June 25th and stopped by Hwasin Department Store. There hung a sign that said it was a state-run department Store. There were not too many things; but they were neatly displayed. I was told that Han Sung Taik *koon* was one of the division heads there, but he was not in his room. The furniture and decorations were impressive in his room. A cute clerk, who must have been his personal assistant, told me to wait, but I left soon after - as the rich and aristocratic environment nauseated me.

Next, I went to the book department and bought five volumes of the magazine, *Several Issues of History*, and a single copy of *Korean Grammar*. There were many thick and inexpensive books, like *Collections* or *The History of the Party,* but they were not available to non-Party members – an obvious act of discrimination. While coming down the stairs with the purchased books, there was an air-raid siren, so I took shelter in the basement. It was nice to observe that the clerks' attitudes and movements in guiding customers to the shelter looked practiced and natural. Among the people in the shelter were some male and female soldiers. Although I'd heard about them, I was seeing female soldiers for the first time. The conduct and behavior of all the soldiers here were refined and polite. My recent experience had been that soldiers of the People's Republic were of high quality and well-trained. My initial unpleasant impression from my first encounter with them at the school was gradually waning.

The air raid continued for about two hours and because it looked as if the top of Hwasin was the main target, I became very nervous. At times, there must have been explosions not too far away because the whole Hwasin building was trembling, and machine gun fire seemed to pierce my ears. They differed greatly from the bombings I used to watch from afar at Jungreung[71].

When I got home, I saw Wife upset in an unusually grieved manner saying, "How can these things happen?" When asked why, she related the story of Jungsook[72] who went to a shop owned by the neighborhood leader to buy some onions. She asked for *damanaeghi* (*Japanese word for onion*) and was rebuffed. "You say *damanaeghi?* If you want to use those words, go to Japan. Even a child from a

---

71 Jungreung (Jungreung-dong or Jungreung-ri) was the village (or town) where the family of Prof. Kim lived during the Korean War. At the time, Jungreung was just outside the city of Seoul towards the north. He used to live inside the city in Donam-dong. The translator believes he moved away from the city to be able to work with soil. He had a love for the land (see Appendix B: My Parents, at the end of the book).
72 Jungsook was a live-in housekeeper, about 18-20 years old. At the time, there were many poor families who sent their teenage daughters to Seoul as live-in housekeepers in exchange for housing/clothing and food, and some small compensation. The translator remembers her.

house of reactionary elements is indeed different." Jungsook didn't tolerate it and she shot back, "Is 'reactionary elements' our house name? Why is our house reactionary?" She said they exchanged more unfriendly words.

When I inquired later, there was no real reason for my being called a reactionary except that they saw this so-called university professor spending his time doing nothing during this wonderful period and there was no slogan posted on his front door like everybody else's. Also, the words 'reactionary elements', were meant to be nothing more than a simple slur.

However, in times like this, it makes me uneasy to know that we had a scuffle with the *banjang*-- no, now a *dongjang*-- of Jungreung-ri, who is known as the model of democratic families and who wields much power.

"Then, very young Women's League members came to our house and said that we need to receive cultural education, etc. They said that 'cultural education' meant jail. How should I not be angry?" She still seemed to need to vent more.

"Such petty people. Now, they just want to show off their newly earned illusion of power. Just entertain them. What else can we do?" I laughed it off, but the damage was done. I was frightened as I had no idea how they would report our house to the Party, or when an unexpected judgment might come. It is such an uncertain time.

July 26, 1950.

Today, there was a so-called People's Committee election in our town that had been long announced through newspapers, radio, roadside propaganda, and local meetings. I had heard about this 'most democratic election of our representatives with our own hands'. The words, 'democratic election' had been repeatedly drilled into our heads. As I saw it with my own eyes today, now I know precisely what it is. It all comes down to the blessing of becoming a citizen of the People's Republic.

For a while, there have been posters and announcements from the Temporary People's Committee that it would hold the election in Jungreung on the 27th and ordered everyone to be there. I have been curious to find out who the candidates would be. But expecting the candidates to be made known before the election demonstrated my ignorance of what a real democratic election was to be. The committee then abruptly announced on the afternoon of the 25th that the election on the 27th would now be held on the 26th at 5 am. Holding it at the crack of dawn in the Jungreung Mountains could be understood as a way to avoid the hot sun and airplanes; but changing the dates quite arbitrarily at the last moment seemed to me that members of the committee were worried about something. I wondered if the situation was not as secure as they led us to believe.

But still, how could I abstain from such an order?

In the darkness of early dawn, our *banjang* pounded on our front gate urging us to come out as soon as possible. With sleeping children on our backs, the whole household took off. The whole town was emptied as everybody headed toward the mountains. At 5 am sharp, over ten thousand people gathered in a grassy place in front of a royal tomb.

Checking attendance was done by submitting a piece of paper on which our names were written, which our neighborhood leader had distributed earlier. Submitting this piece of paper was the only evidence that we took part in the election. The meeting place had no order of any sort with people standing or sitting. Some who were afraid of bombings or worried about children at home were sneaking away in the back, but nobody seemed to care.

The phrase I saw later in the People's Newspaper headline was: "Thus, the historic Democratic election was held with everybody's participation...."

In front of the Jungjakak Pavilion structure, they set up a podium. An election host delivered a short greeting to everyone, and then a junior fellow explained the process that would take place. He went into a long narrative about the international situation and a detailed explanation of recent Korean history. He then said, "Rhee Syngman's traitor group, egged on by American Imperialism, stirred up the hornet's nest on June 25th. The People's Republic had to respond." There was a young man near me who could not suppress an involuntary smirk at this remark. The speaker continued, "Finally the country is ready for a glorious election." This speech took almost thirty minutes.

What he said a bit more in detail is, "The brave and august People's Army, with our best sons and daughters, liberated Seoul within sixty hours of the counterattack, saving a million and a half people suffering under the barbarian rule of Rhee Syngman regime, and continued to march south and took Daejun in less than a month. It conquered the Kyunggi, Choongchung and Chunra Provinces and is now marching toward the Kyungsang Province. Days are numbered for those shameless invading American Imperialists..."

Next was an election of the Chairman's Group. The election host asked the audience how this could be done. There was a motion from the crowd, "Let's ask the election host to take care of it." Shouts of "Good" and "Right" followed.

The election host then called out, with no hesitation, the names of seven people. Seven unknown people then came up to the podium and sat down in a row.

Next came the election of candidates. Someone from the crowd stood up and said, "I nominate such a person." From the recorder's corner someone said, "I favor." They must have been writing down the names. Another person stood up and recommended another person and it was also followed by someone shouting, "Good." By the time this was repeated several times, and just when someone was going to recommend another person, the election host stepped in and said, "We already have nine candidates for seven seats. How about stopping recommendations now?" Once again, there were scattered shouts of approval. In this way, the candidate selection was done. Something that seemed odd to me was that sometimes nominators would loudly yell the names of the candidates, but at other times, their enunciations were so mumbled that, even though I was close by, I could not hear them clearly. Apparently, the young recorders up at the recorder's corner must have heard them clearly enough because there was no hesitation in the process. It was as incomprehensible to me as magic.

It was my first time to learn that there would be seven elected. What an ignorant voter I must have been.

Next came discussions about the candidates. What kind of game this would be now, I wondered.

Nominators brought nominees up to the podium, one by one, and delivered a short resume of each candidate. As if coming from a template, the resumes said that each candidate had once been a poor farmer or a laborer. In very superficial narratives, nominators stated that candidates had struggled to work hard for the people and that they were members of the Workers Party of South Korea (Namrodang). That drew applause here and there from the crowd.

Mr. Su Jungook, a beekeeper, was also nominated and his introduction was unique. His special reason for choosing beekeeping as his living was because he was deeply interested in bees' social lifestyle that was like our longed-for Utopian society: "Fellow citizens, if anyone wants honey, go to him and he will share it free …" Big laughs followed.

In this way, our old *banjang* Mr. Lee Yoon Ki, was also nominated. His sister stood up and recommended a woman fighter. I was told that Mr. Lee's two brothers who had been in and out of jail for their underground activities positioned themselves among the crowd to play an active part in engineering the crowd's approval of candidates. His young daughter in primary school was holding a bouquet and waiting in the background. Such a brilliantly democratic household.

I was wrong in assuming that the forum would be composed only of these dull biographical introductions. When Mr. Gong, the last candidate, was introduced, one of Mr. Lee's brothers called out, "Tell us Mr. Gong's party membership." The nominator who was about to come down the steps, went back up to the podium and said, "It is the Korea Independence Party (Handokdang)[73]." Then somebody else

---

[73] The Korea Independence Party (Handokdang) was established in 1930 in Shanghai, China. It pursued liberation of Korea from Japan and established the Shanghai Temporary

in the crowd voiced disapproval saying, "Handokdang is a party with hostile feelings towards us. We cannot elect somebody who was affiliated with such a party as our representative." Once again, voices of "That's right, that's right," came from a part of the crowd.

There was a youth who raised his hand and got permission to speak from the election host. It surprised me to recognize him as the pale-faced son of the noodle shop owner who was enrolled in the language department of our school. When this youth was attending Yangjung Middle School, there was a wide-spread rumor in the town that he was suspended from school indefinitely for joining the left-wing movement. The ROK police had not looked kindly on him.

I was wondering what he would say. He said, "We should elect our representatives based on the qualities of the candidates; why are we hung up on what party he belongs to? Mr. Gong works hard now as the deputy chairman of the Jungreung Temporary People's Committee, and, furthermore, isn't Handokdang a patriotic party that had taken part in the South-North negotiations?" Before he finished, there was thunderous applause. Some people were even thumping their feet. The police would arrest this naïve youth later, but at that moment, his popularity was sky high.

Another person counter-argued, "No, it can't be. Handokdang collaborated with the American military government in the past. It is obvious that, together with the Rhee Syngman regime, it played a part in selling our country to the American Imperialist robbers. We just *cannot* ac-

---

Government before the liberation. After the liberation, this conservative party in ROK became less powerful.

cept a person who belongs to such a traitor party as our representative. I am not saying that candidates should only be from Namrodang, but we should remember that Namrodang was the only party that fought for the people and is truly the party that can fight for us." Then another person came up and started saying, "The nature of Handokdang's crime...." Mr. Gong stood up and stopped him, "I resign from the candidacy." The vehement discussion thus was ended. Now we had eight candidates for seven positions.

Next came the real election.

I was wondering whether I should vote for Mr. Su, or Mr. Lee, or just abstain altogether. But then, the election host had each of the candidates stand up one by one and asked the crowd, "How do you like this person?" From several corners, voices of approval came. "Anybody who opposes him raise his hand." Somebody raised his hand, only to be rebuked by surrounding people. He then dropped his hand...

In this way, Mr. Lee Yoonki was elected unanimously. Applause followed. The next candidate also got one hundred percent of the voters' approval. The election proceeded quickly in this fashion until it came to the female candidate. There were enough hands opposing her, so a vote count took place. During the count there were hesitant hands that were raised or dropped. There were loud admonishments and directives from surrounding people. It was not a smoothly run operation. The counters appeared brilliant in coming up with the final tallies.

In this environment, it was very difficult to raise a 'no' hand. Here, the tactic of asking first for 'no' hands made sense. At the beginning, many people were not sure of what was happening, and, to an extent, some were afraid to express their opinions. So, they only half-raised and half-lowered their hands. Some were hesitantly raising 'no' hands and then dropping them when glared at.

But when they saw the shabbily dressed female candidate, lots of hands were raised. Many must have been thinking, "Hey, what's going on? Everybody is raising their hands. Maybe I should too." The absolute majority of people raised their hands - expressing opposition!

This female party member's biography was not any worse than other candidates' nor did she lack in hearty recommendations from the organizing group. When the crowd had no clear knowledge nor judgment of all these introduced-at-the-last-minute candidates, where was this sudden bold expression of opposition coming from?

My guess was that her appearance was so shabby that their self-esteem must have been hurt to accept her as their representative. Another reason may be that their simmering discontent and contempt at the entire election process have exploded, expressed in everyone's raised hands. Crowd psychology is really a strange phenomenon. Anyhow, one must look respectable to succeed in this world.

This presented a dilemma to the election host and the organizing group. If the 'election process pushers' -- I gave them this name. After observing them for a while, their actions were obvious, and I could count them. -- wanted the female candidate to fail, everything would have been fine. But it did not appear that was what they wanted.

The election host and other leaders took turns getting up to say, "This comrade fought for the people with her life in the past and she still is fighting." They emphasized repeatedly that she would therefore be the best representative for our people. They presented no concrete evidence how she fought and how she is still fighting. I think it is their specialty to use only superficial, exuberant, and beautiful phrases.

At the same time, the election process pushers in the crowd were reminding hand raisers to be sure of what they were doing, intimating that there would be consequences. This way, they were conducting a brilliant, enlightening and instructive operation. Through these tactics, hands were lowered one by one. They had held their hands high for such a long time that it was possible there was a physical necessity to lower them. The election process pushers then counted the number of raised hands. They stared directly at the people with raised hands as they were counting slowly, one-by-one. Hands were raised and lowered here and there during this process, and people could not really figure out what was going on. Nonetheless, the organizers came up with the tally of opposers to be a few tens. But I couldn't hear the number clearly. An announcement followed -- this candidate was also declared elected by an absolute majority.

Then the seven members elected the chairman. Wreaths were presented to them, and children from primary schools (which are now called the 'people's schools') sang in a chorus. I was incredulous to see how these wee mouths sang so well the song of General Kim Ilsung!

Jangbaek Mountains, blood stains on every ridge,
Aprok River, blood stains in every turn,
Today again on the wreaths of the free Chosun,
The vividly shining holy mark,

Aaah, the name of the general we pine for,
Aaah, the General Kim Ilsung whose name shines.

Just then, I realized something: *What had just happened?* There were eight candidates (one dropped out of nine) and seven were elected. *So, through what procedure did one not get elected?* I was dumbfounded as I had carefully watched the whole thing without leaving my place. I cautiously asked somebody nearby and he said he didn't know either. We were idiots. Opposing votes were mostly cast to the woman candidate, but she was declared elected with an absolute majority and she was among our representatives who received wreaths. *Things were really confusing.*

After the children's song, the historical democratic election ended with three hoorays to General Kim Ilsung and Generalissimo Stalin. During the election, there were American planes in the sky, but luckily there were no bombings. I was positive that the images of General Kim Ilsung and Generalissimo Stalin posted on the columns of Jungjakak Pavillion must have protected us.

July 27, 1950.

News of yesterday's election dominated The People's Chosun News.

It reported, "With every voter present, a historical election was held with grand success. Candidates decorated with bloody fighting backgrounds made an appearance as people's representatives to enthusiastic ovations;" and "With every voter's zealous support, the foundation of the People's Government was created."

They say that the son of the noodle shop owner, who had a moment of fame when he supported Handokdang yesterday, went to Yongin with his family as soon as they released him from the Interior Affairs office. He disappeared quickly and the news traveled just as quickly.

I didn't know much about radios until now. It was not only because I was slow to adapt to modern technologies, but also because I did not have the financial freedom to buy a good machine after starting the family. Besides, programs here were not attractive enough to buy a radio. As the children grew, however, I began to feel a need for a radio. With the money from royalties I received from a manuscript from the last winter, I bought a good short-wave radio. But it was confiscated when Chung Myungkyo *koon,* who was carrying it home, was held up at a checkpoint by the Sungdong police department. At the time, one could keep short-wave radios only with permission from the authorities. Friends told me that people like us could get permission if we went through the proper channels. But in this time of taut apprehension, I did not want to draw any suspicion of listening to broadcasts from the North. I thus made only a few hesitant visits to Sungdong Police Station before I gave up entirely.

Just before June 25th, I do not remember why but I had asked Yongchool *koon* to buy me a non-short-wave radio. These days, it is quite useful. In mornings and evenings, I can listen to 'The Announcements of the Headquarters of the People's Army of the Chosun Democratic People's Republic' and to the conversion statements of those who have changed sides.

I do not believe that anyone can compose their statements made on radio as they wish under the present circumstances.

For example, the ramblings of the former ROK interior secretary, Mr. Kim Hyosuk, were overly obsequious, disgraceful and spineless. In comparison, broadcasts of so-called neutralists such as Mr. Ahn Jaehong, Mr. Cho Soang, etc. were easier on my ears. They placed less blame on the Republic of Korea and heaped less fawning upon the People's Republic. The differences in speeches depend on individual personalities, but these broadcasts led me to re-confirm that neutrality is a valuable commodity in a society.

There had been a rampant rumor that Mr. X (*sic*)[74] employed only people who would curry favor with him. Wouldn't it be natural that a person who would curry favor with A would also curry favor with B when the world is turned upside-down?

It moved me deeply to listen to the solemn broadcast by Dr. Kim Kyoosik against Mr. X. I was moved because the broadcast was not addressed to please a certain party, but instead seemed to be an explosive expression of his dissatisfaction from the depths of his being.

July 28, 1950.

Son Woosung *sunsaeng* paid me a visit. He said there was a notice from the school to report tomorrow for an examination.

He was angry, "Examination? What kind of examination? Can't they insult us and fire us freely without having

---

[74] The translator dares to conjecture that this Mr. X is ROK president Rhee Syngman. .

to come up with any trumped-up excuses?" Although I agreed with him by saying, "Their work and interests are preoccupied with sizing us up and insulting us," I kind of felt uneasy saying so, as I did not know Son *sunsaeng* that well. Even though we lived in the same village, we hadn't known each other before. I didn't even know that he had transferred from Sungkyoonkwan University to our school just before June 25th. Thanks to a recent school intra-communication policy, we got to know where each of us lived and had exchanged a few visits since then. His unsophisticated manner and grave personality made him seem trustworthy enough for me to utter those words.

He had an interesting metaphor, "Communist Party members are like Egyptian slaves building Pyramids."

July 29, 1950.

I went to the school early as we were told to be there for the examination. Almost all professors came. Excluding those people who were still 'marching south', those who were taken to the police or to the political security office and those who were hiding in fear of being captured, it looked like everybody was present. I was the last to join and found a seat next to Mr. Lee Myungsun and Mr. Yoo Eungho. I felt somewhat awkward, but it couldn't be helped.

I was wondering what this examination was about, who was conducting the examination, and how. But Mr. Lee stood up and said that we would not be taking the examination today. It had been postponed until tomorrow by a decision from the Department of Education. Since we were already there, Mr. Lee said, we would have a discussion on another matter....

"Our brave People's Army rose with a righteous sword against the unlawful invasion on June 25th which was recklessly started by the Rhee Syngman puppet regime at the instigation by its lord, the robber American Imperialists. We were going to defeat our enemy and go after those to achieve the holy task of unifying our Mother Country in a short time.

"But the American Imperialist's barbarian military interference has caused additional and needless bloodshed. However, our enemy's largest post, Daejun, has fallen now. We have almost pushed the enemy into the small rat holes of Daegu and Busan[75]. It is just a matter of time before we will push them out into the sea.

"On the other hand, historical elections at various levels of the People's Committee are occurring in liberated areas. Land reform[76], the task of the century, is progressing at a rapid pace. The people who suffered most under the oppression and exploitation by the treacherous imperialists, devious landowners and capitalists are so happy to welcome true

---

75 Busan is the second largest city of Korea and located at the Southeastern corner of the Korean peninsula.

76 During the 35 years of Japanese occupation, many Japanese people and organizations lived and owned land and property in Korea. After they left, there was the issue of how to redistribute lands properly to Koreans. Also, at the same time, there was another issue of how to reform centuries-old, outdated practices between landowners and sharecroppers. These issues were finally resolved with a law in 1949 and its implementation in 1950.

liberation. This can be witnessed in the fact that, in less than a month, 540,000 youths from Seoul and the neighboring areas have volunteered to join the volunteer army. In universities as well, students we used to teach have joined this holy march toward the complete unification of the Motherland. Some teachers are following the students stating that they cannot leave the task to the students alone.

"However, look at us in the Arts and Science College. I haven't heard of any professor among us who has stepped up to join the Volunteer Army. Even during the puppet regime period, we prided ourselves to be the best and highest educational organization, in name and reality, and others also regarded us likewise. However, in the month after the liberation, our contribution is deplorably shameful even to our eyes.

"We should get rid of our old ways and inhale the breath of the new age as quickly as possible. This is our ultimate order which is solemnly laid down before us. If we are the only ones left alone after the Motherland Liberation War, could we remain as scholars of our country? Would our school even be allowed to remain as one to be considered viable? I surely don't think so.

"Then what should we do? Today, we should demonstrate our resolution to the society with everyone's application to the Volunteer Army. Of course, it is impossible that everyone will pass the examination and go to the war front. I personally expect that most teachers would fail the examination against their wishes. The examination is tougher than we imagine. Nonetheless I believe that our announcement of everyone's application is absolutely necessary. Through this act, we can impart tremendous influence on the society which is watching our every move. And this is the only way for the school and its faculty to survive in this new era."

Following him, Mr. Yoo Eungho said, "I agree. I am sure that all of you don't have any objections to this. But if you do, please let us hear them," and looked around. There was only silence so heavy that you could hear a pin drop.

One minute, then, two minutes passed and everyone, with their rigid postures and grave facial expressions, sat so quietly that even their breathing seemed to have stopped. *Pitiful professors, are we going to become mummies in our seats?*

Finally, Mr. Lee opened his mouth, "I see there is no objection. I trust everyone agrees. Thank you. With this unanimous resolution, it will be clearly known to all of society that the Arts and Science College is alive and the accusations that we are counter-revolutionary operatives would prove to be defamations."

Next, Mr. Yoo brought out a prepared stamp pad and papers asking, "Sign here please, one by one." I had been uncomfortable from the start because I happened to choose a bad seat. Now I'm facing a piece of paper in front of me. I can overlook his talk concerning the true nature of this war and the rights and wrongs of joining the Volunteer Army. But calling everyone in for an examination and then forcing everybody to apply to the Volunteer Army offended me. But if I were to reveal my thoughts, what would happen to me was beyond my comprehension. The hope that someone else would speak up did not materialize, and now I felt I was forced to act.

I stared at the piece of paper in front of me and rounding up all my courage said, "There was a motion by the chair, but there was no second motion. How can we say this is a resolution? One might say this is a grave matter and I should therefore think it is important to have everyone be in complete agreement, if possible. It may take time, but how about having a full discussion?" The other professors all breathed out a sigh of relief and said, "Right," and "An excellent idea." Following this, a real discussion took place. I could not fail to notice a deep frown on Mr. Lee's face making my heart flutter.

Many opinions came forth but none of them were forceful enough. The professors, who must have read a book on the study of logic at least once, spoke a bit and then finished without any definite conclusion of yes or no while at same time trying to guess what the Chairman might be thinking. A junior fellow from the English Literature Department said, "This is a personally important matter. How about all of us go home, talk to our wives and then vote tomorrow?" Everybody could not help but laugh and the fellow was embarrassed.

Mr. Choi Inho, the physical education teacher, stood up and with gusto said, "There doesn't seem to be any conclusion however long we talk about it. And this is not the time to hesitate. Let us all agree that we volunteer." Finally, the Chair proposed to do so by raising hands. There were only two *nay* votes. All who had called themselves renowned liberals raised their hands with unsettled looks.

Min *sunsaeng* of Chinese Literature said something ridiculous, "There may be other ways of expressing our resolution than applying to the Volunteer Army. Can we all put our names in a message to UN Secretary General Lie and American President Truman requesting that the barbarous bombing be stopped?" Perhaps he may have thought this may be done instead of volunteering with the army, but as this could be another tricky proposition for us, everybody's heart sank at his suggestion. As the Chair was focused on going in one direction only, this issue was luckily not brought to the formal agenda.

July 30, 1950.

There was an actual examination today. Our willingness to volunteer yesterday was the price to pay for securing a seat at this examination. Like students who are taking oral examinations, they called us in one by one for an interrogation on previously submitted autobiographies and other documents.

The examiners were comprised of a healthy-looking junior person from the Department of Education, a former professor at Hongik University and another person.

The first ridiculously curt question was: "Why didn't you come to the North?" Next came a difficult question: "Please let me hear your view on history."

"Those are difficult to explain in simple terms, and kind of awkward to express here. If you really wanted, I am sure you have other ways to know." They also laughed.

Next was a cunning and unexpected leading question: "You were involved in the One-People Academy[77], right?"

---

77 This was an academy where the one-Korea-one-people concept, proposed by President Rhee Syngman, had been discussed.

At the end of this so-called examination, they stated, "We will continue the examination tomorrow at Kyunggi Middle School[78]. Also, there will be a meeting of professors. Everyone should be there." What more could they want?

July 31, 1950.

A few days earlier, electric cars began operating from Donam-dong but they sometimes took longer than walking as the frequent air raids forced passengers to get out of and back into cars frequently in the middle of a ride. Once an airplane appears in the air, all cars stop right where they are, and passengers get out to hide in alleys or under the eaves of nearby buildings.

It was almost impossible to get to Kyunggi Middle School on time. At the school a long-term lecture series was being held for the mainstay teachers of many schools. From our school two professors, Garam[79] and Ilsuk, and an assis-

---

78 The translator and the two brothers attended this school after the war.
79 Garam is Prof. Lee Byunggee, a respected scholar of Korean literature, Ilsuk is Prof. Lee Heeseung, a respected scholar of Korean linguistics and Park sunsaengnim is Prof. Park Jonghong, a respected scholar in philosophy. Prof. Lee Heeseung was a mentor of Prof. Kim's wife when she went to the Kyungsung Imperial College and Prof. Park Jonghong was a mentor to Prof. Kim since his high school years. During his teen years, as the eldest son representing his family, the

tant from the Korean Literature Department, Park *sunsaengnim* from the Philosophy Department, and Mr. Kim Ilchool from the History Department were attending.

I saw Kim Hanjoo *koon* and Mr. Park Sihyung who were now lecturers at the university. It was good to see familiar faces from the old days, but they were under the banner of the victors, and we were targets of examination whose jobs, and even lives, were threatened.

They had talked about the continuation of the examination, but I learned that the examination would be postponed until later. Instead, there would be a rally by all college and middle school teachers. They should have told us, as it was obviously pre-planned. This has become a serial drama of out-and-out lies. I heard about a rally of teachers earlier in downtown Chongro. *If they did it once, wasn't that enough? What was this rally for?*

Numerous groups of teachers packed the large auditorium. Most of them must have come for the continuation of the examination.

First, Mr. Lee Seungyup, the chairman of the City of Seoul Interim People's Committee, made a long-winded speech. The content was from the usual cookie cutter template, but his manner of speaking made him appear to radiate strength and trust. He looked honorable, reminiscent of an old revolutionary soldier.

---

translator visited houses of both Lee Heeseung and Park Jonghong sunsaengnims on Jan 2nd each year to pay respect to them. He knelt and bowed to them (and their wives), and they would give him a small new year's meal. Lee sunsaengnim would give him a shiny ten-cents coin as well.

Next followed a series of resolutions, declarations, and messages. I snuck out in the middle. As I in advance chose a seat near the door, it was easy for me to do so. I later heard that the rally concluded with another call for everybody to volunteer.

In the afternoon, the History Society invited Mr. Park Si-hyung to hold a discussion session in Chongro. Although it was a meeting of prominent history scholars, there was no discussion on history. Instead, it began and ended with an introduction to the current school system in the North, by explaining how well teachers are treated, even including a story of how much meat and sugar they get each month. I watched Mr. Park's new prosperous and confident look which was a striking contrast to his old haggard look. He also mentioned generous payments for scholastic manuscripts.

Everybody listened to this young historian as if in envy when he proudly declared the Soviet language is an absolute necessity in the North and scholars there are well-groomed. But the minds of the listeners who are worried about whether they would pass the current examination looked discomfited while listening to these fantastic stories of Northern scholars.

August 1950

August 1, 1950.

Mr. Yoo Yul of the Korean Language Society came to see me. He said he had evacuated his Donam-dong house and rented a room from Mr. Hu Namgoo of our village. When I asked, "Now you also must change your name to a new one as Ryoo Ryul[80], right?" he answered, "It's an issue where we have to decide once again which one is right."

I touched his sore spot saying, "As I read the book of Chosun Language Grammar, prominent linguists like Mr. Lee Keugro and Mr. Kim Byungje[81] who had gone up to the North were not allowed to contribute much there. Now that the North occupies the South, would it really listen to people like you and change things? You are in trouble anyway. Would you insist on your opinion for the sake of truth? Or would you rather buckle under political pressure?" His earlier boastful claim - "The People's Republic appreciates scholars and cultured men" - disappeared.

---

80 See the comments below about pronouncing and/or writing the sound 'r'.
81 These people were well-regarded linguists. Prof. Kim is referring to the fact that none of the grammar books from the North showed contributions by these well-regarded linguists, even though they are supposedly respected and treated very well.

The Ural Altai language family[82] does not make an 'r' sound as the lead sound in the first syllable, but in the North, they use words like *rodongja* (*a working man*), instead of *nodongja* and Rhee Syngman[83] instead of Yi Syngman. Although their grammar books write words with 'r' and then allow people to pronounce them without it, Pyungan Province[84] dialects can read those 'r' sounds very well. They even call us counter-revolutionaries when we say *nodongja* and Yi Syngman, stating we cannot shed (*American*) puppet's enunciation habits.

Afraid of being called 'counter-revolutionaries', we now should say 'Ri' Syngman at least in front of other people. If that is not to our liking, we should be careful to avoid words that start with 'r'.

---

82 Since the 18th century, based on similarities, there have been hypotheses that grouped certain languages in the world into the Ural-Altai language family which includes Finnish, Turkish, Mongolian, Korean, Japanese languages and many others.
83 Curiously, the president of the Republic of Korea himself included 'r' in front of his name, but this was highly unusual in the South. People in the South still do not pronounce this 'r' in his name but say instead, 'Yi Syngman'.
84 A province in the North Korea where its capital Pyungyang is located.

August 2, 1950.

A few days ago, I saw portraits in the People's Daily of General Kim Ilsung and Generalissimo Stalin on the front face of the Joongangchung[85] building. We see portraits of those two in front of other government or company buildings these days. Also, inside of these buildings, those two portraits are hung side by side in locations high enough to draw our attention. I heard a story about how Mr. Lee Myungsun humiliated Mr. Sung of the library for not carefully handling these pictures.

People of the Arts Union and the Pictures Union are pouring all their efforts into how to best draw, reproduce and print those two pictures. Thanks to the hard-working people who labored day and night to produce them, every household received two portraits each. We got them, too, but somehow misplaced them in the confusion and now cannot find them.

---

85 The main government office building of ROK, and of the People's Army during the war. After taking over Korea in 1910, Japan began construction of this building inside the Kyungbok Palace, dismantling many of existing palace structures. It was understood that Japan chose this site in order to suppress the cultural, historical and national spirit of Korea. It was dismantled in 1995 by the Korean government. The official reason for the removal was to get rid of remnants of Japanese occupation and to rebuild the national spirit. There were opposing opinions to preserve the historical building with a claim that Koreans should always be reminded of the shameful history.

I was told that Bong-a went to play at Kwanggee's house today and was fascinated by those pictures. I felt a cold sweat on my back when Kwanggee's grandmother asked, "It seems you do not have the pictures of Kim Ilsung and Stalin?"

I replied feeling as if cold sweat was running down my back, "I put them up in my study and he must not have seen them yet," but my words sounded unnatural. An ethics professor of the Koryo University had written in his book, "I should never utter a lie. A lie I made during the Japanese occupation in an unavoidable situation still bothers me." I heard that they labeled him as a counter-revolutionary and expelled him from the school. He now spends his life in a condition of semi-exile. I wonder if he still cannot tell a lie.

A few days earlier, for the sake of the People's Republic, I told Choi Bongrae *koon* about my view asking, "Shouldn't we re-think about putting up Stalin's picture too prominently? Some people may be offended by it."

He answered, "We cannot abide by the people of the South whose awareness level is far behind…. From the get-go, we should show them what is right and push it so they can follow us." It was as if I was listening to somebody from another planet. It appeared that my awareness level is not quite there.

August 3, 1950.

Weather was pleasant, and it felt like May. When I saw in *Life* magazine a picture of fireworks in Budapest on the night of Stalin's birthday, I had wondered, "Really? Should they really do that?" Now I read in a magazine published in North Korea that our People's Republic not only sent a prodigious present to Stalin but also erected celebration posts, conducted flag processions, gave hurrahs and displayed fireworks on every corner in North Korea to celebrate the day.

I recalled reading, in *Yulha-ilgee* by Yunam, a story that a congratulatory delegation, led by Park Myungwon, went to Beijing in order to celebrate the 70th birthday of Emperor Kunryoongje of the Qing Dynasty and afterwards went as far north as Yulha, but I never heard that there had been a celebration back in Seoul.

I was somewhat skeptical when I heard from people who came from the North that there is a Stalin Blvd in Pyungyang and a Molotov Square in Sineuijoo[86]. Now, I see it could be possible from the way Stalin and the Soviet Union are hoisted up by these people. *When will our people stop worshipping the powerful and still survive?*

August 4, 1950.

The bombings are becoming fiercer every day. First, there was a rumor that planes were targeting the Han River. Then, they bombed Yongsan. Gradually they are coming closer to the heart of the city and now they are dropping incendiary bombs and missiles. Earlier, they bombed the areas of Chungryang-ri and the Changdong Train Station and

---

[86] Pyungyang is the capital of DPRK and Sineuijoo is a North Korean city facing China across the Yalu River.

a few days ago, they burned to the ground an oil factory in Miari which was not too far from here. When they were targeting Miari, it was as scary as if planes were coming right onto the roof of our house.

Now, even Jungreung does not feel safe anymore. The Kyungsin School, a mere hundred yards away, is packed with the People's Army soldiers. In the woods in front of the school, there are horses, and they are making some kind of wagons. Occasionally, I see some soldiers – perhaps communication soldiers? – asking about the location of a command center. There must be a command center in this valley town. If this is the case, you never know when Jungreung-ri will become a bombing target. When American soldiers attacked Tokyo, I heard they started from the outskirts.

I don't know where it started, but there is a rumor the American military decided to use atomic bombs. Some say they read leaflets dropped from planes advising people to move ten miles away from Seoul. More rumors say that this must indicate the American military's intention to use atomic bombs. The other day, I saw some people, deceived by the rumor, fleeing from Jungreung-ri, with only a few essential items.

They can't possibly use atomic bombs. Even if they use them, they wouldn't drop them on Seoul. But when everybody is unsettled, my mind becomes anxious as well and I reread books such as *Hiroshima* or *The Bell of Nagasaki*. But then there are people who say, "The bombs nowadays are ten times more powerful than those used in Japan, so what's the use of reading those books?"

I had a small underground shelter dug out and put some toys in there so that when there are bombings, I could let the children play in it. But, if an atomic bomb drops onto Seoul, that would be the end for all. I am sure that would not happen.

But the closeness of the Kyungsin School worries me. If possible, at least sending Bong-a and Mok-a to some place in the countryside would ease my mind. But there is no good place I can think of and, even if there was and I could ask Kyunghee to take them, I doubt the children would tolerate being away from us for so long. In these times, with active volunteer soldiers around, Kyunghee himself may not be safe. This is the principal topic of discussion between Wife and I these days, but we can't come up with a satisfactory solution.

I went out to Wooee-dong today as I heard it is a quiet place. From our village it is easy to pass through the Cheema Bawi Hill and, if we can get a room or two there, perhaps some of us could stay there for a while. It may help to minimize the danger.

With Bong-a and Mok-a in a basket atop a bicycle that Kyunghee pulled, we started our trip. The children were happy with the chance of enjoying the excursion; but the hearts of the adults are heavy as if a chunk of lead is pressing them down. The road on the way was littered with smashed automobiles and all the bridges were broken. Damaged and discarded tanks were seen occasionally. Sporadic fresh mounds of dirt indicated the graves of soldiers - common signs of the war in this town.

We looked around Wooeedong the entire day, but there were already too many former Seoul residents taking refuge here. Then we heard these people were being closely watched by the People's Committee of this town as possible counter-revolutionaries. It didn't look encouraging after all, and we came back empty-handed.

August 5, 1950.

A new office called the Democratic Propaganda Office was set up. In villages, they selected a few meeting places where, morning and evening, they could tell us about current affairs and read newspapers for us. They also teach People's songs to both children and adults.

In our village, one office opened in the town office building and another at the old mill by Mr. Son's house. These days, it is awkward for me to pass by the front of the town office. I fear they might wonder, "Why doesn't that fellow go to the school? Could he be a counter-revolutionary?" In case somebody is watching me carefully, when I go to the vegetable field, I deliberately take the road in front of Dr. Cho's while fewer people are on the streets. It has become a habit of mine to avoid eye contact while I sneak through the streets. Today, while working in the field, I happened to be called into the democratic propaganda office at Mr. Son's house in the adjoining field.

When a member of the Chosun Youth Alliance was to convey interpretations of current affairs, people are all brought in from their homes, from working in the fields and from the roads to hear him. He was a young person of about twenty, plucky looking but still quite youthful. I wouldn't know about his personal struggle history, but he did not look cultivated.

Even when he tried to show his conviction that the North army will prevail, using cliché phrases like 'Robber American Imperialists,' 'their running dog, Rhee Syngman's traitor group,' 'the People's Army going south unhindered,' 'would finally push the enemies into the sea,' etc., he stumbled occasionally and had to get help from a few young members of the Women's League nearby.

The most interesting story was: The reason Seoul residents are missing meals so often is because the South puppet gang dumped all the food stored in Seoul into the Han River when they ran away because it was too heavy, and they didn't want the enemy to benefit from it. Therefore, there is plenty of rice spread out on the bottom of the Han River now. In a way, re-directing the unbearable agony of hunger to anger toward the South may not be too bad of an idea. But the question is whether people would believe such an explanation on face value or not.

I did not know whether this fellow is speaking such nonsense at the direction of his boss or by his own volition, but I felt as if he was giving me side glances, trying to figure out my thoughts. *Am I showing a certain attitude that he detects?* The feeling worried me.

August 6, 1950.

Myung Daemok dropped by to see me. For long he had been a malnourished person. He was now looking very haggard as well. As I always do when a visitor like him comes, I took him into the far corner of the house, hid his shoes and closed any doors facing the gate. Facing him, I could not feel but tense and tight.

He told me how Myung *sunsaeng*[87], whose fate I had been wondering about, had been taken to the Political Protection Office, and how his son Daesung was taken to the Volunteer's Army at school. Now his own family got an eviction/transfer order from their Myungryoon-dong house....

I asked, "Why on earth did a person like Myung *sunsaeng* not go to the South, but remain here instead? It would have been hard to avoid troubles here, am I not right?" He answered, 'Yes of course we tried hard to persuade him, but he wouldn't listen. He would say, "A government that threw away Seoul so easily could not stay alive too long. Eventually, it would be exiled to Japan across the ocean. I cannot let myself to go to the land of the enemy (*Japan*) against which I have been fighting for sixty years of my life and expect to pick up whatever vestige is left of my life. I would rather die in the hands of my own people and get buried in this land.' He would not budge. If Dr. Rhee Syngman provided him a car to help him move to the South, perhaps he might have ... But while the government was occupied only in making its own haphazard-and-fast runaway, abandoning even the vice president and not bothering to warn the foreign embassies, it would not have had time to consider arranging such things. So, what could we do? Even if he had decided to move, a seventy-year-old elderly person would have had to face competition with younger refugees for a space in boats and roads, he would not have endured such things even if he were threatened with imminent death.

---

87 Myung Jese. He was a liberation (from Japan) fighter and the first president of Simkyewon, the ROK organization that oversaw the government budget.

Even if he should have started off for the South, he would not have gone far." Saying this, his eyes watered.

"Then why did he just sit there to be captured? Couldn't he hide someplace?" I was sorry for the tone of my voice - It sounded as if I was accusing Myung Daemok.

"Well, we talked about it... But he said, 'What big crimes have I committed that I need to look for a hiding hole? My life is no longer so important, and I do not worry about being captured and of dying. Perhaps it's better to die, rather than live and see all these things. Let's say Kim Ilsung will capture me! If I am captured, I will be able to meet him or his subordinates. When I meet them, I will tell them this is not proper and honorable. Does this infighting of thirty million of the same people make sense? If they like communism, they can do it themselves. Why do they take direction from another country and aim guns at their own people? After forty long years of Japanese exploitation and hardship that left us with just skin and bones, aren't we all supposed to help each other? What's the reason for raising swords against each other and killing one another? Are you asking me whether the North would listen to these words? Whether they listen or not, it's up to them. But shouldn't I say these words?' Then he passively surrendered to the arrest. I worry that my father's attitude may harm him more." His eyes were wet.

Even while he was speaking, we felt shaking of the house and reverberations of the window papers[88] probably from

---

88 Most windows in Korea didn't have glass panes. Instead, reinforced (with starch) semi-thick Korean papers were used. They were light, opaque, semi-resilient but allowed some light into a room.

some nearby bombings. Whenever that happened, I read a slight hope in his eyes while staring at me.

"Sir, what do you think? Is there still hope for restoration?" Standing up, he cautiously asked me the last question.

Already accustomed to these types of questions, I answered, "The war is decided only when it ends. Not being an expert in this area, how could I predict?" It was a canned answer, but putting myself in his position, I wish I could have provided more substantial opinions, at least to him.

August 7, 1950.

Mr. Choi, Hong *koon*'s brother-in-law, who has a construction material business in front of the Donam-dong firehouse, was arrested by the Internal Affairs Office. The reason was that he had been the vice president of a local branch of the People Protection Organization (Minbodan) before the war. His brothers ran to Hong *koon* for help the same day as he is the president of the Court Self-governing Committee. But Hong *koon* curtly said, "I am busy today, I cannot come," with a cold face.

When Mr. Choi's brothers, trusting him to be close and reliable, begged him further for help, he got irritated and said, "They do not kill people there, nor torture people indiscriminately like ROK used to. Rather, it could be an excellent opportunity for him (*Mr. Choi*) to learn. Everybody who had been loyal to ROK should go through the process at least once." The Choi brothers became really enraged.

I doubted if Hong *koon* actually said those words. I didn't think the relationship between Hong *koon* and the

Choi brothers was like this. Theirs was a sweet brother/sister relationship. Hong *koon* had been in unfortunate circumstances since the liberation. His brothers-in-law had been providing Hong *koon*'s family with rice, fuel twigs, and even some clothing material. Wife and I noticed this ourselves, and his wife told us they had been doing this for all five years since the Liberation.

When Hong *koon* was arrested twice, it was moving to see how the brothers went about trying to help him. Perhaps that's why Hong *koon*'s own family had not been much help to him. The brothers were busy seeing prosecutors and judges and buying lawyer services, etc. As I understood, the relationship between Hong *koon*'s wife and the brothers was a very special one. Hong *koon*'s mother-in-law loved her only daughter, her last child, very much and the brothers helped their sister eagerly, honoring their mother's wishes.

I didn't know the Choi brothers before, but I met them often since Hong *koon* acquired an office in a corner of their building. When Hong *koon* was arrested, I saw them going about town, trying to save him. They were all honest and diligent businessmen, showing no indication of political colors. The crime they accused one of them of committing was that he was involved with the People Protection Organization. But, during those confused times before the war, anybody who had any means to contribute to village affairs could have easily lent his name to the organization. Now they faulted him for not having turned himself in earlier. To me, it doesn't seem to be such a big deal to arrest anybody.

Hong *koon* may have had reason for his cold response, but the brothers were so disappointed with him, given their strong feelings toward him as a family. The person who agonized most was his wife. Even when she cried and begged, he would say, "What would your brother do at home doing nothing? He may actually learn something there." If she said, "In this hot weather, such suffering he must endure...", he'd say, "Anybody who prospered during the time of the Republic of Korea needs to go through such an experience," as if talking about some stranger's affairs. His wife told Wife this sad story.

The power of the party to change even a person's character impressed me anew.

August 8, 1950.

When I went to my brother-in-law's house in Donam-dong, I decided to stop by the school. They told me there was an inauguration ceremony of a Professional Alliance, but no professors were there. After we were all forcefully volunteered to the People's Army, I'm told that nobody comes to the school anymore. When there was a call to come to the Baeje School Auditorium for volunteer soldier examination, I skipped it and wondered if I was the only one, but I learned later that most of us boycotted it as well except Mr. Lee Byungdo, Mr. Kim Sangkee, Park *sunsaengnim*, Mr. Kim Ilchool and a few others. Mornings and evenings, they were fed only millet balls. Having spent three days with younger volunteers in this way, they became sick when they got home. According to a person who was there, the examination was not at all well-coordinated. It was so slow that they were kept in quarters like a pig pen for three to four days. It would have made new patients instead of soldiers.

At the Professional Alliance inauguration ceremony, Mr. Lee Myungsun said, "The reason we dismantled traditional organizations such as the Educators' Association and the Teachers' Cooperative (*both were labor organizations*) and unite them into the Professional Alliance is because our approach toward the government and its organizations is changing. We have been fighting against the ROK government but now that we have established our dream society, we must cooperate with the new government and its other organizations so that their policies get executed effectively."

Listening to Mr. Lee's words, I realized that our conventional understanding of the goals of labor organizations to enhance the socioeconomic welfare of laborers has been misconceived.

They elected Chae Heekook, Im Jinsang and Chung Chanyung. All of them came from the offices of the Teachers Union or the Scientists Union. No professors were elected. During the few days I was absent, the school had changed completely.

A North Korean soldier returned a saw he had borrowed from me. I had assumed that any articles they took were as good as gone. Considering that, I really appreciated he remembered and returned it. Not that the item was so important, but his attention and care were to be appreciated. Not just because I liked him, but because I could begin to have hope for our whole country. I hope these new fresh shoots of the country do not become a sacrifice to benefit some misguided politicians' ambitions.

August 9, 1950.

Kim Sangkee *sunsaeng* made a special visit to me with some school news: I was 'withheld' at the last examination. This is a euphemism for being fired through the examination. Mr. Lee Myungsun said he was very sorry. He said he argued very hard on my behalf, but most of the professors of the departments of Social Sciences, especially because of their historical views on socialism, were given the 'withheld' notices. To me, there was no reason for Mr. Lee to feel sorry at all. After the Volunteer Army show, we were already far apart.

Kim Sangkee *sunsaeng* told me that he could have sent somebody else, but the reason why he came himself was because he wanted to tell me in person to be especially careful as there may be some further actions to be taken against 'withheld' professors.

These days, newspapers keep publishing stories about Americans and South Koreans massacring many innocent people in places like Suwon, Daejun, and Yungdong. He said these stories may become justification for certain future harsh actions to be taken by the People's Army. I took his comment as a penetrating observation by a historian.

Lee Bonryung *koon*, who is now the head of Dankook College, sent a person asking, "Now that you are out of the Arts and Science College, how about coming to our school? When the time comes, there will soon be a fundamental reorganization and teachers will be redistributed. Once you are in Dankook or any place, things will get easier." I told him, "Thank you for caring for my sake. But, taking this window of opportunity, I want to leave the education field for good. You know there is a saying: Teachers do not get respect. Even dogs would not eat teachers' dung. I already have been thinking about giving up my teaching career as it does not suit my temperament, but I didn't have the chance. I will work more vigorously for the country in other areas, so please always vouch for me in the future." I mumbled my way through with this answer.

I knew he would see through me with a smile on his face[89]. But I also believed he would stop there with a simple smile and not pursue it any further.

August 10, 1950.

When I heard that Daekyoo got a job at Kyungdong Middle School and was forced to volunteer to the army the next day, I visited my sister in Myungryoon-dong. She had gone out with Yungkyoo to sell things. Jungkyoo was alone at home and was so happy to see me.

"What are you eating these days? Have you been hungry?" I asked.

His explanation made me sad. "We ate what you sent us earlier, and we received a cousin's share of food distribution once. After our big brother was gone, we sold a bicycle to keep us going. Mother told us not to eat all that's left. She buys and sells vegetables to keep us holding on. In the

---

89 His friend Mr. Lee was a recognized leftist. The translator's interpretation of this sentence is that he didn't want to associate himself with a leftist and that he and Mr. Lee were both fully aware of the true reason why he was rejecting Mr. Lee's gracious offer.

morning we eat rice soup and then vegetables at lunch and dinner."

These brothers have not had too many chances to eat to their heart's content since they were young. My sister has always been struggling to support them alone and without money, and hunger has always been with them. Now that we are going through these hard times, she may not eat even one full meal a day.... My sister's situation must be more lamentable than her children's.

Hot and exhausted, I was lying down on the floor for a while when Jungkyoo brought something from the kitchen and asked me to eat it. It was boiled cabbage mixed with bean sauce. "You eat it. If I eat, your portion will get smaller." Although starving, I could not take their food.

He said, "It's all right. There were a lot of leftovers at the market yesterday, so we boiled enough to eat today."

I asked again, "Really?" To prove it to me, he showed me a large, full basket.

I was hungry. I ate almost a bowlful. He watched me curiously and said, "You don't have much food either, do you?" He is only about ten years old.

"Right, we don't have enough either."

"Then, even college professors are not any better?"

"It's the same for everybody."

"My cousin says he gets more food distribution than they need." His cousin must be Lee Suk.

I have known Suk as multi-talented. He joined the communist movement while he was in middle school and has worked underground for twenty years. Now he is the head officer at the headquarters of the Volunteer Army.

August 11, 1950.

While cleaning up a corner of the room, I found a few quarts of barley grain in a sack. Students who used the room before must have left them there. When I showed it to Wife, she was happy with the news. Without the owner's consent, we decided to eat it now and deal with the consequences later. Living through the war must be hardening our hearts and minds.

War and morality. Was there any scholar who connected those two together? I have come to feel earnestly these days that the war changes people. Morality therefore should change accordingly both in its meaning and practice.

A stranger came to our pumpkin patch and was busy picking them. When asked who he was, he said that he was so hungry that he could not help but come in. His face was pudgy and yellow with famine. I certainly could not claim ownership of resources against these people and their basic needs.

August 12, 1950.

Now that I am out of the school, lest something happen to my person, I thought I should let Hong *koon* know of my situation. I went out to the orchard around the time when I guessed he might be home. He is now sporting a mustache which makes him look like a different person.

I don't know why but I have not been able to bring myself to feel close with people with mustaches. I am not sure why I have such a bias against those with a mustache and do not treat them with high regard. I don't know if it is because they look presumptuous, or perhaps because I happen not to like people with mustaches around me. When an ignorant person from my hometown got an undeserved position after the Liberation, the first thing he did was to grow a mustache. I didn't know this Mr. Lee, who previously was the vice chancellor of our school until recently and now is a congressman. I didn't have any reason to like or dislike him. But I somehow kept thinking that both his position and his mustache are not appropriate for him and hence I never developed a good impression of him.

Now Hong *koon,* a freshly appointed chairman of the Court Self-Governing Committee, also sports a mustache. I looked at the mustache for a long time but couldn't say what I wanted to say. It made me feel miserable that I must act from now on as if I am still with the school in front of him or any other village people.

August 13, 1950.

In the afternoon, somebody came on bicycle and told Wife that I should come to the office of the Chosun Youth Alliance, and urgently too.

These days we lock the front door all the time. When somebody visits, Wife tells him/her I am at the university. Then I remove my shoes from direct sight and hide myself in the back of the house. My scheme worked today, and he urged, "If he is not here, then somebody else should come as soon as possible."

I got scared wondering if the event we have been dreading has finally come. Considering the gravity of the issue, the person looked rather shabby and there was no reason the Youth Alliance should look for me, at this time in particular.... Anyway, we decided that Wife would go instead of me. What she relayed when she came back in the sweltering heat was, believe it or not, that they want our dog.

She complained, "If that was all they wanted, he could have told us when he came. Telling people to come and go in this hot weather was ridiculously insane."

I could only answer, "That's how they show they are not to be ignored." My mother-in-law, who came at the news, said, "It may be better this way. Beeru is taking the edge off an evil fortune."

Beeru had been with us for three years and was a very loyal member of the household. He was a silly dog though, responding to each siren with a long wail. When we fled to Donam-dong last time, he was the one who minded the house, all alone. He is finally becoming a casualty of the war.

Shortly, the same junior guy from before came back to take the dog. The dog must have understood what was going on. He thrashed violently and kept looking back with his leash tightened around his neck. Sad wailing trailed behind him as Bong-a and Mok-a followed him with tearful faces.

"Pyungan Province people like dog meat stew so much," says my mother-in-law, as a rebuttal to the claim that they would use him for military purposes. After losing him, the house felt emptier than if we had lost a person.

August 14, 1950.

A handful of rice in a light porridge cooked with zucchini, zucchini shoots, and lots of greens is our daily meal these days. Not because we would run out of rice today or tomorrow, but because we do not know the future and the children's appetites are vigorous, so we need to take this extraordinarily wary measure. We feel awful that even this is too much when compared with what our neighbors eat. But the children don't understand the desperate lives of other people.

"I did put in some grains of rice, but can't see them among the abundant weeds," Wife says smiling sadly. For the first few days, the children ate with little complaint. I mistook their response and thought, "Perhaps they now understand we are in a war". Nowadays they turn their faces away from the rice porridge table. When we explain this carefully, Bong-a picks up the spoon, but Mok-a is completely uninterested. If we talk more, he starts crying. How long do we have to suffer like this? It is truly bleak.

August 15, 1950.

As today is the anniversary of the Liberation (*from Japan*), we greeted the day with fear expecting there to be fierce 'memorial bombing'. But bombings today ended up to be not too much different from others. The authorities also must have worried about these as memorial ceremonies were held in each *dong* individually and either at the break of dawn or after the sunset. They were held in places like under big trees so that the bombers could not see them easily.

According to Wife who came back from one of them, they told the group of mostly ignorant women, "Daehan Minkook (*ROK*) started the 6.25 War, so the responsibility of bloodshed between brothers from the North and the South should be borne by Rhee Syngman and the gangs." But Wife said the women didn't appear convinced. She also said she would imagine that Seoul citizens would not be swayed any more these days by the repeated propaganda such as "The reason why Dulles came to the 38th parallel was not to pick flowers[90]," or "Kim Hyosuk testified on the South's Invasion Plan to the North."

There was a countless number of August 15th memorial slogans in the Chosun People's Daily (dated August 12th). The government developed these slogans and told the public to memorize and post them on walls, etc.

---

90 A week before the breakout of the Korean War, President Truman asked John Dulles, a consultant to the Secretary of State, to go to Korea to assess the situation. The crucial question was whether the United States should include the Republic of Korea within its defense wings. Dulles went to the 38th parallel. A photo of him at the 38th parallel was taken, and North Korean authorities used this photo to 'prove' that Dulles ordered South Korean troops to attack the North.

August 16, 1950.

This world is a funny thing. I don't remember committing any crime, and there was nobody particularly looking for me. Nonetheless, I became a pitiable person trying to avoid other people's attention. It is very unclear what types of people are labeled as counter-revolutionaries and, once they are labeled as such, how they are punished and, through what procedures? It could therefore mean that anybody can be labeled as such at any time based on the needs of politics or the emotions of so many political pawns.

Once labeled as such, they will most certainly be punished according to the ever-changing political needs. What is even more scary is the possibility of being punished by the judgment of a particular person in a particular office, or to use an even worse phrase, by his caprice. There are so many rumors floating around that are seeding deep fears in people. Until now, some prominent people from the Daehan Minkook (*ROK*) era have survived relatively unscathed. But at the same time, many people were executed whose crimes were not well understood by the public. Anybody who doesn't have any connections now lives in fear.

I think this may be the real strength of the People's Republic. Everybody is in a near-death situation with hunger, so they need to dance to the Party's music to survive. Everybody has a certain amount of fear, so they must endorse unconditionally whatever the Party does. This may be the perfect political technique when it comes to governing by fear.

It is safer to stay in the house, but I now learn nothing about the affairs outside. I want to see Choi Bongrae *koon* but am afraid to travel to his house. Choi came from the North as a key person, so his safety is guaranteed. He can listen to Japanese broadcasts and have access to other sources of news. He and I have been relatively close to each other since our school days. We also trust each other because we are very open and honest about most issues.

What could happen to me? I tried to conjure up the courage, but I didn't have the gumption to walk openly in the streets. I found my way through a ravine in front of the Yaksoo-am Temple and, mounting the Jungreung Hill through the rear of the Shinheung-sa Temple, arrived at Choi *koon*'s house in Donam-dong. Looking down from the top of the hill, all the streets were deadly quiet. In Donam-dong or Jungreung-ri, there was nothing moving, not even a dog. I was wondering if there was a raid alert, but there wasn't. I heard of 'streets of death' and wondered if they meant these streets. The power of politics is indeed fearsome.

Choi *koon* was very pleased with the news that the People's Army succeeded in crossing the Nakdong River[91]. In his words, on the East side, Pohang was now secured and Kyungjoo and Ulsan were presently being attacked. In the West, Jinju and Masan were also being attacked. And Daegu and Busan are in a precarious situation as well.

---

91 The Nakdong River separates a tiny Southeastern part of the Korean Peninsula from the Southwestern part. The UN and ROK forces were pushed into the Southeastern corner of the Korean peninsula. See the Korean War Map at the beginning of the book. It contains the cities of Daegu and Busan of Kyungsang Province. The crossing of the river was a crucial step for the People's Army as it is the major physical barrier for them. Daegu is very close to the river.

For a Korean fighting against the mighty Americans, it could be an exhilarating story to listen to, but where on earth is this strength of the People's Army coming from? As we learn of the increasing number of captured American soldiers and see more bombings by American planes, it is clear that America is involved in this war. Didn't a world power like Japan eventually surrender to America? The fact that Chosun (*Korea*) is facing such a powerful country and continually winning against them stirs feelings of exhilaration within the Chosun people. I cannot deny that I come to have a certain amount of nationalistic pride in seeing the immense power we can generate regardless of whether it is right or wrong and regardless of my own current situation.

His story about the well-being of the Republic expanded to that of no corruption in the government and no corrupted officials in the North. I told him, if that's the case, Chosun would finally be freed from a feeling of national despair. In his excitement, he narrated actual stories of the people's harsh judgment of corrupted officials in the North.

But when I implored him for more information, I found there were no professional judges involved and no law books consulted. Many different judgments seemed possible for the same crime. When I asked, "Then how can one guarantee objective fairness in their judgments?" He, who once studied law, said that this was an issue only capitalistic countries would address.

His conclusion was, "If the result of a trial serves the political power that best reflects the current situation of the society, then that would automatically be the right trial for the people."

A while ago, I read a story in a magazine that criticized the North: "In the North, depending on the political colors of a plaintiff and a defendant, exactly opposite judgments for an identical issue can result. Laborers or poor farmers will always win lawsuits against landlords or business owners. And then, when the bourgeoisie collapses once and for all and its businesses become the property of the country, laborers and poor farmers would be stripped of all previous freedoms and turned into slaves who cannot but obey." This criticism seems well justified if trials are indeed held the way Choi *koon* describes.

It would be really a good thing if they can completely wipe out social corruption by identifying and prosecuting all the corrupted officials. However, I don't think that is the full answer to preventing social corruption.

Choi *koon*'s story continued. He said the political organization of the North was carefully built. It enforced the people's identification system strictly and its neighbor-watch system was so secure that no defiled elements could penetrate into society. Even visiting an uncle in the next village required reporting it to the authorities.

Sometime in the spring last year, before he went to the North, we ran into each other. He said then that the province ID card system being implemented in Kyungsang-do was a cruel one, harassing people unnecessarily. He also said that the traveler-reporting system implemented in Seoul only exposed the weakness of the political system of ROK. I suddenly remembered these words of his and couldn't suppress a wry smile in my mind. Should he catch my smile now, I could be labeled as a counter-revolutionary. I knew it was not in his character, but the thought, "*Who can I trust in this world?*" never left my mind. This preoccupation, bordering on paranoia, is definitely a tragedy.

I remember that Chung Heejoon *koon* had said some time ago, "I see machine guns, barricades, and yellow lines in front of police stations. If they are so afraid of people, why do they hold on to political power?" A question I have now is: "How much does the People's Democratic Republic trust people and, in turn, allow people to trust it back?"

August 17, 1950.

At the summon of "One grown male per household come to the People's Committee at 8:30", Wife obliged[92]. After verifying attendance for each neighborhood, they went to do some work somewhere. The direction and the character of the work itself were held completely secret. Kwangkee's grandmother and a teacher of the Kyungsin School verified Wife's special situation of having a nursing baby, so she could come home. All the other women came back at dawn. I later learned they went far, about 4 - 5 miles, and moved bullets or some such things on their heads. But how worried the families at home would have been, not knowing what had happened?

I heard that the work didn't amount to anything significant after all, but how would this midnight mobilization af-

---

92 As the reader would know by now, the reason his wife went was because he did not want to be caught outside of the house after he was kicked out of the University. He was now in essence an 'outsider' to the People's Republic.

fect people's mindsets? It can only be described as a derailment of governing or poor governing at best.

August 18, 1950.

Although there is a rumor that, with the June 25th War, a schism was created within the American leftist people, and now even a person like Wallace[93] decided to support the (*US*) government decision. This rumor reached us clandestinely and uncertainly, in quite a similar way to how we got to hear about the existence of the Cairo Declaration[94] during the Japanese occupation.

The People's' Daily and the Liberation Daily still pour out reports every day of work strikes in America, of demonstrations against American military intervention, of absolute support by people in every country of the Stockholm Appeal[95], and of protests by stevedores in America and Japan

---

93 Vice President Henry Wallace, who was from the United States Progressive Party, a left-wing political party.
94 In 1943, US president Franklin Roosevelt, UK Prime Minister Winston Churchill and Chinese Generalissimo Chiang Kai-shek met in Cairo, Egypt and declared that territories and countries Japan had occupied would be liberated from Japan. Korea was also mentioned in it, but Korean people got this information only through rumor mills as the Japanese government suppressed it. The rumors that reached Korean people may not have been completely accurate.
95 On 15 March 1950, the World Peace Council approved the Stockholm Appeal, calling for an absolute ban on nuclear

against the shipment of military supplies to Korea, etc. Perhaps some of these rumors are true but obviously they are excessive exaggerations.

I am not surprised that these manufactured propagandas could occur. The news that Jungsook relayed to us after she went to Kwangwoo's house topped the list: That many of the American bombs and cannonballs these days are duds, so even when hit, people come out unscathed. When opened, the bombs contain scrap paper, sawdust, or sometimes vehement anti-war leaflets. There was a saying during the time of the farmers' uprising of 1894[96]: "Believers did not get killed even when they were hit by bullets." Times are changing but incredible rumors are standard elements during any war.

August 19, 1950.

Time passes fast. Not that long ago, the People's Army came into Seoul overnight. Underground communists appeared as heroes in front of people, and anybody and everybody pretended to be leftists boasting their past struggles; but now their golden time seems to have passed. People do not show it, but they all avoid communism. No political directives are met with willing hands, and, out of sight, they stick their lips out with contempt.

---

weapons.
96 An 1894 armed uprising in Korea mostly by farmers who followed a new Eastern (vs the 'old' Western) religion in Korea.

First, their so-called 'Government for the People' is very harsh to the people. Second, they suspect that, with American involvement and the ever-increasing bombings, the world will eventually be turned upside-down. Sensing this, the Bolsheviks became more impatient and the people, in their turn, pretend to be dumber.

Hong *koon*'s household is typical of a household that is tragically divided. Hong *koon* first proclaimed himself not a Bolshevik, but now acts as one most ardently. He demands for his wife go to the Women's League and teach the children, Yoonja and Namsuk, the People's songs which are riddled with harsh phrases. Compared to the time around June 25th when they were always hungry, nowadays they look quite well with regularly distributed grain in large sacks. Kibong (*Bong-a*) also seems very envious and says, "Yoonja's family has a large sack of rice."

But the brain of Hong *koon*'s wife still doesn't quite catch up with that of Hong *koon's*. Whenever she sees Wife, she utters those unspeakable words like: "The world will now be turned over again?"; "I am sure they cannot win over America."; "What will happen to people like us?" Wife, who cannot answer freely either, says, "Really, what would we know? What does Mr. Hong say?" But according to her, Hong *koon* hates bringing up such talk and says, "If we lose, everybody in Korea will die, so don't even think about it."

But Mrs. Hong just cannot believe those words and suspects America will win. Hence, she not only refuses to go to the Women's League but also urges her husband to extricate himself from his current work. She gets severe tongue-lashings in return. However, the stronger his conviction of victory is, the stronger her premonition of defeat becomes.

His attitude towards her brothers is so harsh that her situation became insufferable, rendering her heart torn. She says she can't help but feel that the society in which her husband is an important member is immoral and unjust.

She is a mild person who cannot voice her opinions strongly, so she is alone in her agony and tears. Although we understand we are the only people to whom she can speak her mind, because she is Hong *koon*'s wife, we can only murmur. It is not something an empathetic person would do, but to survive in this world, it is the only way.

August 20, 1950.

When Mok-a starts singing, "Till the water of the East Sea dries out and Mount Baekdoo wears out / God will protect our country[97]", Bong-a joins. As I had told them that this song should not be sung now, Bong-a doesn't start it on his own, but when Mok-a starts, he follows, unable to control himself.

I tell them, "Please no, not that song." But Mok-a pretends not to hear me and finishes the song. "… Three thousand leagues of roses of Sharon / Daehan[98] people continue in Daehan forever." Although the tune is not quite correct, he finishes the song with a full, throaty voice. I am terrified, lest a neighbor or passerby hears it. Looking at the adults' frowning faces, he may also feel uncomfortable, "Dad, we

---

97 Starting words of the ROK national anthem.
98 Another name for Republic of Korea

shouldn't sing this song, should we?" It looked like he deliberately finished the song while fully knowing that he shouldn't have.

"Certainly not."

"Why not?" He asks, but I cannot answer. If somebody nearby says, "If you sing that song, the police will take you away," he would immediately respond by asking, "Why would they?" He has always been like that.

Then he raises his voice and sings, "Courage, courage, let's go forward / A gun in one hand and love in the other." This time Bong-a helps me, "Mok-a, that song is not good either." Mok-a is almost three and Bong-a is five.

"Then what should I sing?" Mok-a complains to his big brother and sometimes bursts into tears. Those are the only two songs he knows. Being forbidden to sing both songs has ruined his spirits. "Sing instead '*Jangbaek Mountains, blood stains on every ridge,*[99]'" Bong-a says, but Mok-a doesn't know the words, and that further aggravates his mood.

August 21, 1950.

The August 15th memorial speech by General Kim Ilsung that appeared in the Peoples Daily emphasizes, "The month of August should be made the month of liberation." When General Kim Ilsung delivers a speech, every word of it is printed in five-point font that covers the front and back side

---

99 Starting words of the DPRK anthem.

of the newspapers. It is another unique custom of this country to push out all other stories. People must worship every segment of those words and every turn of phrases as if they are the most precious rules.

Then, days after his speech, every organization in all walks of life responds. Brown-nosing stories about the speech, and articles about all occurrences of the society that support the speech's viewpoints are featured in all pages of the newspapers. The reason why farmers are working hard; why students are studying hard and not playing; why trains are running on full steam is all because they had welcomed General Kim Ilsung's speech and were moved by it. At least for now, they have not yet attributed the rising sun and twinkling stars to his speech. However, things like rain falling at the right time, and pigs producing a lot of piglets, etc. may still happen because an omnipotent god looks after our People's Republic, and he is so impressed with General Kim Ilsung's speech.

One thing I cannot forget from his speech is that he repeatedly emphasized to the public and to the front-line soldiers that the month of August should be designated as the 'Month of Liberation'. I thought the implication of the speech was, "If we don't conclude the war within this month, we may lose the opportunity for the victory." If you think about it more, it can also mean, "We don't have any more strength to hang on past this month." At the least, I can detect an impatient mindset behind his strong speech. This is an important data point in our assessment of the current situation.

August 22, 1950.

Son *sunsaeng* of the French Literature Department visited me. He had been to Ichun, Yujoo, and other remote places looking for food. He was limping with swollen feet and his hand was wrapped because of an injury from a bomb fragment. As he said himself, he looked like a defeated soldier.

I think he is around fifty years old. Thinking about this precious scholar of our country, walking a good hundred miles around the countryside under the scorching August sun braving many dangers, wearing a rucksack containing about half a bushel of barley, my heart ached. But he was rather composed, saying, "I am actually in a better situation. As an older fellow, I can safely go around scrounging up food. In the beginning, I was completely helpless, but I have gained confidence in life. Now I feel I can even do daily labor… anything.

"You ask why I went that far? It's because there is no way to get food within twenty-five miles of Seoul. People quicker than us have already scoured neighboring towns, leaving not a single grain available. However, there are lots of goods around. People from Seoul brought so many things like cotton cloth, velvet skirts, wristwatches, and other things that the farmers in the neighboring villages enjoy luxuries now.

"The toughest thing was crossing the Han River[100] on a ferry. American planes seem to have cut off even this primitive means of transportation. They target only ferries.

---

100 The north side of Seoul is more mountainous and grain production is low. It is better in the south side, but then one

When it appears there is a lull in air activities and the ferry starts moving, they somehow know and come back to attack us. If they fly low and circle around the boat, I am told that the swirl alone is enough to capsize the boat. Still, they fire machine guns, drop bombs... The loss of lives on the Han River is ever increasing. You ask why one wants to cross the river? What could I do? I cannot let the children die of hunger, so it is life or death for us. Back when we studied, who would have ever thought we would risk our lives on a ferry for a sack of barley?" Son *sunsaeng* said, laughing.

"There are planes bombing Seoul, but they are nothing compared to the bombings in farm villages. They are determined to cut off all supply lines, small or large, I imagine. All bridges were bombed, so oxen or horse carriages cannot move around anymore. They are pretty good at finding and bombing anything resembling a car. Use of oxen backs or horse backs is treated all the same. So, soldiers must move ammunition and food all on people's backs. I don't know how one can win a war under these conditions.

"If a person wears white clothes[101], they are safe to move around. They can skillfully distinguish military uniforms. How can they see such small details from so far above in the sky? The planes are no longer like those old planes. They even seem to maneuver in between tree branches and in between grass leaves. So, when we come across oxen, horses or soldiers, we stay away from them. It's not because we

---

has to cross the Han River to get there. The only bridge on the river was already destroyed at the start of the war.
101 Korean civilians typically wore white clothes. Other colors were rare.

are afraid of the oxen, horses, or soldiers, of course. Nowadays, I hear that many People's Army soldiers go about wearing white Korean clothes. Some say that the airplanes can see these soldiers even when they change their clothes, but that story may have come about because a regiment of soldiers wearing white clothes were bombed somewhere.

"There is one tragic story related to clothes-changing by soldiers of the People's Army…. On a mountain road somewhere in Kwangjoo, refugees gathered and sang the ROK anthem. No, not '… *the glorious morning in this country / full of silver and gold resources*[102]', but '…water of the East Sea dries out and Mount Baekdoo ….' How could they do that, you say? They certainly could and did. There may never have been such a time when the loyalty of people of the Republic of Korea was so aroused. Now, having been citizens of DPRK, everybody now is yearning for ROK. It is not that they are sentimental. 'Being sentimental' are words too luxurious for the refugees now. Constantly hungry, soaked wet by deluges, sleeping outside, their hardships go on. Why wouldn't they become desperately hopeless?

"Suffering is suffering, but on top of that, you never know when you might die. So, their sense of danger has been altered. Perhaps it could be a longing for the lost Republic of Korea, or perhaps it could be a reaction against the Democratic People's Republic of Korea, which started a civil war against its own people, burning their homes and belongings, pushing all of us into this life-and-death situation. When one person starts singing loudly with feelings of self-abandonment, *'the waters of The East Sea… the*

---

102 Verses of the national anthem of DPRK.

Mount Baekdoo...,' everybody joins him as if there is nothing to worry about and then it ends with wailing. Once, a disguised People's Army soldier saw this and took out a pistol and sprayed bullets - killing many people. Even though we had heard this story, we sang the same song and cried together when we were alone in the mountains."

August 23, 1950.

On the streets, there were posters claiming, "A Complete Liberation of Daegu." *As there is no news from the radio and newspapers, what was the source of this news?* When asked, the leftist people would say, "Daegu was liberated for sure, but our People's Republic of Korea would not officially announce it unless the occupation is so complete that the enemy cannot touch it again. That's why." It sounds like a made-up story to me.

When Bokkyoo said she was told to go south to Daegu as an advance party member of the Women's League, I admonished her, saying, "Even the announcements from the headquarters of the People's Army seem to show fighting still in Daboowon (*a town about 10 miles north of Daegu*). Why are you going there?"

She retorted, "No, there is a person who actually saw the liberated Daegu and came up last night. What more proof do you need?" I had more to say but kept quiet because even though she is my niece, at the same time she is also a cousin of Lee Suk.

August 24, 1950.

My father-in-law, who lives in the South side of the town, borrowed a bicycle from Kyunghee and went to Kwangjoo looking for food, but he came back empty-handed because the People's Army soldiers took the bicycle away. As similar stories were rampant, I had asked him to be careful when he left. But it happened all the same. As I know full well that Kyunghee invested all his belongings to buy this bike, we are now in a very embarrassing situation.

He had said as he was leaving, "I will not lose somebody else's property. If an old man like me plead with the police, they will listen to me unless they are not humans." He was caught on the road, resisted losing the bike and was taken to the People's Committee.

He wouldn't budge even when they said, "I don't want to hear any more. The army needs it urgently. So, if you don't listen, I will have to kill you as a counter-revolutionary." When the soldier pulled out a pistol, he still clung to the bike braving death until the guy pushed him aside and rode the bike away.

August 25, 1950.

It has already been a few days since the news about the liberation of Daegu. But the front line must be stuck in a stalemate as announcements from the Chosun Democratic People's Republic are not as lively as before and sound somehow subdued. Normally, the communist public relations machine makes grand claims spelling out town names:

"It's Poonggi in the morning and Yungjoo in the evening..." But they now use ambiguous and abstract words only.

'The Month of Liberation' which General Kim Ilsung boasted about has only a few days left. Announcements from the headquarters claim that they 'inflicted a severe blow to the enemy's survival capability'. They must be trying extremely hard to come up with different words only to talk about the same thing every day.

The fighting situation must have come to a turning point, but being isolated in this small town, I don't hear any news. Frustrated, I want to go out somewhere, but it wouldn't do any good to be captured on the road. Then a thought occurred: if I use the hilltops of our town to go to Sungbookdong, I should be able to reach Lee Byungdo *sunsaengnim*[103] without being seen.

I saw Kim Sanggee *sunsaengnim* there as well. I spent an enjoyable day with them exchanging information about current affairs and the whereabouts of some of our fellow scholars after June 25th.

"They misjudged the character of Anglo-Saxons in a big way. Once they hold on to something, they do not let it go until they see the end. Trying to tackle them can only be called naïve," said Lee *sunsaeng*.

---

103 A highly respected history scholar. One of his grandsons, Lee Jangmoo, was a classmate and good friend of the translator in high school and in college. He retired as the president of Seoul National University some years ago. Another grandson of his, Lee Woongmoo, worked with the translator for a while in US.

Kim *sunsaeng* forcefully said, "A few days before the North Koreans leave, we should hide someplace. They keep saying that Americans and South Koreans massacre people every time they retreat - I fear that must mean something ominous."

It is interesting to note, however, that even facing this uncertain future, the characters of those two people are in such a contrast. Lee *sunsaeng* relayed a story about a Mr. Han Kilun of North Korea who came to say that he agreed with Lee *sunsaeng*'s scholastic theory (about Samhan and Sagoon[104]) but could not speak out loud because of political pressure. Using this example, Lee *sunsaeng* appeared to not want to definitely take either side. On the other hand, Kim *sunsaeng* is emphatically opposed to the People's Republic.

At lunch, a rice soup with squash vine was served. The family buys and sells squash and they survive on soups like this with whatever is left over. Kim *sunsaeng*'s family did the same with melons, but they had lost their investment capital. For now, they say they survive by selling watches and clothes. However, if this goes on for another month, everybody will die of hunger. Both are such incomparable figures in our country. *Can a country survive with such abominable mistreatment of its scholars in this way?*

---

104 Old tribes in the Korean peninsula prior to the three Kingdom era which started in the first century BC.

August 26, 1950.

The land reform that has been publicized for more than a month is now completed. They had said that lands would be taken away from landlords and distributed to farmers without lands or to hired farmers. Personally, it didn't affect our vegetable field as I had changed its ownership to my in-laws beforehand. The orchard is okay as well because it is an orchard.

Still, it had been very hard to get a land certificate. farmer's co-op fees, certificate issuance fees, and land reform celebration fees, etc. were too costly for those of us without an income. Then there were investigations, meetings, and other such things that almost forced me to give up the land when the law was finally announced.

Our life, however, is getting more difficult. Today, there was an order that we should plant radish and cabbage seeds. Can't we farmers do our own farming without such orders? I listened to a person from local authority in disbelief. He said, "What should we do if even a person like you does not understand and help us? Everything in our People's Republic is based on a planned economy."

I said, "As you know, radish and cabbage seeding time has already passed in this area. If the land is moist, we could certainly plant those seeds now, but it has been dry for more than a month. Seeds planted in this dry and dusty field now are going to burn up and, if we wait for rain, we will miss the planting time completely. My land was originally a stream bed which cannot hold water for long. Every year I planted some of those, but it yielded no harvest. This year, I gave up on them and tried to plant squash instead so we could eat them until late in the year."

"Your situation is nothing more than your own, but the country's business is not handled just as you all wish. The government sets up a definite overall plan. It said that Jungreung-ri would plant radish seeds in so many hectares and cabbage seeds in so many hectares. We follow this plan and allocate this seed planting equitably among farmers. Whatever your situation is, you must plant them according to the plan, and then deliver your harvest allotment in the fall. Only then can the people working in government organizations and factories make *kimjang*[105] as well. We call this a planned economy." The official keeps insisting on the planned economy.

I said, "We are not trying to beg for our own benefit. It is past the seeding time; the weather is impossible for seeding and our land is not the right kind of land for planting radish and cabbage. Seeding is not the most important thing. We will have to produce the items we plant in the end, but all conditions are against planting those seeds right now. How can the planned economy possibly do the impossible?"

Getting annoyed, he rebuffed me saying, "We all know that, too. But we can never alter the nation's plan based on an individual's situation. Then the planned economy would

---

105 Kimjang is a large amount of Kimchee for each family made with cabbage and radish, fermented with salt and red pepper, prepared in the fall for consumption until the late spring. It was sometimes stored in a big earthen pot, buried underground, exposing the top part aboveground for daily access. It used to be a very important (and almost only) source of vegetables and vitamins during long winters in Korea.

go haywire. Destroying the planned economy is the same as destroying the nation. Therefore, an individual's comfort/discomfort, profit/loss cannot be allowed to create a crack in the planned vegetable production plan, can it?" He must be trying to elevate the level of our discussion to silence me.

"I never intended to talk about either a person's comfort and discomfort or profit and loss. If we take upon an objectively impossible task and then fail, it would be a loss to the nation. In these hard times, when food is not available, squash could be a good replacement. If we turn over the squash field to plant radish/cabbage seeds and then yield nothing, it would not be considered just an individual's problem." I reasoned.

He said, "If you really cannot turn over the soil yourself, the People's Committee will do it. Do understand." The discussion was terminated.

August 27, 1950.

Newspapers these days are laying the groundwork for enforcement of labor laws. First the land reform, now comes the labor laws... According to them, "Glorious democratic reform is being successfully completed one-by-one." In the papers appear analyses and pledges from representatives of every organization who do everything in their power to increase the efficiency of their work.

The main points of this law, according to the papers, are 'eight-hour workdays', 'uniform wages regardless of sex, age, or nationality', a 'labor insurance system', and 'special protection of pregnant women'. There are many good aspects of these laws, but we cannot understand why they are anxious to enforce either the land reform or the labor law so hastily. I don't understand their 'section-by-section implementation of the law', either. In China, the land is so vast and the war between the nationalists and the communists was so prolonged that they could want to adopt this 'enforce-where-possible' policy. But rushing the policy here as if there is no tomorrow is beyond my comprehension.

The land reform might be urgent, but how can one implement these laws when bombs are being dropped? Even in Jungreung-ri where people's consciousness level is considered high, a few embarrassing things have happened. *How can things be properly executed in some backward towns in the middle of the war? Is reform possible only with guns and machetes under the ominous sounds of bombs?*

Also, as frequently announced in the papers, do people really 'send their sons to the front line now that they got their lands?' I heard that this happened in China. But the situation here is different. I hear stories that some people who got land do not feel very comfortable now as they hear American planes overhead every day. I heard other stories that some people despise this hastiness in our small, palm-sized country.

I ask here: "When can you throw away your by-the-rulebook approach? The labor law is particularly a problem. In the turmoil of war, what kinds of factories are running other than those that are nationally run for military supplies? Are you going to insist on the eight-hour labor law even there? Can you actually do it? I am not an expert, but the eight-hour clause must be one of the most basic elements of the labor law. Why are you in a hurry to execute a law that you plainly know you can't execute?" *There are too many things happening in the politics of the country. Our brains cannot catch up with them.*

August 28, 1950.

In the People's Daily, there is an article with a picture of 'food transportation commandos.' The story goes like this: "Farmers from Yujoo, Kyunggi-do, enraged by hostile feelings against the robber American Imperialists and their Rhee Syngman traitors, thought hard for an idea about what they could do to defeat the enemy as quickly as possible. They decided they would collect food and deliver it to Seoul. People, including a seventy-year-old, a thirteen-year-old, and a woman with a nursing child carried two or three sacks on their backs under this scorching August sun and walked fifty miles to Seoul. Some died of sickness and others were killed by bombings on their way. But the more these tragic things happened, the stronger their resolve to defeat the invaders became."

I cannot tell whether such articles were prepared by a communist reporter as a boast, or by a secret counter-revolutionary who wanted to expose the hidden follies of the People's Republic. Could there be any stupid reader who still thinks the politics of the People's Republic are something commendable?

August 29, 1950.

Once the world changed, newspapers changed with it. In our obtuse thoughts, we wondered, "The old papers probably can just change their tone and remain as what they used to be?" At least a few left-leaning ones that struggled and did not enjoy freedom of speech under the Republic of Korea could have stayed and seen the new world. But they all were collectively forced to close overnight. The rightist ones may not have much to say on this, but how would the leftist ones feel when they seemed to have celebrated only to receive the death penalty? Because they were closed down overnight, there was no time for them to raise such issues as freedom of speech.

Taking over their buildings and equipment, the *Liberation Daily,* the *Chosun People's Paper*, the *Labor Newspaper,* etc, replaced them. These are all the party newsletters. Also, we seemed to have returned to the old time of having morning papers only. I don't know how to explain this complete control over the press. I didn't like the many useless newspapers during the ROK era as they seemed to waste paper in supporting sly businessmen or politicians only. I now rather longingly remember the old days of so many useless newspapers.

Contents of the newspapers are despicably awful. However big the papers are, they are no more than vehicles for propaganda. In more specific terms, they are no more than government PR flyers, combined with office announcements.

With no exception, the first page is allocated to the government's announcements, in particularly big letters. Examples include decisions made by the Chosun Democratic People's Republic and the Supreme People's Committee.

The names of Chairman Kim Doobong and Secretary General Kang Yangwook appear in big letters regularly. Articles include regulations concerning how to name 'heroes', definitions of 'meritorious services', and speeches by General Kim Ilsung, and contents of messages between General Kim Ilsung and the heads of other Soviet Union satellite countries. They also include laudatory remarks and dedicatory letters to General Kim Ilsung or Generalissimo Stalin.

In the remaining sections, reports from the headquarters of the People's Army, stories of the military feats of people who they call heroes, various political success stories from communist countries, inflammatory descriptions of demonstrations including labor strikes in liberal countries fill the space.

Occasionally, there appear articles about the UN General Assembly or the Security Council. But they, without fail, are centered around speeches by Malik[106] and their interpretations. They do not include any other general news. For example, if there were some recommendations from both Malik and Austin[107], Malik's recommendations are shown clearly while those of Austin do not appear at all.

In these situations, most of the time one could only guess the general context of Austin's message through the paper's abusive interpretations. Still more puzzling is that even Malik's speeches do not immediately appear. They appear in the papers three to four days or even a week later. It makes quite the contrast to practices in liberal countries where news appears on the same or next day and opinions from

---

106 Yakov Malik, the ambassador of the Soviet Union to the United Nations.
107 Warren Austin, US ambassador to UN.

both sides and from the world are clearly presented at the same time.

And it is rare to see the papers every day. If I go into town, I could buy one, but if you wait for delivery to your house, they'll bundle up several days' worth of papers into one package. Newspaper distribution centers and sales offices of the old, outlawed papers have been labeled and thus abolished as 'exploitative middle organizations'. Newspapers are now distributed only through the People's Committee. I sometimes chuckle at the similarity between this system and the way the Japanese Governor's Office used to distribute its newspapers.

This is how we would learn about world affairs a week or ten days after they take place. Furthermore, it is folly to try to learn all about world affairs. Day in and day out, the DPRK newspapers report only beautiful and benevolent politics and with utmost praise and tribute. This country is always full of ecstatic cheering these days and there are neither accidents nor iniquities found anywhere - even if we try our hardest to find them. At least that's how it is in the social section of the papers.

August 30, 1950.

Rain seems to have forgotten us completely and the moon is very bright every night. Taking advantage of these moonlit nights, they call frequent compulsory labor duties these days. They have us turn over the fields that did not follow the 'planned seeding' of radish and cabbage. This is undoubtedly done to force such seeding. The women willingly participated. The reason is that there would be edible by-products when fields of squash, pepper, and other vegetables are turned over.

"As the days are dry and as we don't know when we can seed radish and cabbage past their season, my hands trembled with guilt while raking up those thriving squash vines. The squash could have saved a few starving souls right now," Kwanggee's grandmother said.

Following several days of a lingering sickness, an elderly member of the neighborhood passed away. According to town rumors, he died of hunger.

I read the book *The Gods are Thirsty* by Anatole France. The world of the 18th century during the time of the French Revolution is so like our current affairs that I was able to finish the book with renewed interest.

August 31, 1950.

Oh Doosoo *koon* paid me a visit. It gave me a great pleasure to see he had survived, and I welcomed him warmly. He has a friend who listens to a short wave stealthily and, according to this friend, MacArthur had demanded that General Kim Ilsung surrender under uncompromising conditions, declaring that he would finish the 'Korean Affairs' within a couple of weeks. There are only a few days left in those two weeks. The Americans not only severed the land supply routes of the People's Army with their aircraft bombings but also sealed off all the coastlines. The North Koreans no longer have the strength to continue the war anymore. Soldiers from the UN and the Republic of Korea turned the war into a total counterattack and have made victories continuously. One story says that they have already crossed the Choopoong-Ryung Mountain and reached Yungdong[108].

"How do you see this war, Sir?" he asked.

"First, it is sad that people of the same bloodline have killed each other; second, it is sadder still that when Americans and Koreans are fighting against each other drawing blood, there is an increasing number of Koreans who root for the Americans," I replied.

---

108 This means that the UN and ROK troops are now pushing back North away from the Nakdong River.

September 1950

September 1, 1950.

September 1! It's already autumn. The weather is cool with no rain. It seems like a dream to have survived the summer. Actually, it was more like a nightmare than a dream. Awakened by the noise of bombings, a man nearing his forties is wetting his cheeks with tears while watching a particularly bright moon. Considering the future of our people, I feel like bursting into wailing. Amid fratricide, foreign forces have joined to turn our country into a field of slaughter and destruction.

Even at this moment, how many are killed or become beggars; how many houses are destroyed or burned down? During the past 5 years, how much did we add to the houses and factories the Japanese abandoned? Now we are destroying them.

Even if the war ends right now, what are we going to do to clothe ourselves and what will we eat to survive? If the situation favors the side of the allied troops, there may be relief food available; but if the favor shifts to the other side...the knowledge that I myself would die of hunger makes me indescribably desolate. *Either to become a beggar or to die of hunger. Is this our fate?*

If an outside force invaded us, we could at least have a target for our indignation. Instead, it darkens my heart when I consider how we, the South and the North, were manipulated by other countries to start killing our own brothers. There are undoubtedly conflicts everywhere in the world these days, but why should we be the ones suffering the most? I question the people who had insisted, as if reciting Buddhist invocations, that this was the only way for all people to live better. Does this way have to go through murder and arson, brother against brother and total destruction of the country?

It's possible the North didn't know at the beginning that it would turn out this way. They probably thought the Republic of Korea would be finished within a few days if they pushed the South very hard with the tanks and cannons they got from the Soviet Union. As for America, following a similar example in China, it would hurriedly leave the Korean peninsula. Unification would be much better than two separate states. They should unite the country regardless of the sacrifice to follow as a consequence. And if unification is to be accomplished, they should be the one to lead the way. If not, there will be no place for them. This is how the upper echelon of the North might have viewed things.

They also probably thought that unless they acted, Chosun would become spoils for the Imperialist Americans. They must have been quite anxious and fretful. When American newspapers and magazines reported around the beginning of the year that it was the policy of the American State Department[109] to exclude Korea from the American Defense

---

109 "Secretary of State Dean G. Acheson's speech at the National Press Club on January 12, 1950 was among the most important and controversial US policy statements in the early history of the Cold War in East Asia. In it, he defined the American 'defensive perimeter' in the Pacific as a line running through Japan, the Ryukyus, and the Philippines. This denied a guarantee of US military protection to the

Line, they must have further strengthened their resolve to attack the South.

Whatever their reasons were, their crime should never, ever be erased not only from our memory but also from history, considering they made an erroneous political judgment and acted rashly and recklessly, butchering fellow countrymen and burning our homeland to ashes. If they are living animals with blood and tears, they should be shedding the bitterest tears of remorse now.

But I say this only after having seen the results. Thinking back on their original motivations, I find no difference between the People's Republic and Republic of Korea. Didn't both of them raise and shake their flimsy fists, advocating either the invasion into the South or the conquering of the North respectively?

There is no need to mention DPRK's ceaseless planning and propaganda regarding the invasion to the South as everybody already knows about them. They became more obvious when they turned them into a reality. On the other hand, some people in important positions in the South had always advocated for the conquering of the North. I still remember their rants that, if there was nobody holding us back, we could take Pyungyang within a week.

The only difference between the two sides should be that one used whips upon their people to prepare for the war day and night while the other just made loud but hollow boasts without preparing for the North's invasion. The overlord

---

Republic of Korea (ROK) and the Republic of China (ROC) on Taiwan." -- James Matray, The Journal of Conflict Studies, 2002.

states -- China and the Soviet Union -- of one side gave an irresponsible order to their puppet -- the North -- directing it to wrestle with the South regardless of the consequences. In the meantime, the overload state -- the US -- of the other side aggressively dissuaded any unprovoked actions of its puppet -- the South -- presumably concerned with any unforeseeable consequences.

Another difference is that, on one side, once an inviolable directive came down that was reverently supported by the puppet, no one could express any second opinions however reasonable they might have been. Officials in the government or general citizens could only join their voices and recite in unison, "We are completely awe-stricken as it is what it is to be." Even if one is convinced that a mistake was made in the assessment of the political situation, he would have risked his neck first if he insisted on his conviction. Thereupon he had to follow without fail the order of 'Our Most Brilliant[110]'.

But then, how about the other side? Was there really a firmly established democratic principle of freedom of speech? We can't say for sure. When Dr. Cho - - (*sic*) presented an article in the Seoul Daily, publicly advocating the conquering of the North, how many university professors who frowned on this article wrote back begging to differ? Not even one. Of course, given the political passivity of professors who are steeped in the force of habit, there may not have been many who would've been carried away by a 'rash impulse' to rebut the article. But, even if there were

---

110 A title bestowed upon General Kim Ilsung.

somebody, would that person have been accepted under the political atmosphere at the time?

September 2, 1950.

Somebody said that one can hear broadcasts from places other than Seoul using even a primitive radio. When we tried, we could catch one from the Republic of Korea and one from Japan. "We wish we knew of this before." Wife and I smiled.

When we heard the words, "The voice of freedom, the broadcasts of the Republic of Korea," we choked up. *Really! Were we attached to ROK this much?*

"People who remain in the communist world, please do not go near military facilities and stay alive so we can enjoy better days together." Wife and I cried, holding hands. We have become quite sentimental.

As we listened to the different broadcasts, our lives seem to have brightened a lot; but listening to them is very hard work indeed. Even though the weather has cooled a bit, it is still a hot summer. We take turns listening under heavy blankets. As we listen for a prolonged time, our knees become numb and sweat flows; but hoping to catch some fantastic news, we are not aware of the pain. Now and then, one of us will go outside the house to make sure no sounds leak out.

First, we adjust the frequency and control the volume so that it is neither too high nor too low. As if there is somebody interfering with it, it flips to a different broadcast every now and then. This happens whenever a story comes to a really meaty part, without fail. We turn the knob around frantically, but sometimes a horrendously loud and high sound blares out and scares us.

The broadcasts of the People's Republic, as Mr. Yoo Yul said, are forceful but disgusting because they repeat the same stories every day. What they repeat these days are: the anger against the invading American Imperialists and the resolve to defeat them; results of elections at various levels of People's Committees; the progress of the land reform project; the gratitude of farmers who received land; touching emotions regarding the execution of the labor law; signature collection movements for execution of traitors, etc.

Names of speakers change daily, but the content is so identical that it is as if they had come from the same template. After listening to them twice, I felt like throwing up by the third time. If they really think about it, they could do better. Even if only one person writes all of these stories, he could add a bit of different slant each time.... This is unfortunate for the People's Republic.

It perhaps may not be because of the inadequacy of the writer, but because the freedom of expression is so severely limited?

September 3, 1950.

Already, several of the village youths who had left as volunteer soldiers have come back as wounded soldiers. Some are limping, and others have lost hands. Others came back in wretched shape with bandages wrapped around their shoulders. Still, they said they are in a better situation compared to others who are nowhere to be found - some have died or could not come back because of their severe injuries. Hearing this, the entire village suddenly turned into a sea of tears. The misery of the war now feels as if it is cutting deep into our bones.

All of them were injured at the Yungdong front line. It is amazing that they walked some one hundred and twenty miles in this hot weather with little medical help. This provides us with a few hints.

— *There are more wounded soldiers than they had expected; hospital facilities are in short supply; there is no way to build new facilities while transportation systems are completely paralyzed.*

Returning soldiers would not say anything openly but listening to stories given only to their family and friends, the current front line is a fight between men and machines. Unless there is some kind of new development, they cannot sustain this type of war any longer. This is what we had expected.

I could hear public anger on why they are providing noble human lives as limitless fodder for American cannons.

September 4, 1950.

A school messenger came to get my stamp on my July salary document. They prepared a document for July but with no cash payment. The method to calculate the salary amount could not have been conceived by anybody other than the People's Republic.

As we were kicked out at the August screening and had therefore been regular employees until July, it would be reasonable that they would pay us for July. But their method of calculation is to pay a fraction of our 20,000-*won* monthly salary based on the number of days we were actually present at the school. For example, as I went to the school for eleven days, they would pay me 7,095 *won* only. We were being paid salaries on a daily basis. This was not in the contract....

But if this is the way of the People's Republic, I give up on raising an issue. While we, who have been with the school from before the arrival of the North army, are treated in such an unheard-of harsh way, sixteen new professors such as Chung Chanyung and Chae Heekook will receive their full pay of 20,000 *won*. It was the first time I had heard they were hired, en masse, and they only began working at the school in late July at the earliest *or* in August. I knew this, and it was also confirmed by the words of the messenger who went to the school every day. What's funnier is that many of them had not even shown up at the school yet. I would imagine that, regardless of the actual initial attendance, they can assign any employment date and pay full salaries starting from July. But how could they pay full salaries to those whose names were not in the July attendance book while paying daily salaries to those who have been at the school from long before? I don't understand how this can happen. Nobody but the People's Republic could think like this and no one other than Mr. Lee Myungsun could even dream it up.

Mr. Lee Myungsun has frequently remarked that we should reconfigure our brains, but it will be impossible to bow our heads and say, "You are absolutely right," to this. We are the ones who got kicked out. We did not even expect any money from our July salaries. Even if they offered, not many would go to the school to collect. *Isn't everybody kind of shying away from the school now? However much we want to get our salaries, how could we go to the school and request payment?* It has left us with a really bitter taste in the mouth to be insulted this way while they knew full well they didn't have to pay us anyway.

I told the messenger, "As I haven't been a day laborer from the beginning, I have no reason to receive daily salary. I will therefore give up the July salary."

He said it was hard for him to have walked three miles looking for me and begged while smiling, "Please stamp the document so I don't have to repeat the visit again. What can you do about it, Sir? In this kind of world, don't make an issue of it and just close your eyes and stamp it." I relented.

September 5, 1950.

The leftist propaganda has been explaining the situation as follows: "The reason the front line has not been moving faster is because the moon was clear, and the days were bright. If we have three rainy days, we could wipe out Daegu and Busan, no problem…" The rain has been the leftists' object of longing for a while.

"When it rains, whether it be September or October, plant radish and cabbage seeds according to the assigned areas. Whether it is a bit early or late is not an issue. When one makes possible the impossible, it shows the fervor of the people." To enforce the planned seeding, they had made us turn over the squash and pepper fields. *Oh, how we all longed for rain!*

That rain came today. We planted the radish and cabbage seeds in the rain. It is obvious that it will not work, considering the local weather, the type of soil, and the characteristics of these vegetables, but I went along anyway begrudgingly, not wanting to raise any unwanted flags with the authorities. But the actual problem is not with the planting. We can tolerate the fact that we cannot eat the squash that would have been a help with the food supply right now and the extra expense in tilling the fields… but it would be a big problem if they require in-kind taxes on this in the fall.

The rumor may not be groundless that the farmers who had received land earlier are also agonizing over the planned planting, in-kind taxes and 'voluntary offerings.'

September 6, 1950.

I have heard so many times that it is now ingrained in my head that, once one volunteers to the Volunteer Army, they will supply their remaining family with special food distributions. It did not stop there as the story went that the People's Committee would also take care of all aspects of their livelihood. However, up to the time when volunteer soldiers came home after getting injured on the front line, I have not heard of any food distribution—not even a single grain—to their families. Daegyoo brothers went to the front line, but my sister's household of women and children still subsisted on the soup of dried radish leaves.

In my neighbor Yoo's household, two young working men went to the front line, leaving a couple who are in their seventies, a sick woman and children at home - seven all together. They have been starving for so long that they all just lie in a row, bereft of any strength. The household of Mr. Lee Yoonki, well known as a 'democratic family', brings in food in big sacks although none of their several brothers has volunteered for the army and gone to the front line. I am told that the smell of roasting food turns their neighbors' stomach upside-down every evening.

American planes visit Seoul's night sky with no worry of anti-aircraft guns these days. As a consequence, the control of lights on the ground at night has become very strict. If there are any small lights that leak out, the town gets excited with fear and volunteer soldiers stationed at the Kyungsin school rush over and threaten to shoot the offenders. But the above-mentioned Yoos deliberately turn their lights on and do not turn them off regardless of who comes to the house.

They say, "Shoot if you will. Rather than enduring the agony of dying in this way of hunger, it would be better to die of a gunshot. If a bomb comes down and kill us all, it would be far better." Even the People's Army soldiers could not do anything. Neighbors are very uncomfortable too but cannot say anything. There must be many people nowadays who could not care less about their own lives anymore.

September 7, 1950.

There is no household in our neighborhood that does not pick and dry acorns. Climbing up to the Bookhan Mountains and picking acorns has become a full-time job for everyone. There is the additional recruiting of volunteer soldiers in the mountains probably because they know they will find many people there. After a few days, young men have decided not to go there anymore. Thus, this hard work is again taken up by old people, women, and children.

After picking acorns, we peel and leave them in water for a long time to leech out poisonous elements. We then dry and pulverize them to make cakes or jelly to eat. This used to be an age-old traditional measure to prepare for lean times. But we are now suffering from a famine in the middle of the 20th Century. After a full day of peeling, the undersides of our fingernails become numb and painful. The pain itself is not what we cannot bear but it is the thought of it that brings tears to our eyes.

I remember what Jungkyoo, who is only thirteen years old, had once said: "You Uncle said you will just study, but you starve even after you studied. I will therefore not study but will join the Communist Party."

September 8, 1950.

It has already been more than a week after 'The Liberation Month' that they used to tout so much. The two-week ultimatum date America is said to have given the People's Army to surrender has also passed. For the past month, it appears that the front line has been moving back and forth near Daboowon. The occasional broadcasts from the South and from Japan that we listen to in hiding do not offer any special news. The headquarters of the People's Army repeat their claims that they have destroyed the enemy's ability to survive. When the bombings stopped completely a few days ago, we were beginning to nurse a secret hope that some change might have occurred. But fierce bombings have come back again these days.

As I have become so curious about everything, I set out to see Mr. Kim Ilchool with the hope of hearing any recent news. I climbed Jungreung Hill, went through Sungbookdong Valley, and knocked at the gate of Mr. Kim's house in Hyehwa-dong. Mr. Kim had gone to Pyungyang on a long training mission, but his father, Mr. Kim Choonmyung, gave me a joyous welcome. He had always been concerned about not having enough space in his house. A next-door neighbor happened to be forced out by a transfer order recently. He was able to secure this empty house and opened a pharmacy and a small shop as well.

This older gentleman holds strong hostility towards America. He bitterly lamented, "If they had not come in but had just left us alone, we would have been unified a long time ago and we all could have started new lives together with our fellow countrymen. Now this enormous sacrifice is brought upon us because of their unnecessary meddling...." In a way, his words made sense.

I asked, "Do you have news about your second son, Taehong?" He answered that, in the beginning when the People's Army came down, he was told they had found him. But no matter how hard his family tried to visit and communicate with him, he could not be located and then his trail disappeared. He must have died, but it is not clear whether he died at the hands of the Republic of Korea or of the People's Republic. He had ample reason to be hated by either side: Mr. Kim Taehong had come down to the South as one of the three-member team[111] of the North with a peace appeal document a few days before June 25th. They were arrested and then 'defected to the South and turned against and accused the North'. This 'news' was broadcast by the Seoul Broadcasts.

An interesting story by Mr. Kim:

"Daegu is completely surrounded by our (*the North*) troops and no supply lines exist. American planes drop food and ammunition there, but sometimes one of those packages drops into our camp. The People's Army soldiers eat as many chocolates as possible."

September 9, 1950.

Whenever I have to go out these days, I do so only after we send the children out first to make sure there is nobody in the alley. When I come back, I hide in the trees and watch the town before coming in. In case somebody from town comes looking for me, Wife would say, "He went to the countryside looking for food."

---

111 Please refer to the diary of June 25th. They were DPRK envoys to ROK with an 'insincere' peace proposal who 'defected (possibly by torture)' to ROK.

We forbid the children from speaking the word, 'Abba (*Daddy*)'. I spend my days with my books in the back corner of my study or on the backside veranda of the main room.

Kyunghee, my cousin who used to work at the Chosun Financial Union, cannot obtain food at his boarding house. Because it is worrisome to leave a young man on streets, we brought him in, and he now stays with us. Things are more dangerous for him than for me. But for now, even the neighbors do not know that he is with us.

I made a little hideout out of a pile of bricks in the backyard and when a suspicious person comes, I'd go there to hide. But as it is not comfortable, I lifted a small section of wooden floor in the house and placed a straw bag and pillows inside. We two cousins hide ourselves lying down when there comes a knock at the gate. We are living a pitiful life in every sense of the word.

Then, I was accidentally discovered by the People's Army soldiers today. Wife went with the two boys, Kibong and Kimok, to a nearby stream to wash diapers while Kyunghee stayed inside the study. I was lying down on the back veranda keeping an eye on Kihyub who was playing by himself inside. I heard some murmuring from Hanboon's house (*next-door neighbor*) in the direction of soy sauce crocks. When I looked up casually, two soldiers were up in a Chinese date tree eating dates, looking down my way as they were talking to each other.

At that moment, I felt a shudder flowing through my body. In broad daylight, they saw a young man doing nothing without making any sound as if he was trying to avoid attention. *What suspicions would they harbor, wondering what my status is and what I'm doing?* Just a couple days ago when they mobilized the town people to dig an air raid shelter in the front yard of the Kyungsin School, they complained that the work did not progress much because only women and children had come.

The People's Army is a fighting unit, but it does not seem to operate alone, it seems to have a symbiotic relationship with the Women's Union and the Chosun Youth Alliance, as they always move together... When I thought of the possibility of being found out by any of the others, I feared as if everything had been for naught... I felt as if what strength I had was deserting my body.

After worrying about it with Wife when she came back, we opened the front gate and made some noise as if somebody was leaving - we had an excuse prepared in case something happened later. She pretended that a guest had visited. We moved into a room and started opening peapods with the children. We were all still unsettled when we heard loud noises coming from Hanboon's house. I moved quickly into the hole under the floor and asked Wife to check on what was happening. Later, she related to me what happened ...

When Hanboon's family returned home from their outing, they saw the soldiers in the tree eating un-ripened dates and Hanboon's mother screamed at them. But the soldiers, with the audacity of thieves, slapped the cheek of Hanboon's mother berating her, "What kind of hostility do you have against People's Army soldiers? You scream like hell in the middle of town just because we had a few dates?" They did not know that she had been beside herself after her husband had recently died of starvation.

In the evening, Hanboon came with a large bowl of green dates. When asked what it was for, he said, "Because Mother got slapped on the cheek because of the dates, she picked the tree clean in anger. When they ripen, we planned to exchange them for food. But they may not stay there now even if we leave them there."

September 10, 1950.

One practice I like most of the People's Republic is their use of Korean words only. They do not use Chinese characters at all. However, a strange thing is that the number of Chinese-character-derived Korean words [112] did not decrease at all. They rather chose to use newly manufactured

---

112 Korean words fall into two different categories. One is indigenous Korean, with the sound and meaning totally different from any other language. Examples are namoo (tree) and baram (wind). These words are written in Korean letters and of course is spoken in the Korean language. The other type of words originated from Chinese characters and their meanings. Individual Chinese characters are combined to form new words that reflect a certain combined meaning of the individual characters.

When Chinese-based Korean words are used, South Koreans print them either in Korean alphabets emulating sounds of Chinese characters, or in their original Chinese characters. North Koreans had decided not to use Chinese characters at all in all of their communications and printed everything in Korean alphabets only. Prof. Kim liked this Korean-alphabet-only approach in that Koreans can use their own language alone, without the cumbersome practice of switching words from Korean to Chinese back and forth.

However, according to Prof. Kim, the North had recently coined words which are more difficult to understand. For example, I hear the word *dokbohoe*[113] all the time, without being able to guess correctly what it means. There are many such words, such as *kyungkaksung* or *changbalsung,* and they all sound strange to my ears.

Some scholars criticized this practice saying, "The policy of 'Korean alphabet only' is the inevitable result of a 'keep-people-ignorant policy'. To be more precise, after eliminating educated people from the system and working only with

---

many new words using Chinese characters, sometimes with awkward or unclear combinations of Chinese characters. A syllable in a Korean-letter-only word can represent multiple Chinese characters. Readers are reminded of the earlier example of one phonetic syllable 'mi' that can mean beauty, rice, or many others. As a consequence, meaning of a new awkward combination of syllables may become difficult to decipher if it is hard to guess which Chinese characters were meant to be used in the new word.

So, people who are not familiar with newly manufactured North Korean words can easily get confused. People who don't know how to read Chinese characters have tougher times.

113 Another example of the confusion is shown here. Look at the word 'dokbohoe'. According to Naver Chinese Character Dictionary, the Korean syllable 'dok' can represent at least 29 different Chinese characters and meanings. 'bo' can have 40 different meanings. 'hoe' has 60 different meanings. Unless one can guess all three syllables correctly, one cannot understand the meaning of the word. If the word was not put together rationally to begin with, it creates real confusion. Prof. Kim, who had translated Chinese books into Korean, could not guess what this word 'dokbohoe' meant.

ignorant laborers and farmers, they cannot but use only Korean. The reason why they are still using Chinese-derived Korean words is because ignorant people can only recite directives using these words like parrots without clear understanding of their precise meaning, and they are certain to recite 'incantations' as if they are hypnotized." I don't like this kind of thinking because, like the communists, they are looking at world matters from a distorted point of view and interpreting them in the worst way.

In the North, there are people like Mr. Kim Doobong, Mr. Lee Keugro, and Mr. Kim Byungje; and writers like Mr. Lee Kiyung, Mr. Lee Taejoon, Mr. Han Sulya, Mr. Ahn Hoenam, Mr. Kim Namchun, Mr. Lim Wah, Mr. Lee Wonjo and many other talented scholars and writers. So why do they sustain such an old-fashioned method of expression? In time, even without exerting much effort, our ways of speaking would get smoother and gentler if one chooses to keep using Korean characters only. *Why do they keep on using so many convoluted Chinese-derived words?*[114]

Only recently, I began to possibly understand why. Moscow-published Korean language books such as *Communist Party History* or *Lenin Selections* use exactly the same expressions as now does the North. Words like *kyungkaksung* or *changbalsung* must have come from there. These words

---

114 Prof. Kim's major field was Korean and Oriental histories. But Korean language was almost as important to him. He had organized a study group of indigenous Korean words before the war. His wife, a Korean language scholar, started working in this field as a professor after the war. Some thirty-five years later, she would publish a four-volume treatise, 'Study of the Origin of Korean Language'.

must have been translated by local Koreans in Moscow who might not have been familiar with the current polished style of the Korean language. They must have used a version of Korean language that is two or three generations old. Since the North Korea directly imports the culture of Moscow and considers it sacred, it can neither criticize nor improve upon what is handed down to it by Moscow.

September 11, 1950.

After they took Beeru away, we ate the chickens one by one while giving some away to friends. There is no more chicken left now. It is with the same idea as was had by our neighbor who was getting rid of un-ripened dates. We sent a goat to Jungyong in Donam-dong and a rabbit to the in-laws across town. As there was nothing to feed it, we let the cat free, too. Our 'zoo' house is now deserted. Only four ducks remain. Because we had worked hard to hatch them in the spring and the children are still fascinated by them, we just kept them.

It was past midnight. Somebody was shaking our gate and yelling. At night, we normally pretend to sleep and don't open the gate regardless of visitors. But the knocking was so loud and prolonged, and because the visitor kept saying, "Kibong-a, it's me, me.", that Wife reluctantly went out.

In the meantime, I did not have time even to go under the floor, but only to sneak under a bunch of burning bush branches leaning against the fence. I guessed nobody could see me in the dark. The Wife's conversation at the gate must have gone on for a long time. I had not known there were so many mosquitos under the bundle of burning bush branches. They were biting my face, neck, arms and feet indiscriminately. In short time, I developed blisters all over my body. Their bites are immediately painful and itchy. There must be many types of mosquitoes in the bush. Still, I had to stay quiet and endure it.

After a while, Wife came back and took the ducks out. Then I heard the gate closing and the latches being bolted. I finally felt liberated, but my entire body was in ruin.

The person who visited was the daughter of Mr. Wang across the street. She had brought a cook of the People's Army who needed to prepare some drink and food for Army officers staying in her house. The officers wanted a chicken and when they were told there was no chicken, they wanted a duck instead. The deal between her and Wife for the ducks must have taken a long time. For the ducks, she brought dried seaweed. The deal was not a bad one, but I went through an unpleasant ordeal for it as a consequence.

The daughter of Mr. Wang used to work for the Korea Youth Organization. Now she is running around looking for drink and food for the officers of the People's Army. I am sure even she may not resist a wry smile.

September 12, 1950.

Wife went to a meeting to elect a 'people's judge.'

Here a 'judge' is like a judge in a jury system. Koyang-koon[115] is chosen to elect one judge for the state of Kyunggi Province. It, in turn, named Soongin-myun as 'its democratic *myun* of Koyang-koon' and asked it to do the honor of selecting a judge. Soongin-myun, in turn, named Jungreung-ri as 'its democratic town' and asked it to do the job. For our town it is such a glorious honor, but the election was quite strange. *After this, they would say we elected our judge with our own hands....*

I do not know the details of the election process as I didn't see it myself. According to Wife, it was once again the same method used when they selected the People's Committee members. Two candidates came up. One is our *ban* leader, Mr. Lee Yoonki, and the other is a person named Mr. Cho. The election committee must have favored Mr. Lee and introduced him first for a vote. More than half of the people raised their hands. At Mr. Cho's turn, there were more hands raised than for Mr. Lee, but the committee crushed their votes saying one cannot vote twice. In the end, Mr. Lee was the winner. People were dumbfounded because Mr. Cho was superior to Mr. Lee in age, education, personality and experience.

Regarding Mr. Lee, I am surprised we have had such an 'honorable person' in our own neighborhood.

---

115 "Here, "*koon*" is not a title for a person as used in the diary elsewhere but refers to a geographical area. This is another example of a Chinese-driven Korean word having different meanings. Koon, *myun* and *ri* refer to jurisdictional geographical areas of successively smaller sizes. For example, a province has several *koons*, a *koon* has several *myuns*, and a *myun* has several *ris*."

He is around forty years old. According to the introduction at the time of the People's Committee election, he had not even finished primary school. He is our *ban* leader, and I know him to be nearly illiterate. His experience is only the work as a *ban* leader and his occupation is the owner of a small store. He does not seem to have much of any revolutionary fighting experience. His two brothers and a sister had been in and out of prison before, but after June 25th, his family became very powerful as a 'democratic family.' He is now a member of the Jungreung-ri People's Committee and also our town leader. He has often been intoxicated these days but now he will be the judge of Kyunggi Province. What a meteoric rise in the world!

He will not be able to understand lawsuits even if they are written in Korean. *How are people like him going to preside over trials?* Perhaps it may well be possible if we follow Choi Bongrae *koon's* edict, "The fairness and validity of a trial is not the issue."

Mr. Lee is now called the "King of Jungreung-ri." He actually is, indeed.

September 13, 1950.

Read *Various Problems of History* today.

September 14, 1950.

After the breakout of the war, another challenging issue for us concerns doctors. Dr. Kim Sungsik of Soongin Clinic who had been treating our family's ailments disappeared early with his family. Being a gentle man and a faithful Christian, he imbued his patients with a feeling of relaxed comfort. But he disappeared at the start of the war like smoke.

In our village, he must have been the only one who had moved to the South with his family before the war. According to rumors, Hanmindang (Korea Democratic Party) had told all its members to evacuate before the fall of Seoul. Could it be true he was a member of Hanmindang? I know he aggressively supported Mr. Cho Byungok during the August 30th election, but he has always kept Mr. Kim Koo[116]'s picture on his table which kept me wondering about his political inclinations.

There was another person we used to visit in emergencies, Mr. Cho Kwanghyun of Severance University, who used to live close to our house. I think he had a degree, because he was known as Dr. Cho in town. He has been missing since June 27th after he went to the school. His wife spends her days in tears assuming he is dead.

There was a rumor concerning him: "When the People's Army came down, he was treating wounded South Korean soldiers at the school. Northern soldiers came and demanded the patients to be handed over in order to kill them off. When he refused, he was shot on the spot being branded as a counter-revolutionary." The wife fainted at this rumor. She was born in a well-known, very wealthy house in Chosun, the Kims of Anak, and she did not know any hardship

---

116 Mr. Cho Byungok and Mr. Kim Koo were prominent politicians in ROK who didn't see each other eye-to eye before the war.

while growing up. She is now struggling with the care of her young children with no food. She miscarried a baby at news of her husband and now lies in a sickbed.

There are certain things we thought we knew, but it turned out we were wrong. I thought Dr. Cho and Mr. Suh Kwangwook were very close to each other in this town. Dr. Cho would react vehemently against anything related to communism and, whenever there was an opportunity, he would convey his feelings against them to us. So much so we would sometimes point out to him that he was leaning too much toward the right. Now he disappeared while the war was going on and Mr. Suh is the Chairman of the People's Committee and a big shot in the Communist Party.

Dr. Cho was a forthright person in nature and, beyond offering criticism of the left, he would also have unloaded all his ill feelings against leftists to Mr. Suh. Mr. Suh must have put up with him going along with these curses day and night while remaining close friends for years. Anyway, I wonder what would have happened if Dr. Cho was still with us here.

Another doctor, Mr. Koh Heebong, the Obstetrics Department Head at the Red Cross Hospital, is a descendant of a noble family. Being educated in Japan, he speaks Korean like Japanese people do. His young wife, often wearing a blue skirt, is a student at a women's medical university. These two stayed in Seoul when the war broke out. Both have now been conscripted by the military and are working there. They are not with us anymore.

There used to be a clinic called Jungreung Clinic in the north of Soongin Clinic. We never had any contact with it before. Now that all the other clinics are gone, Wife must have taken Hyub-a to that place. Returning home, she said both the husband and the wife there worked as doctors and so they must be 'commies' (*communists*). Asked why she thought so, she said, "A Republic of Korea flag on the wall map has been erased." I quipped, "Wouldn't everybody do that nowadays?" and she laughed, "I know, but somehow they looked so to me."

The sound of the word, 'commies', had not been that offensive until only a while ago. I was secretly hoping the communists would be something that could straighten out the ever-corrupt government of the Republic of Korea and thus give our people some hope. *What could be the reason for such a drastic change in the feeling that word gives me in just two or three months?* According to Wife, the doctor couple in Jungreung Clinic must indeed be communists as their treatment of patients is not very focused and, even while holding stethoscopes, they always seem to be waiting to answer the call of political horns and to march out drumming. She could not trust them as doctors.

In the meantime, a new Inmin Clinic opened. When the owner of Soongin Clinic, Mr. Kim Sungsik, fled during the war, his older brother, along with an anemic nurse from Wonjoo, began receiving patients. They were branded as counter-revolutionaries in early August, and the People's Committee took over their building and all of the equipment to open this new Inmin Clinic. All of the chairs and beds had been taken away by the Committee, and important machines were shipped away to other places. The newly opened clinic is just a shell.

Before, it was just the doctor and two nurses who had adequately managed the hospital and were always greeting patients with smiles; but now there are additional workers: an administrator, an accountant, and an errand boy. I did not know there were so many young men still around in the People's Republic. What is their status and why are they not taken to the Volunteer Army, despite doing little work? These individuals look quite healthy, as if they are from another world while most people are weak, suffering from severe hunger.

As these plump and menacing-looking youths have little work, they sit around chess boards even during working hours. If someone says, "I came here to collect a bill," they would say, "This is lunch time. Come back after one o'clock."

After one o'clock, they say, "We are eating now. Wait outside." And if somebody brings an urgent patient early in the morning, they would say, "This is before opening time. Come back after nine." When they get there after nine, they say, "The doctor is not here yet, so wait here." If somebody requests a home visit, "A home visit? When things are this busy?" If one gets there just past five, they say, "We are closed. Come tomorrow," even though the doctor, the nurses, the office person, the accountant, and the errand boy are still there.

This kind of bureaucracy may not necessarily exist everywhere in the People's Republic and the Inmin Clinic might be a case of an extraordinary exception. However, I feel this 'nationalization of all businesses' begs further study.

September 15, 1950.

There is a new word we have learned: 'self-surrender'. When order was restored after the People's Army came into Seoul, there were posters everywhere in the streets conveying the following message: "Anybody who once worked as officers of the Republic of Korea, including soldiers, policemen, members of the Korea Youth Organization, members of the People Protection Organization and any others who worked for ROK, please self-surrender. We will receive them unconditionally and their safety is guaranteed." Mr. Choi, brother-in-law of Hong *koon*, was arrested because he had worked as the deputy chief of the Protection Organization and did not surrender himself. I do not know his current whereabouts.

Many people prepared self-surrender documents and reported to police stations. Some of them have been released quickly, but there are also many who are still incarcerated. Among those who had been released and felt at ease thereafter, were some who were taken in again. In our town, a man who was the head of a certain department in the ROK Department of Business and Technology, self-surrendered and has never returned since. His family cries all the time, "Didn't they say, if he self-surrenders, there would be unconditional acceptance?" But there is no place to plead his case.

September 16, 1950.

Gentle cannon sounds are coming from somewhere. I can hear them more during the night. With such intense excitement, I can't fall asleep.

Food is almost gone. I am out of work. I have lived the long summer without seeing the sun. Whenever I hear the squeak of the gate, my heart sinks and I hurry into the hole under the floor, but even that is not safe. Here and there, many innocent people are being taken and rumors of gruesome slaughters are circulating in town.

As the autumn winds blow, my anxiety grows worse. I may look composed on the outside, but I am seething with anxiety inside.

To begin with, I was not very loyal to the Republic of Korea. Every action it took did not seem right. Its way of handling issues was so inexperienced and unreliable that I had even anticipated a day would come when I would end up being a citizen of the People's Republic. I never went about in a Jeep with an army sign, and when the Korea Youth Organization (*of ROK*) had asked me for a cultural lecture, I had feigned sickness.

Did I then ever harbor a special longing for the People's Republic? That is not true either. My anticipation for the People's Republic was dampened several years ago when I read an article in North Korea's Minsung Magazine about a discussion among North Korea's cultured elite. People like Lee Kiyung, Han Sulya, and Lee Taejoon gathered to praise the exalted leader, General Kim Ilsung. At the end of every sentence, there were comments that all social phenomena and even the gentle rains and smooth winds were attributable to the grace of Exalted Leader General Kim Ilsung.

They turned me off so much that I brought it up with Chul later, "Have those guys really taken leave of their senses, or were they politically pressured? How can so-called cultured people be in unison with such adulation?"

The People's Republic had still been agreeable to me, mostly because there was absent such rampant corruption as witnessed in the Republic of Korea. I also felt relaxed in thinking that, even if I ever became a subject of the People's Republic, I did not see a strong reason not to be won over by them.

Some who hear these words may accuse me of sitting on the fence or call me an opportunist, but my opportunism never depended upon who was on the winning side. I compared the two in order to judge who is right, but never tried to follow one rather than the other in order to rise in the world. My conscience is therefore clear.

I now feel my life is threatened in the People's Republic and am hiding underground filled with trepidation. But nobody has come to take me yet nor have I heard anyone mentioning such a thing. In a sense, I may be acting like a criminal out of a self-imposed fear. However, when I hear that another person is taken away and shot seemingly out of the blue or at random, I cannot let my guard down.

As I was kicked out of the school, it may be possible some could label me as a counter-revolutionary. When one is labeled as such, it will be easy to punish him/her in any arbitrary way. If this situation persists for another few months, I will certainly die of hunger before being captured and killed. All my lifelines are now cut off and any friend who I thought could be a help in this new world refuses to see me.

My insomnia and anxiety come from enduring these situations and from my surrounding atmosphere. One Japanese broadcast boasted the day before yesterday that forty thousand more UN troops would be deployed: twenty thousand in September and October and another twenty thousand in November and December. I was never more disappointed than when I heard this news. *For those of us who are struggling to survive day by day, how long is this war going to drag on?*

Is Seoul going to be recovered after we all die? Wife and I smiled a bitter smile. "How would unification be useful to anybody after they kill off everybody?" I remembered the words of Dr. Kim's brother.

Nevertheless, I distinctly heard cannon sounds last night. Even now, if I listen intently, I think I hear the sound of distant booming. There is a rumor the UN troops landed at Inchon (*a large Western port city near Seoul*). If I can hear the cannons this close, how far away could they be? Anyway, the front line is not focused only on Daegu and Busan anymore. The headquarters of the People's Army also announced it had crushed the enemy's attempt to land at Koonsan[117].

Some speculated saying, "Who knows? They may pretend to attempt a landing at Koonsan to divert the North forces while they really are aiming to land at Inchon."

Others also said, "They announced the Koonsan landing attempt after more than ten days. Even if the UN forces had

---

117 Koonsan is another Western coastal city, far South of Inchon.

landed at Inchon now, there may or may not be an announcement until ten more days have passed."

These are our futile back-alley debates. But we also hear some eye-opening news. A person who used to live on a small island beyond Wolmi Island[118] is said to be taking shelter in the next town. As a gag order is placed on this, no details are available. But what does it mean that a person from the area near Inchon is taking refuge here?

September 17, 1950.

There are so-called 'round-table talks' involving the families of South Korean soldiers these days. They use the airwaves of broadcasting stations to persuade South Korean soldiers to surrender. Their scripts are sometimes published in newspapers. A mother would address her son or a sister to her brother, "We are in the comforting hands of the People's Republic Army and live a comfortable life, wanting nothing. But when we think about you who betrayed the country and our people, aiming your gun directly at our people, it is unbearable. It is not too late. You can come back even now. The People's Republic would welcome you with open arms." Among them, today's appeal by Dukwha's mother to her husband has penetrated people's hearts to the core.

"When you became an enemy of the people by joining the American Imperialists and the Rhee Syngman puppets, we could no longer raise our heads high. Dukwha joined

---

118 An island off Inchon.

the Volunteer Army, saying she must atone for your sins. Every night, I cannot go to sleep imagining you and Dukwha aiming guns at each other or thrusting swords at each other. Please come back and as soon as possible. Come back to the side of the People," she pleaded.

Her husband is an officer of the ROK Army. She and her daughter under DPRK spent day after day in unbearable fear. Finally, the daughter was forced to join the Volunteer Army with the possibility of eventually turning her gun on her father. *Is this tragedy limited to Dukwha's family only?* No. In some cases, fathers stand against sons, or brothers are pitted against brothers, only to kill or be killed. Wailing until the end of the world cannot drown this tragic reality.

September 18, 1950.

A platoon of the People's Army has been staying at our house since yesterday. It is the Communications Battalion, the Second Platoon. There are sixteen soldiers including a leader. The leader is the only one from the regular North Army. All others are volunteers from Kangkyung. A young one, about sixteen or seventeen years old, said he used to be a student at Kyungsung Electricity School and is now a liaison soldier.

The platoon leader does not look particularly dignified nor very cultured. When he spoke to his soldiers at a meeting, he was loud, but his content was all messed up. He used complex words like 'awareness' and 'creativity,' but he didn't appear to understand them correctly. His sentences were a string of disjointed words. However, when he asked them afterwards whether they understood him, the answers were all 'yes'. I marveled they could understand him at all. The education level of most of the soldiers seemed higher than that of the leader. One of them was educated at a good school and may be a party member. He is supposed to teach them about the party. His gentle attitude made a good impression on me.

When the People's Republic Army went into their town Kangkyung, all the youths there volunteered. After two weeks of training, they were transferred to the regular army. Considering it is only about a month since they became soldiers, they are well-disciplined, and their technical education is thorough. When asked if any had prior experience in communications, the answer was no.

One of them said he had read many books in Chinese and was overjoyed to see many Chinese texts in the house. This chap was so excited that he began relaying many stories to me. At the end, he said, "There are still many Southern soldiers in the mountains wherever we go. They shoot signals into the air above and solidify their bunkers. We ourselves were once surrounded by them in Anyang but narrowly escaped." He was going to go on with more interesting stories until the possible party member gave him a sign to change the subject.

The platoon leader was so enamored by our record player that he played it continuously as if his life depended on it. He played a few records of ours and then asked the platoon members to go around the block to collect all records available. Among them were some vulgar popular songs and comedy shows that made me ill, but he played them over and over with even more enthusiasm. Some platoon members also frowned at them, but the leader was completely oblivious. I was worried about what some passers-by or other People's Army soldiers in other houses would think of the noise. He almost forgot about his food and slept with the machine.

I really regretted that I answered yes when he asked, "Do you have a record player?" But the cat is already out of the bag.

When he asked, "Do you have a radio?" I lied clumsily, but I felt I did well. I was scared to death when, as I hurried to remove the cords before they saw them, Bong-a saw me and blurted out loud, "Why are you taking out the radio cords?" A cold sweat ran down my back.

September 19, 1950.

The soldiers had said they would stay only a night, but they don't show any sign of leaving and this was the third day of their stay. I was uncomfortable with their watching me doing nothing at home every day, so I told them I was going to the school and then went up to the attic space over the main bedroom. If I sat down, I had to bend my head, so I lay down there, reading books or sleeping.

Although it was easier on my body to lie down, lying down all day long was quite boring. I could sympathize with people who are bedridden for lengthy periods of time. I ate a ball of rice for lunch. I was going to have my dinner after the children went to bed, but they played around even after dinner today. Probably because the soldiers were huddled outside, making noise, they were too excited to go to sleep.

Bong-a must have remembered me, "Why isn't daddy home yet?" Mok-a followed, "Yeah, where is he?"

Wife told them, "Daddy may not be home tonight. Why don't you go to sleep first?" But they said, "I can't go to sleep yet."

What a predicament! I had been holding off urinating for a long time, but now it was urgent. I should have brought in a chamber pot, but regret is of no use now. I peeked at the children through a gap in the door anxiously and their eyes were as bright as ever.

I am not the only one suffering from the difficulties caused by soldier transfers. Kyunghee went out to the orchard through the back door when the soldiers came in. It is also extremely hard for him because he cannot alert the people who live in the orchard to his presence either. Speaking of the people in the orchard, Hong *koon* was somebody I could relate to on any subject. But now something tells me our relationship is not like what it was in the past anymore.

Even though Hong *koon* said he was not a real Bolshevik and would not act unruly like the others, he started working the morning of that very day. I thought it must have been unavoidable perhaps because of his prior history... Even when I heard he was forcing his wife to work at the Women's League and was teaching children songs of the People's Republic as part of his work, I allowed myself to think he must be putting on a show. After all, he had said he was not a real Bolshevik. I also thought he is acting perhaps because he was anxious about his past. He once had joined an anti-communist news federation before the war. But how can I ignore Hong *koon*'s icy attitude when his third brother-in-law was arrested and also when I heard of the cursing and berating he gave his wife because her younger brother and nephews did not join the Volunteer Army? Considering all of this, I cannot let him know about Kyunghee's hideout in the orchard.

Even if he knew, I still believe he would never do such a thing as to report him to the authorities. But I cannot allow him to see my cousin as a persona non grata because of this. Whether his way of thinking is right or wrong is another issue. I just do not want to let him know about Kyunghee.

The distance between him and me is already so vast. He must know by now that they kicked me out of work, and I am now staying at home doing nothing. However, he never brings up the topic. Perhaps he may think I would feel awkward and chooses not to talk to me about it for my sake, but our relationship was not like this before.

Knowing that we are without work or rations, he may ask with some concern how we are doing with food if just in passing. But there is no hint of concern either from him or his wife. They might think we are okay with food because when they were in a real bind earlier, we shared bits of food with them. But what could be the reason for their trying not to show our family members that they are receiving large sacks of food?

We used to criticize the wrongdoings of the Rhee Syngman government or point out wrong approaches of the Communist Party on current events. Our viewpoints had always been quite similar and there had been no gulf between us. Now, there is an endless number of current affairs to talk about with each other these days. But he has sealed his mouth and does not express himself at all. It seems like he has no desire to talk and wants to avoid me.

I do not think he looks askance at me, nor has he labeled me a counter-revolutionary. But he seems to expect that talking to me now would not be like before and that our thoughts would not converge. We may not conclude a discussion with a violent argument, but he might be afraid of an awkward parting from each other.

I also think the more we discussed topics the clearer our opposing views would become, and we would grow even farther apart. *Are friendships really like this? Is this acceptable?* I think about these questions over and over every sleepless night, but I am left only with a deep sorrow. I cannot help but feel despair about life. Kyungsuk[119] is gone, Chul is gone, and now Seungkee is also gone. *Who really is left for me?*

Has our friendship always been weak and fragile from the beginning? It may not have been weak at the beginning, but has it taken a beating over the years? If it was neither of those things, are friendships supposed to weaken as we get older? Perhaps it is not a matter of friendship itself after all, but that the power of politics is simply too strong? Why have all of my friends become communists? At the beginning, they were not like that...

Jungsook brings a lunchbox every day to Kyunghee who is hidden underneath a growth of beanstalks. In the daytime, he reads books in the shade underneath peach trees and at night he goes into an empty pigsty to sleep. Abundant leaves around him are helpful to shield him from prying eyes, but he says it is hard indeed to sleep because of the mosquitoes. I remember the time when I hid myself under

---

119 See the diary of November 3.

a bundle of burning bushes. If the mosquitoes are anything like those, I wonder how he survives even a single night.

September 20, 1950.

The sound of cannon fire is getting closer every day. Our hearts are swelling with hope.

The People's Republic would not relinquish Seoul as easily as the Republic of Korea did as soon as the war broke out. There will more than likely be fierce fighting in the streets. The danger to the citizens of Seoul would increase. However, what is this intense anticipation and desperate waiting we feel as the sounds from cannons get closer? It must not be simple fear of death from hunger nor a yearning for freedom. It must be coming from some mixture of sensations and feelings that are much more complex and difficult to articulate.

Now, the story of the Inchon landing is more than a rumor and the close sounds of cannon fire seem to indicate that they are at least near Kimpo. Another rumor is that American soldiers are already in the Yungdeungpo[120] area. Perhaps it's a made-up story, but the UN soldiers supposedly distributed a flour sack to every hungry citizen as soon as they entered Inchon and Yungdeungpo. It sounds quite generous even if it is only a rumor.

The soldiers in our house also seem to be a bit bewildered. They keep discussing how far away the cannons might be. It must be a specialty of the Communist Party to

---

120 A district in Seoul just south of the Han River.

not let even their own soldiers receive information from the front line. They boisterously argued whether it is ten or thirteen miles away when the party member confidently said, "It's at least twenty-five miles."

His face belied that he may not exactly believe that himself. The platoon leader came in then and rebuked them saying, "Twenty-five miles or two miles. What does it matter? They're all practice sounds." Nobody would take these words at face value, but it must be the custom of this country in the North to pretend to understand.

A message came to them stating, "Finish preparations and be ready." They dismantled and cleaned their guns, packed communication gear and their clothes in a sack and then shared a shovel each. They had nothing that could be called a backpack. If no leather was available, a cloth backpack would be nice. But all they had was a small knapsack. The platoon leader has a fine leather bag which must be a spoil of the war. It would go better with a gentleman's suit—not suitable to carry around in battle fields. He must have understood at least this much as he did not carry it, but instead he let the liaison soldier carry it as a knapsack on his back.

He seemed to be thinking about something intensely and then asked the liaison soldier to inquire if he could have one of the children's backpacks hanging in the main hallway. Wife persuaded Bong-a to let the army soldier have it with a promise that he will get a better one later. The comrade platoon leader was incredibly happy as he attached it to his side and stuffed pencils and papers into it. For the backpack, he said he would give us four shovels. We told him he did not have to, but he said they were extras anyway and the soldiers put them into a storage hut.

Even during this time, American planes appeared above in the Jungreung sky. The tempo of the bombings seemed to have accelerated. Whenever the soldiers heard the airplanes, they hid underneath the eaves. While on their way, they are ordered to move quickly to the sides of the road, lie down and stay still when they hear airplanes.

The order was, "The current destination is Mapo[121]. But when they get there, wait for another order regarding whether to move elsewhere." They must be going to the front line. Because they have deluded leaders, these pure and innocent youths, whom I could not hate even if I tried as they do not differ from my younger brothers or nephews, with only a knapsack, a shotgun, and a shovel will become cannon fodder when they encounter the highly mechanized American troops. As I lie in the attic, tears fall down my cheeks.

Do they know their fate will be decided in a few hours? Does their passivity come from their knowing and accepting this fate? But they are too young and innocent to know what's coming which make them look even more pitiful.

Having observed their education for several days, I realize their education consists only of monotonous repetitions of stereotypical phrases of communism. Current affairs and military news are kept in the dark and never mentioned. Only the usual knee-jerk exhortations of hostilities are repeated. Even as they are leaving for the front line, I hear the relentless words of the communist regime such as:

"Daegu and Busan are now completely liberated."

---

121 A Seoul district just north of the Han River, facing Yungdeungpo across the Han River.

"The enemy that landed at Inchon was completely crushed. Although crushed, they still repeat their futile attempts to land. They were completely pushed into the sea. Once in the water, with the mindset of trying to grasp even a floating straw, they repeatedly make desperate attempts. But every time they fall under the guns and swords of our smart and brave soldiers."

"The invader's evil hands that soaked our beautiful land with blood are now finally getting their due. Now we are going to the front line to kill every one of them."

"The holy task of unifying our Mother Country is now at the last moment of success. The hands that tried to kill so many of our brothers and sisters and destroy our factories and houses are now receding. We will have the honorable duty of finishing them off."

These are their words of encouragement. Their propaganda is really masterful. The only problem is that they lack truth and honesty, the essential elements of any propaganda.

Using their remaining time until they were ready, they sang songs. The platoon leader directed and corrected their mistakes. Bong-a and Mok-a were giddy with excitement.

September 21, 1950.

Wife came back from the orchard reporting that the Hongs are packing their things, perhaps intending to move away.

"I am sure you are mistaken. If they intend to move, they will tell me." Still, a move is plausible. While we are listening and waiting for the ever-approaching sound of cannons with inflated hearts, those on the left must be worried to death. Mr. Lee Yoonki, known once as the 'King of Jungreung', is not as drunk anymore and looks very flustered to me, considering the situation.

Wife asked Mrs. Hong as she was packing, "Are you now moving somewhere?"

"Husband is not talking about it, so we can't move. But I am too uneasy to not do anything."

It was an ambiguous answer. Therefore, Wife asked again, "As we don't hear any news and are staying put at home, we are thirsty for any news. What does Mr. Hong say?"

"He won't let me talk at all. When I ask him whether the world is going upside-down, he yells angrily saying, 'If so, all Koreans would end up dying. Is that what you wish? Why do you say such things?' These are his replies. However much I am worried there may be a calamity in a couple of days, he gives nothing away. So, I really don't know what to do."

"Why don't you go to your parent's house?"

"Our parents' house? We don't know what happened to our brother who was taken away. Hong *subang*[122] acted so

---

122 Subang is a word used by a wife to mention her husband to her elders or people she respects. It is not used in front of her children, for example. A husband, on the other hand, would use words like jibsaram (the house person) to designate his wife in front of his elders. Koreans use same words differently depending on to whom they talk. They emphasize respecting the elders in everyday conversation.

cold and nonchalant about it… I don't know how much I cried. My older brothers tell me they will cut the ties between us, and they are right. Mother keeps crying all the time. How can I step foot in my parents' house ever again?"

In the afternoon, Mrs. Hong left with the children. She did not say where she was going….

Hong *koon* indeed left me saying nothing.

Can this be possible? Are all Bolsheviks like this?

Perhaps he believed that seeing me would come back to hurt me one day—and he wanted to be extra cautious.

Looking up the autumn sky, I feel profoundly sad.

September 22, 1950.

Bokkyoo came. As she seemed waiting to see how the wind was blowing, I asked, "Is the work at the Women's League still busy? You had time to come out today?" She said there was not much work at all these days.

I inquired, "Why in the world are you working at the Women's League? Did your brother tell you to do so? Did your mother? Or do you yourself like to do so?"

One example is 'meal'. For elders, it is 'jinji', and for children, it is 'bap'. Another example is 'to eat'. For elders, it is 'deusinda', and for children, it is 'mugneunda'. So, it's like 'jinji deusinda' vs 'bap mugneunda', depending on to or about whom you talk.

"Nobody told me to do it and it's not that I wanted to. It was only that some in town kept urging me day and night...."

"Just because somebody pressures you, you obey and go there? Does every girl in town go out to work then?" But it is already spilled milk... And Suk (*her communist cousin, See the August 10 diary*) may not like hearing our discussion anyway. I continued, "They must have landed at Inchon. What are you going to do now?"

"They say it is all rumors, - their landing at Inchon or moving into Yungdeungpo. The day before yesterday, a person came back from Inchon saying that he saw all the enemy that landed at Inchon was shot or drowned to death. Inchon is now peaceful."

"Is that person from Inchon not the same person who came back from Daegu a month ago? Why do you only listen to people like him?"

"He may have been wrong then, but they say Daegu and Busan are all liberated now."

"Who says that?" I pressed her.

"There are posters on the streets and the Women's League is planning a celebration parade."

"Even while listening to those cannon sounds?"

"They say they are drills. Really." She seemed convinced.

There is no medicine for these people. On the other hand, I envy the narcotic power of the People's Republic.

September 23, 1950.

We have heard rumors that cars and transportation trucks keep moving toward the North over the Miari Hill at night. Now it is many nights already, but I do not know how many people and things have moved out.

A heart-wrenching story is that every night, they take many prisoners away on foot who look to have been of high stature and position. They bind these prisoners by rope as if they are dried fish bundled in a row and force them to walk quickly. If any of them are not well or not willing to follow orders, they are cursed and beaten. Once they pass Moonumi Hill[123], they shoot the prisoners on the spot if they can no longer follow orders.

In the afternoon, Bokkyoo brought along with her a lady whom I have not known. She is said to be the wife of Mr. Lee Suk and asked if we can keep a sack of items for a while. We worried whether there may be some trouble later if the authorities find it, but I readily said yes when she said it was full of clothes and sleeping blankets.

But thinking about it again, even if she had said the contents were not clothes and blankets, I do not think I could have refused. Once I'd accepted them, I could not possibly report it to the authorities later either. Being a citizen in this country is quite challenging.

---

123 This is a hill just north of Seoul, about 2 miles north of Jungreung-ri.

September 24, 1950.

I was told that Mr. Shim Hyun, who ran a kindergarten by the police station, was shot to death. Another person was also killed in Chungsoojang which is nearby. Mr. Shim was at home when he was dragged out to be shot in front of a weaver's house. His wife followed them and when she tried to stop the shooting, she was also shot and one of her cheeks was torn apart. Their children are young, and their neighbors did not even dare to look out at the scene. He was covered in a burlap sack for the night, truly a pitiful event.

I was told that Mr. Shim did not respond quickly enough to the demands of the guerillas who asked him to vacate the kindergarten. I do not know, however, the details of the real story. He was said to have graduated from a certain engineering high school in Japan and had a sign that said, 'Shim Hyun Monotype Research Institute'. I do not know what that means. He was always out in the garden taking care of vegetable plants and fruit trees. He was old, never spoke much and was not seen often outside. He could not have been much of a counter-revolutionary even if he tried.

Not only that, but there are also rampant rumors that massacres continue downtown. The words of Kim Sangkee *sunsaengnim* must come true[124].

---

124 On August 9 and on Aug 25, Prof. Kim Sangkee told Prof. Kim Sungchil that DPRK newspaper stories reported Americans and South Koreans massacred many innocent people during their retreat. Prof. Kim Sangkee warned these stories may be used as an excuse for the North to take harsh

September 25, 1950.

Fighting in the street seems to get fiercer since yesterday. Not only do we now hear the cannons, but we can see flames, too. From the direction of Dongdaemoon[125], thick smoke rises high into the sky as if it rises from a straw pile. Gruesome red flames are seen in the smoke at night.

Airplanes are dropping bombs twenty-four hours a day. There are too many to count as they take turns dropping bombs on their targets, crushing them one by one. Even in the Jungreung valley, bright red rocket bombs are pouring down.

Top level leftists seem to have already escaped while leaving only soldiers behind to offer resistance. I wonder if it wouldn't be better for them to just run away without creating unnecessary casualties and destroying streets. Maybe the top-level members are trying to gain time for themselves this way.

The family of Mr. Lee Yoonki is also busy packing things. The young plump sister had volunteered for the army around the time when there was a rumor of the Inchon landing. There was a rumor that even party members were called upon at the end. She went out saying that she wouldn't return if we cannot drive the enemy Americans

---

actions when things turn against their favor.
125 The East Gate of Seoul. One of the four big gates of Seoul, about half a mile south of Seoul National University.

out. I am envious of these people who are blindly committed to their beliefs.

September 26, 1950.

Kim Choondeuk *koon* came with a bundle on his back just before dinner. He is a movie actor with the screen name of Dok Eunki. We shared a room when we were in middle school. He had not been too keen about ideologies. As many artists had turned toward the left, he might have been influenced by them. Like everybody else, he had also suffered long under the cruel oppression of the Japanese. He had high hopes after the 8.15 Liberation but was deeply disappointed by the pathetic cultural policies of South Chosun (*Korea*). Even after the Republic of Korea's government was established, this disappointment only got deeper and he began to long for the North. Then the North's active propaganda was effective enough to turn him to their side when the 6.25 Incident broke out.

Now he must leave for the North. He said he'd been sick with lung disease for a few years, but now is cured. He still looks weak. I wonder how he will manage walking more than a hundred miles at night with that large bundle on his back. He is now asking about a mountain road. If he ever reaches Pyungyang, it may not be as bad, as his daughter Soonshim is already there getting educated.

In this way, we are continually sending away these cultured and educated people. We lose overnight these people who had decades of education under their belt. *How is the Republic of Korea going to manage now?*

Many talented writers, painters, musicians and movie producers have gone to the North. Even in the academic field, many young and energetic people have left and only old, listless people like me stay around.

If those people who have gone to the North were originally Bolsheviks, that is a different matter. But many people who maintained a neutral position or who were conscientious idealists also went north. This is something on which we really should self-examine ourselves.

I am sure there may be some fault in those people who went north. Peas in my neighbor's field may look bigger than mine. The North's propaganda may have been an effective method to prey on those that are young, who focus on unhappiness over the realities of life and seek ideals only.

But then, is that all we can say? Was the atmosphere in the South ever conducive to their working happily? Considering how poorly their rights had been guaranteed and how unstable their lives had been, it looks as if we had almost pushed their backs to the North over the 38th parallel.

As I send off another conscientious artist to the North, I think about his long-suffering illness, his hardships in life, and the threats of torture he endured. I can't help but lament grievously the paucity of cultural policies in this land.

September 27, 1950.

The sound of gunfire in the streets is coming closer every hour. It is not just cannon sounds, as now I also hear the crackling rattle of guns. It looks like the front line has moved away from downtown and is now coming closer to us.

Large numbers of defeated People's Army soldiers, guerillas and leftist civilians are passing through our town and snaking through the corners of Bookhan Mountain. I notice how shabbily they are dressed with anxious expressions on their faces. I cannot help but feel they are still our brothers and sisters. *Why do they have to leave?*

In the afternoon, cannon sounds were surprisingly close when Wife came running from the vegetable field saying bombs were being dropped at Kyungshin High School (*one block away from the house*) and we should leave the house now. We hurriedly took care of the kitchen fire[126] and went out. All the townspeople are also moving out, wide-eyed.

From across the field, we can see the smoke rising from the bombs falling near the school. Airplanes are busily flying above our heads. Maybe they are guiding target points for the bombs. They dropped one bomb into a thatched cottage near a stream and pulverized it into powder. Was I mistaken to feel that the townspeople's faces look more alive in this midst of these bombings?

---

126 In every household, a wood burning kitchen fire is almost always kept going while people are in the house. This fire, via under-the-floor air passages, also delivers heat to rooms in winter. Rooms are heated through the floors above these passages. The floors are basically dried mud slabs with thick water-proof oil papers on the top. They retain heat very well.

September 28, 1950[127].

At daybreak, townspeople plundered the military supplies left by the People's Army. The People's Army has retreated while ROK and UN soldiers have not moved in yet. Everybody sensed this lack of authority. People went in to grab as much food and clothing as they could -- creating a pandemonium. We were worried about Jungsook who went to the vegetable field with her breakfast and did not come back for hours. When she returned, she had a piece of silk with an telltale injury on her hand. Chosun people have become horrendously materialistic.

After lunch, we wondered what was happening when we heard a disturbance in the alley and loud rifle noises. Now the American soldiers were here and engaged in a clean-up operation. I became worried because Wife had taken the children out. For several hours, bullets were zinging by so thick and fast that I couldn't raise my head even inside a room. One of the bullets came through a wall in my study and broke an ink bottle scaring me, but luckily it went over my head. I could not fathom how this one came in, piercing obliquely through the kitchen door.

Eventually, the clean-up operation was over and Wife came back safely with the children. After all this time, I once again could step outside the door. It feels as if I had come back to life after my own death.

---

127 The day Seoul was fully liberated from People's Army. It's called the 9.28 Recovery Day.

September 29, 1950.

A commando group of the People's Army raided the town at dawn, and there was fierce fighting with the American soldiers. As they came down unexpectedly, there may not have been enough time for the Americans to use their superior firepower, and as a result there were heavy casualties. All who saw it praised the strong attacking spirit of the People's Army. Regardless of which side they were on, I simply liked that the Chosun people showed such bravery.

A curious phenomenon - somebody must have instructed the children to do so, or they might have come up with it by themselves -- they are clapping their hands and expressing warm welcome when the Americans pass by. But when they clapped their hands and expressed happiness as the Americans were moving their dead and wounded in stretchers, the Americans got upset. They couldn't express this to the children, so they threw rocks at them instead. The children were welcoming them but in return, had rocks thrown at them. Of course, it baffled them. This is still another tragic part of our history during the war.

September 30, 1950.

As we had been cooped up for so long inside the house, I took Bong-a and Mok-a to Chungsoojang for a picnic. My legs felt a little wobbly and even the familiar scenery felt less welcome and more dangerous, lest an enemy jump out at us from the woods. We didn't go far.

I sent Kyunghee to the Union for the first time in three months. Ever since June 25th, I had restrained him against his will from going out although he was listless while staying home all the time. As a result, he missed his examination and had heard a hearsay that he was kicked out by the Union. Now I feel much happier for him as he rejoices that it was all worthwhile to suffer and endure during the last three months.

Recovery of Seoul, and Escape to the South

October 1950

October 1, 1950.

As I was working in the vegetable field, Kim Yongchool *koon* came by. His face revealed what he had endured during three months of hiding. Nonetheless, we are both happy we were able to stay alive and can now see each other.

He relayed to me the news of Park Chaneung *koon* and Chung Myungkyo *koon* who went down to their hometowns to work. I regret we might not see these promising young people anymore. I still can visualize in my mind how Park *koon* was so eager to study and how witty and lively Chung *koon* was. *What fault was theirs in this?* There was no fault, it is just the fate of the unfortunate people of this country.

When Yongchool *koon* said he wanted to work now, rather than studying, I sternly warned him of the folly. "I do not fault you for changing the course of your career. If you are convinced what you were doing was wrong, it is good to change into another direction. Also, I am not saying this because I think joining this new work may bring danger to you eventually. But do not forget you are a student who is learning some very important skills for Chosun. There are plenty of people who can and will work out there even if you don't. But studying technology should not be postponed even by one hour. Isn't that the supreme calling of our people?"

October 2, 1950.

I went out to go downtown. I could react to what my eyes witnessed there only with tears and sighs.

The Chongro intersection was now all in ruin. I couldn't find even a glimpse of Chongkak[128]. Its bell had fallen to the ground. Even after a week, from the basement of the structure which was left with only a skeleton frame, burning smoke with an indescribable smoky smell was belching out. Blackened and burnt-out electricity poles and gnarled cables made it hard to find a pathway.

I found it weird to look at the blackened facade of the damaged main Joongangchung building looking like a ghostly shell. The once-busy Yookjo street has turned into piles of burnt ashes with broken bricks and roof tiles. During the last five years what did we Koreans add to this once-Japanese-occupied Seoul and now why on earth did we bring this destruction to it? This anguish I feel cannot be mollified even with banging the ground and wailing… my legs are shaking as I walk.

---

128 A small Korean style open structure that houses a big bell on Chongro.

The Beekak [129] has been crushed to the ground at Kwanghwamoon[130] and Namdaemoon[131] has a big hole in it. The Severance Hospital has become ashes and the Seoul Train Station looks like a miserably crushed cigarette pack in a trash can. With wobbly legs and a weary mind, I turned back from the station, crying.

A Platanus tree with its vigorous leaves was burned mercilessly. Oh, when will you have a new gloss on your body and healthy shoots again?

October 3, 1950.

As expected, the University was ordered to vacate all its buildings for the UN troops. This school was built by the Japanese as a part of their colonization policy. Although it stood on our land, the student ratio of Japanese to Koreans was five to one. Because of this, many youths had viewed it with indignation and resentment. Many students had to

---

129 A small open structure that houses a monument.
130 The largest street intersection, centrally located in Seoul. Joongangchung, the main government building, is a couple of blocks to the north. Chungwadae, the Blue House, where the ROK president currently lives and works, is another few blocks directly behind Joongangchung. The largest street in Seoul at the time, Chongro, runs east-west between Kwangwhamoon and Dongdaemoon.
131 Another big gate of Seoul, the South Gate. It is National Treasure No.1. It is located several blocks south of Kwanghwamoon. The Seoul Train Station is another several blocks south of Namdaemoon.

cross the East Sea (*to Japan*) or the Aprok River (*to Manchuria and China beyond*) to study. After August 15th, American soldiers moved in to use its buildings.

When they left in the following spring, the new Kyungsung University was established. But the deplorably thick-headed education policies of the military government and the destructive fighting tactics of the leftists created the unfortunate 'National University Plan - Kookdaean' (*see comments on June 26*) movement on campus that left many issues unsettled for a long time. Before the confusion was settled in one way or another, the war brought in the People's Army soldiers, soon to be followed by the City People's Committee. As soon as they ran away, and before any cleanup could take place, it now is occupied by the headquarters of the American 8th Army. *Ah, sad is the fate of the campus on this land!*

October 4, 1950.

I sorted the books in my study, returned library books and brought personal books home. Sedon brothers (*his nephews*) and Hyunchul (*his brother-in-law*) worked hard all day.

There are certain differences between the People's Army and this American army in their use of the buildings. When the People's Army came in, they had told the school administrator: "We will use the building starting today, so move out. We will keep everything as is and will disturb nothing." But then we know only too well what happened in the end. On the other hand, this American army says, "Vacate the school by this time on this day. Take all of your belongings with you. We will never touch your property, but sometimes we may not know how to keep them properly...."

I don't know whether this could be ascribed to either an individual difference in culture or a difference in thinking, but when the People's Committee told the citizens of Seoul to move out of the city, it said, "Leave with what you are wearing now. Where you are going, there will be a house, furniture, and food—everything. As for the things you leave here, we will keep them safe and send them to you later." I don't know what the places to which they took them look like as I haven't seen them, but their furniture and knickknacks are now being circulated at secondhand markets. Even if they did not lose the war, based on hearsay concerning the character of the People's Committee members in our towns, I have strong reservations about how conscientiously the items were stored and kept.

October 5, 1950.

The American soldiers who were stationed in our town for a few days retreated yesterday. In their stead, Korean soldiers have moved in. The Americans seem to have slept outside in the cold, but the Korean soldiers are pestering townspeople for rooms to sleep in. We vacated the study and the gate room last night. The faces of these weary young men, covered with the dirt of one thousand leagues (*about 250 miles*), looked as familiar as if they are my blood brothers.

Still, I can't help thinking about the North Korean soldiers who stayed in the same rooms only a few days ago. These two groups fought against each other. I don't know whether those North Korean soldiers are alive or not. My heart is torn with sadness for the brave youths of both countries. There shouldn't be either enmities or hostilities between those who now do not have any place to hide as defeated soldiers if they are alive at all, and the strong-looking Korean soldiers sitting in front of me now. They should be on the same side. *What did they do wrong, other than having bad leaders?*

I can still manage to smile while listening to their stories... "At the front, the two sides got into hand-to-hand combat. When I was just about to thrust a knife into an enemy soldier, I realized he was my second elder brother! As I called out, "Brother!" and threw away my knife, I started crying."

But when I hear such stories as, "All the UN soldiers are amazed by the fearlessness of our soldiers. In hand-to hand combat, we even crushed their faces and bit their noses," my heart burns with pain and aches—they are the same people! Looking at the Korean soldiers in front of me now, I can imagine the North Korean soldiers, who were in the same room just a few days ago, coming in through the gate to arm wrestle or just chat with these soldiers. It pains me to imagine them crushing and biting each other's faces or noses.

At night, I spent a good amount of time with the wine they bought.

They continued, "When the enemy first came down, our equipment was pitiful. It was like fighting tanks with handguns. There was no contest. We had to retreat, biting back tears. The Americans didn't trust us at first because they thought if they give us weapons, we would soon hand them off to the communist army just as General Chiang Kai

Shek[132]'s army did. But as they fought next to us, they saw we were brave and strong and not a single unit would talk to the enemy nor defect to the other side. Then they began trusting and supplying weapons to us." My heart warmed to hear this kind of story.

"Once we got the equipment, we were unstoppable. But the American headquarters kept ordering us to retreat. Once we took an important enemy post after fighting against a formidable enemy, we received an order to retreat unconditionally. There was even a time when some young officers pounded desks with fists crying. While being pushed back, how could we have known it was part of their grand strategy? Sometimes we were angry, believing these guys intervened into others' fight with drawn swords but cared for their own interests only. But, after reaching a predetermined line, the order of a counterattack finally came down and we were able to forcefully attack the enemy like a roaring wave. We felt very proud of ourselves." A confidence-generating story.

"Before the war, when we were soldiers stationed in Yongsan, did anybody even care to look at us when we came into the streets? When comparing our treatment to the respectful treatment of soldiers during Japanese rule, we were quite upset. Considering that, Seoul citizens' hardships may

---

132 A Chinese leader who fought against Japan during World War II. He fought against Chairman Mao Zedong of the Communist Party of China after the war and was defeated. He retreated to Taiwan and became the president of the Republic of China in Taiwan.

be deemed as what they deserved." This may be a bit of an overstatement.

October 6, 1950.

Wife hoisted on a pole a national flag we had hidden until now. We hoisted it on the same pole on which the unfamiliar North Korean flag had been flying for three months. We felt relieved and refreshed, but at the same time I also felt pitiful like a man who posts this flag and then the other, as sunflowers would turn their faces to follow the sun. Even more pitiful is my small and fretful mind worrying if a guerilla hiding in the mountains might come down at night and create problems.

In the evening, somebody was banging on the gate with authority. A soldier brought a worn-out flag made of poor clothes and asked to exchange it with our flag. *Sir, just like you, we know what's good and what's not. This is an unreasonable request. You may not know it, but this flag carries our sorrows and our tears. Asking us to exchange it with that scrap is a crushing blow to our feelings. This is too much.* I wanted to say these words, but I exchanged the flags saying nothing. Because he had a gun.

October 7, 1950.

I went to the university. The school was moved to the university president's office building. They mobilized nearby townspeople to move books from the offices to the library. Together with Koh Byungik and Jun Haejong (*his fellow history professors*), I oversaw and helped with the work. Seeing the books, in English and Chinese, piled up with no order and at random in the library's hallway, I wondered when I could ever sort them out properly and study again. This image made me sigh.

Already a generator was running in a corner of the playground and Americans dropped in while we were cleaning the rooms. They may be assigning rooms to themselves or anxious about our slow work pace. When I went to the reading room, soldiers were crushing the bookstands with their boots. They may want to bring in beds or tables, but when I saw these good cultural facilities, which contained our fond memories and could be used by young students for a long time, being mercilessly destroyed, I became unglued and didn't have enough strength to work there anymore.

October 8, 1950.

Jungyong came by and parked his bicycle outside the gate. A youth who seemed to be a military informant made an issue about the ownership of this bicycle. He berated us and took us to a house next door. Even though we explained the situation earnestly, we were severely and unreasonably chastised. The officer there seemed quite drunk, and it was hard to answer him.

An uncle of Mr. Lee Keunmoo came over and asked to see the house in the orchard, so I went out with him. In front of the old neighborhood leader's house, a patrolman questioned us. He asked us to show our IDs and I brought mine from home. We had to suffer a long lecture about carrying our IDs all the time. He repeated himself once, and then again, and as he spoke, his drunken breath made it very hard to listen to him.

October 9, 1950.

There was a faculty meeting at the school.

Mr. Lee Byungdo, assuming the role of chairman, explained recent developments. He said that, according to a directive of the Department of Education, all professors would be investigated and examined again. This time under the direction of the ROK government. He said our school had set up an investigative committee, but it needs to be more inclusive in its membership with a broader spectrum of professors.

Following him, Mr. Cho Yoonje expressed concerns about the selection of committee members. He said this investigation must be thorough and severe to punish people who erred during North Korean rule. He added that he was pushed out during the first purge after June 25th, hence he was different from those who stayed on at the school. Then a few others, who were also pushed out in the first purge along with Mr. Cho, reiterated that they were the only ones proven to be genuine patriots and were not happy the new committee members included some people who were not like them.

In the meantime, Mr. Kim Sunkee came in. After he asked a person sitting next to him what was going on, he started saying there might be some people among the investigators who had been Northern sympathizers during the time of the People's Republic. How could they investigate him who is so clean? It is as if a criminal was judging an innocent man. He repeated himself over and over, flashing his enormous eyes. Many told him repeatedly it was not the case, but he would not budge.

Mr. Shin Dosung, in frustration, said although we are working for democracy now, we are currently under martial law and therefore this is not the time to decide everything through an exhaustive opinion-gathering process. He further stated that we should refrain from initiating trouble with partisan views on already decided facts, and also that whether someone had been purged in the first purge or in the second really didn't matter. He was in the first purge himself, but he didn't have any intention of faulting those who were purged later. He added that trying to find what little difference exists between the two is nothing but nonsense.

Mr. Cho Yoonje said that Mr. Shin, with his unique style of sophistry, was trying to block a fair and open discussion and blamed Mr. Shin as the one that was partisan. Mr. Kim Sunkee again reiterated that people who were already corrupted could not investigate clean people like him.

Kim Sanggee *sunsaengnim* rebuked him and told them not to disturb the meeting with abstract words but bring out concrete facts if they want to impeach improper investigators. Mr. Kim repeatedly gave vague answers, saying he didn't mean there was really an improper investigator, but that if there were indeed people like that, it would be a grave matter.

The College of Arts and Science, are you still boasting of yourself as the college of colleges?

October 10, 1950.

The new *banjang*, preparing the *ban* members list, emphasized, "Use Chinese characters." I have been worried about such a reaction to the Korean-only policy of the Northern puppet regime. Now I know my worries were valid.

A good practice is good regardless of who implements it. So why should we reject a Korean-only (in writing) policy just because the North started it?

It would be better if more Koreans could understand posters in the streets, and this would happen if only Korean is used. Nowadays, they use 'highbrow' Chinese characters and among them are such nonsensical expressions as 'Justice should won[133]'. What is that supposed to mean? More extreme leaflets say, 'Hooray to enter units the 7th Division the 8th regiment clobber enemy ringleader Moojung Corps[134]'. They post these leaflets everywhere. I don't know if they make any sense. The bad practice of not attaching suffixes to invocations or funeral orations[135] is overflowing in the streets of Seoul. It is beyond being simply regretful.

---

133 A transliteration of Chinese characters by the translator.
134 A transliteration of an ill-expressed phrase of serial Chinese characters without any space or suffixes.
135 Often, Chinese sentences or phrases can be confusing to the readers. Therefore, Korean suffixes to Chinese words are often used to bring better understanding. In invocations or

October 11, 1950.

My father-in-law in the next town was on the road with a pushcart to get some food when a policeman asked him to help move some items. He was unable to refuse such a request, so he followed him to a house where a downtrodden woman kept sighing. The policeman threatened her, "As you are all leftists, you had better out pack your clothes and bedding and hand them over to me."

The policeman had him bring out her belongings and load them with other furnishings onto the pushcart and move them to a house in Sungbook-dong which the policeman had already taken from somebody else. Although my father-in-law was in his sixties and labored hard to move those items, when it was done, the policeman just said, "That's it. You can go now."

I was wondering how such a thing could happen… But then, Shin *koon*, who was a teacher at Kyungsung Agriculture School, had taken refuge in the countryside and hasn't come back yet. A policeman took his house and all of his belongings and loudly announced, "Shin is a leftist. If he comes back, we will kill him." Shin *koon* not only lost his house and his belongings, but he was also falsely accused of being a leftist. *How will he feel when he comes back?*

---

funeral orations, it is customary to use suffixes for better understanding by all in attendance.

October 12, 1950.

I think there was a line in Yunam[136]'s writing, "Whenever scholars and politicians had a chance, they criticized Emperor Jin's[137] burning of books and burying of scholars alive. However, their actions copy those of Emperor Jin these days as if they are afraid of not doing the same thing quickly enough."

After the August 15th Liberation, with the tips of tongues or tips of pens, people have constantly cursed and spat at Hitler and Mussolini. But I sense the trend here and now is coming close to that style of Hitler and Mussolini. Even now, while saying the Northern puppet regime was the worst enemy ever, people's actions seem to follow the same template as that of the communists. *Is it coming from an 'openminded' mindset that one should learn special skills even if they are the skills of thieves?* I can count more than a few examples.

* With nothing much to be done, we are all urged to come to work anyway even on Sundays. There isn't proper transportation available, though, so are they attempting to increase the productivity of people by making them tired instead?

---

136 See footnote 20 on June 27th.
137 Emperor Jin of China in the third century BC burnt books and buried scholars. Since that time, the event has been cited in China and Korea as a symbol of oppression of press and culture.

* They also get rid of people through 'examination'. "You cannot be included in the examination if you don't come to work, whether there is work or not." And "If you don't submit such-and-such documents now, we will exclude you from the examination."

How well they copy even the diction and speech of the regime of merely a few days ago.

October 13, 1950.

I was told that Lee Heeseung *sunsaengnim* suffered a horrendous loss during the war.

In the morning of the day the area of the West Gate was liberated, many bombs came down in his neighborhood. He and his family were all huddled in a room covered with a thick quilt. When a nursing granddaughter complained of stuffiness, the daughter-in-law lifted the edge of the quilt and was taken aback by a heavy, destructive sound. When they realized what had happened, the main area of the house had already collapsed, and fire had reached the room they were in. They rushed out with whatever clothes they had on and without shoes. His wife was slightly injured by a bomb fragment, but everybody came out alive.

The ladies lamented that they could not save any clothes or bedding, but *sunsaengnim* lost all of the books he had collected throughout his life. He lost all of his manuscripts together with research cards and wondered if he had any strength left to recover from the loss. He said, "I saved my life well enough, but half of my life has gone up in flames."

Sunsaengnim said, "The horrendous sights in the streets don't seem like somebody else's problem anymore and when I spot a house with no war damage, I wonder how much goodness and virtue the owner must have had accumulated."

October 14, 1950.

Myung Daemok, very much alive, visited us. I marveled at this wonderful event. It was around the first of July when he came by and told me his father, Myung Jese *sunsaeng*, had been captured. He had wondered in despair, "There may not be any hope of restoring the world again, right?"

I couldn't answer honestly then as it was such a dreadful time, "Who can tell precisely what will happen? Let's see what develops. According to an ancient saying by a sage: A cyclone will not last a whole day and squalls do not fall all day." He had sat quietly and then left without a word. I didn't know whether my words had any effect on him.

Later I heard that he was picked up as a soldier of the Volunteer Army and I imagined I would never see him again. Surprisingly, he ran away from the North. I was more than happy to hear of his escape.

He shared with me news about the North: "Maybe because it is summer, but people are mostly walking around barefoot, men and women. People who have shoes are less than ten percent of the population. They have only one set of summer clothes and one set of winter clothes. Houses with proper Chosun papers on their windows can be counted with one hand and most of the others have newspaper covering the holes.

"Their living is tough, but things can't be accomplished unless they go through tough times, right? Here in the South people seek too much freedom and are corrupted. Being in the North was like having a wake-up call. Here in the South, I think we also need to restrict what needs to be restricted.

"Wherever the Volunteer Army went, local Women's Leagues provided them with food. Their thorough discipline, training and organization were enviable. Shouldn't we copy and learn from them?"

We should learn about good practices even of the North puppet regime. And its organization and training seem to be superior to ours. However, its policy of considering humans to be machines, and driving them ruthlessly into war preparations, cannot be a good practice. This is not something to learn or emulate. But it is also a nightmare that such a group is here, right next door, always looking for ways to take us.

October 15, 1950.

The fellow who created the ruckus at the last faculty meeting refusing to be examined by the people he claimed to have been corrupted themselves under the leftist administration brought the same argument to the Department of Education, threw out elder investigators and became an investigator himself. I lack the desire to go to the school, after noting he acquired a petty helper from some investigative organization and swaggers around like a hooligan.

Still, I cannot choose not to come to the school simply because I feel sick to my stomach... A notice was posted that all staff members should come to the school at least once a day, with or without any work to do. They produced an attendance book. Transportation is not available these days, so we must walk many miles each way. But that's not all. Now and then, they require us to prepare 'activity reports' or 'personal history documents', saying, "One must submit these by the end of the day. Anyone who doesn't will be eliminated from the examinations." These are now the most dreadful words coming after us from nowhere and anywhere. With an empty stomach, one has to trudge to school to witness these detestable scenes.

It would be nice to give up the whole thing, stay home and just farm, or if that is not possible, go into the mountains to become a monk. But that's not possible because if someone fails an examination and loses his job thereof, they may label him as a leftist or an enemy informant. Then you may be at the mercy of the authorities. It therefore is still best to swallow one's pride and endure indignities.

Sometimes I can't help but mock myself thinking of these 'human devaluations'. *If I continue this habit of swallowing my pride, what will become of me when I get old?*

I also worry about my career. *With my pride taking a beating, it's even affecting my role as a teacher... how could I face my students again?* I feel profoundly ashamed. But when I heard that a drunken soldier came to the house asking threateningly what the man of the house does and where he is now, I realize I should bear it and attempt to put up with everything.

< A note to myself >
- Staff personal history examination sheet (3 copies)
- New personal history examination sheet (1 copy)
- Civil servant activities report (5 copies)

< Civil servant activities report >
Name of directorate, division and department, position, age, address, name.

< Investigative items >

1. Relationship with the self-governing committee: Date of enrollment/duty/number of workdays
2. Any items of assistance to the puppet government organizations: Date of employment/duty/number of workdays (monthly)
3. Status of membership in political party organizations: Name of the party or the organization/date of joining/name(s) of introducer or exhorter
4. Self-surrender status: If submitted, date of submission/submitted-to organization/name(s) of introducer or exhorter
5. Others

October 16, 1950.

During the time of the People's Republic, the phrase *kyesok namjinjoong*[138], had been used as a joke, but now a

---

138 It means 'continuously marching south', a North Korean propaganda phrase. After a while, people did not believe

new word *namha*[139] is used with a dignified grandness.

On June 27th, two days after the war broke out, radio broadcasts were repeatedly announcing, "We are all working at Joongangchung as usual like any other day while our soldiers have already taken Euijungboo back and crushed the enemy everywhere. The enemy is running away as they are defeated on all fronts. Citizens should take it easy, stay and protect your workplaces." But the government did *namha* – ran away south clandestinely.

The political party of the government cheated and left people under enemy gunfire with bombs dropping all around. It secretly alerted only their party members to *namha*. Some quick-witted people, even though they were neither highly ranked in the government nor members of the party, also headed south early. Having more or less followed the government's movements to Daegu or to Busan, they came to join the elite government group of the 'honorable *namha* patriots' who proudly avoided the 'disgraceful association with the North'.

Examples of these *namha* people in our town include Sangbok's uncle who is easily scared and was one of the first ones to join the *namha* group. Myungsoon's family, horribly scared, did *namha* at the first sound of cannons abandoning their four children including a nursing baby.

On the other hand, many 'dumb and foolish' citizens - more than 99% of the Seoul population - followed the government's exhortation to 'protect' workplaces and homes.

---

these words anymore.
139 It means 'to move south', a phrase used by ROK authorities and citizens.

They encountered the Red Army and went hungry, were treated inhumanely for ninety days, trembled under threats to their lives, and by some luck survived to greet the Korean and UN soldiers in Seoul. They are now treated harshly by *namha* patriots: "We who did *namha* with the government are the only patriots. You all who stayed in the enemy-occupied territory are tainted." *In the history of this entire world, could there be a more unfair accusation?*

All of the government investigative organizations are already restored. Because all of the communists had shown themselves very clearly in every town and in every organization during the period of the North's occupation, it should be easy to identify and punish them accordingly.

The government should then say to all others, "You have suffered much. We are sorry we fled from the war." Instead, there are widespread examinations and personal insults, copying line-by-line the practices of the People's Republic. To make things even worse, there are rumors of instances where people have made arbitrary accusations to eliminate their rivals or people they don't like. *Holy are the ones who claim to be namha patriots.*

October 17, 1950.

Hyunchul experienced a police interrogation yesterday at Arirang Hill. When asked, "Where have you been?" He answered, "I am coming home from a *dongmoo*[140]'s house."

---

140 The original meaning is 'young friend'. However, North Koreans used this word politically to mean 'a communist

The policeman said, "As you use the word *dongmoo*, you must be a commie." The word *chinkoo*[141] is an agreeable word at my age, but at Hyunchul's younger age, *dongmoo* is actually a better-suited word. I must figure out an alternative word.

October 18, 1950.

Although we were hungry during the People's Republic era, we were so desperate and anxious that we didn't even know we were hungry. After the return of the government, perhaps our minds have become more relaxed because we now feel hunger. Along with a month-long examination 'game', there is neither salary nor distribution of food. Now we worry about dying of hunger as winter is coming close.

We were hoping the Americans would let us eat at least some flour porridge, but our disappointment grows with the shrinking of our stomachs.

It was nice just to hear them talk about distributing to each family a sack of flour or five cups of rice. Then five cups became two cups, and then two cups became one and a quarter cup, and finally even that stopped. The price of rice hasn't come down from 16,000 *won* a bushel. We all sold everything, including our clothing, during those three months under the People's Republic. Now we are left with no choice but to die of hunger.

---

comrade'.
141 Another word for 'friend'.

One load of firewood is 60,000 *won* in Mapo and transport to downtown Seoul would cost additional 10,000 *won*. If we don't die of hunger, we will freeze to death this winter.

These are what the university professors discuss amongst themselves. *Pitiful lives!*

October 19, 1950.

I saw the temporary head of the school, Mr. Bang Jonghyun, and talked with him about the examination of Lee Heeseung *sunsaeng*.

"I speak because you, Mr. Bang, know better than I that Lee Heeseung *sunsaeng* is neither a communist nor even slightly leaning towards the left. Everyone would agree without a single grain of reservation that he is a fine nationalist.

"The so-called head of education slyly wanted to take advantage of Lee *sunsaeng*'s reputation. So, Lee *sunsaeng* was allowed not to fail the examination and continued to stay at the school. But you must have found during the current investigation that he never took sides with the enemy, right? You did *namha*, so you probably don't really know how things were here. It was impossible to refuse to pass the examination when they offered one.

"When one's family is going hungry, the promise of salary and food distribution might have been too irresistible of a bait. Furthermore, if he refused, they could have accused him of being a counter-revolutionary and his life would have been in grave danger. As he had already lost the chance to do *namha*, how could he possibly refuse the offer to pass the examination? With their hands on their hearts, people need to ask this question of themselves.

"Anyhow, this is a tragedy of the nation. How can we fault Lee *sunsaeng* only? Furthermore, Lee *sunsaeng* suffered horrendous damage during the war—losing everything including clothes, food, and house. He will now be worried about how to survive the winter. If he were to be separated from the school, how miserably desolate would he feel? Also, if we lose one conscientious scholar at the highest level in his academic field, wouldn't it be an enormous loss for the country? Even in a political sense, I firmly believe the Republic of Korea is not so prejudiced and intolerant as to not embrace a scholar like Lee Heeseung *sunsaeng*.

"Furthermore, if you, Bang *sunsaeng*, as the responsible person in this situation, who used to sit with Lee Heeseung *sunsaeng* in the same department, cannot save him, how would you explain this to later generations?

"I am not mentioning Garam *sunsaeng* who is in a similar situation as he was involved in a gratuitous rumor about the Literature League. I refrain from speaking for Park Jonghong *sunsaeng* although I know him very well, but don't know how well you know him. But I believe you should settle things at least for Lee Heeseung *sunsaeng*.

"Of course, I know well that you have the same, or even stronger, concerns than I on this matter. I just wanted to let you know there is another person on the faculty who has the same views as Bang *sunsaeng*'s."

After I spoke, Bang *sunsaeng* said, "Very well, thank you. After I took this job, many people visited me, but you are the first to offer words of support for a colleague which gives me great delight." He said this, smiling.

October 20, 1950.

There was a story that Mr. Shin Sahoon had moved into the schoolhouse in which Mr. Yoo Eungho used to live. But a man with a gun came by at night and threatened him to vacate the house. He therefore cannot come near the house anymore. This led to another story about people wearing armbands with the words, 'Self-Protection Committee,' coming and taking away school furniture such as beds and chairs.

Eventually, the books left by Mr. Yoo became a topic of conversation. I put a word in saying, "It may be better to move Mr. Yoo Eungho's books to the school library." But, as I heard others saying, 'Yoo Eungho', I felt uneasy because I realized I was the only one who used the honorific title of Mister with his name.

Immediately after June 25th, when everybody was denigrating 'The Traitor of All Ages, Rhee Syngman', I tactlessly uttered the words 'Mr. Rhee Syngman'. I remember a philosophy department graduate reprimanded me. I became worried to death this might be the basis for being accused of being a counter-revolutionary.

October 21, 1950.

Jungsook went to the field yesterday and noticed somebody had already moved into our orchard house, and arranged his belongings, claiming adamantly that he is a family member of a soldier. I went there myself after breakfast to find chalk writing on the wall, 'Chung Hanyung, Army

Intelligence Office'. He was not there, but instead, there was a filthy old man, making breakfast with our wood and pulling our vegetables from the ground as if they were his own. Even when discovered by me, he kept claiming he is with 'our soldier'.

Upon prodding, he told me that an intelligence soldier of the 903rd Unit had used his power to take our house and had given it to his mother-in-law. By the way he emphasized the words, 'intelligence office' and 'intelligence personnel', he seemed to be hinting that unless I surrender my house completely, I may be taken in to suffer severe punishment.

When I asked, "If you want to move into somebody else's house, you have to talk to the owner first. How can you do this?" His answer was the soldier is the only one who knows such things and he, the old man, knows nothing. I didn't know what to do as it seemed the soldier hadn't been there for days. "How can you burn dried bean leaves that were left for the goats to eat as if they are yours?" He answered, "They are used to cook the soldier's meals." However, the solider in question was nowhere in sight.

October 22, 1950.

I visited Dr. Cho when I heard he had returned. Dr. Cho used to be a doctor at the Severance Hospital. On June 28th, he did *namha* while he was at the school. His wife had been worried to death for his life. She lost an unborn baby and endured severe suffering with their children.

He had been a rightist from the beginning, but after coming back from *namha*, his ideological views seem to have become stronger. He said, "For a while now, we should throw away any notions of democracy or what-not. There should be severe and ruthless cleansing and suppression." His stern vigor overshadowed the listener's spirits.

I smiled wryly as I recalled his prior best friend, Suh Kwangwook, had been elected as the Chairman of the People's Committee under the People's Republic and ran wild with his power for a while. Dr. Cho said, "I know everybody is impressed by the bravery of our soldiers during the war. As a doctor, the unflinching spirits of wounded soldiers also surprised me. When we were cutting arms and legs with no anesthesia, our hands trembled. But the soldiers closed their mouths tightly and suffered through the operations. There was nobody crying about pain." I had an involuntary smile.

October 23, 1950.

Lee Taeksik *koon*[142] said he needed a recommendation letter from either a congressman or a high-ranking government official in order to get a job at the Army Weapon Man-

---

142 He was a younger friend of Prof. Kim. He was a professor in the mechanical engineering department, at Seoul National University. Much later, he became an advisor to this translator when the latter was a graduate student in the department during the late sixties.

agement Office. I took him to Parliament and saw Lee Jaehyung[143] *koon*. It has been my principle to not visit a congressman or high-ranking government official to ask for favors. But as this was a request by Taeksik *koon*, I could not help it.

Jaehyung *koon* said, "There is no hope. As foreign assistance is plentiful and people are now united, this is a once-in-a-lifetime opportunity. But what can we accomplish with this top-to-bottom corruption?"

I encouraged him saying, "Despair is a self-destructive word for the incompetent. Was there a time in any society when there were no adverse conditions? So, wouldn't it be the responsibility of a capable politician to overcome adverse conditions and build new things?" Still my heart was as miserable as his.

He said, "I saw it in front of the Busan train station. While injured soldiers from the front lines were walking dozens of miles with their arms folded or limping on wounded legs, high-ranking government officials zoomed past in cars spraying dirt onto them and not feeling remoseful at all."

This demonstrated to me that his thoughts are still keen on seeking the truth.

---

143 He was an old friend and boss of Prof. Kim when he worked at the Chosun Financial Union. He was now a congressman and would later become the Chairman of the ROK Parliament.

October 24, 1950. (The UN Day).

When I went to see Cho Kyunghee *koon* yesterday, his father told me, "Whether our country will turn out better or worse depends on how much we embrace or exclude people now. The real fanatical leftists should be thoroughly identified and punished severely, but they have already run away. If we search for all the people who merely pretended to help save their lives, you will never stop searching. What would be the benefit of persecuting the people who thought, 'I wasn't a bad person. Nobody would care about me.' and stayed quietly where they were? Doing so would be like confessing their own poor statesmanship. We can always turn those people into good and loyal citizens of the Republic of Korea.

"As I witnessed during the October 1st Incident[144], and during this war, the ones who suffer the most are the innocent, middle-ground people. The worst offenders run away because they know well what they did while the people in the middle were caught defenseless and thus suffered.

"Before us, there lies a lot of work to be done including restoration, construction, and so much more. Why do we have to push away those people treating them as enemies when we can embrace them? There is nothing more stupid than this.

"During this war, houses were burned, and factories were demolished. However, the loss of people is a much bigger problem. We can rebuild those buildings or borrow somebody else's. But one engineer needs dozens of years of training. We can't borrow such skilled workers.

---

144 See the footnote 64 on July 20th.

"The country didn't have too many educated people to start with. After the August 15th Liberation, many people did not have clear political views. Because the leftists were very active, many capable people followed these leftist ideas and especially after June 25th, the world turned lopsidedly to the left. Many of the people who had previously been in the middle ground happened to turn toward the left.

"It is regrettable both on a personal and a national level that many intelligent people made connections with the leftists for this or that reason. They therefore lost the opportunity to work for our country in the present. Trying now to push even those people who are still remaining the middle can only be described as outrageously reckless. In its extreme, one might call this 'national suicide'.

October 25, 1950.

On the road to Samsunpyung, I saw Mr. Kook of Sungbook-dong. During the Japanese rule, he used to be associated with the Dong-a Daily and lived a proud, lonely life with his bees in Sungbook-dong Valley. When I was in school, I had occasion to visit and impose on him one summer day. It has been a long time since that visit. As he looked quite anxious, I asked if there was something that worried him. His daughter had been working at the Donam Elementary School. The Political Security Office took her husband, who was also a teacher at the school, on a trivial matter after June 25th. To save him, she joined and worked at the Women's League to show her willingness to help the

People's Republic and to show they were not a counter-revolutionary household. She has now been arrested by the ROK military police because of that.

"My son-in-law was taken by the People's Republic, and we don't know his whereabouts. Then the Republic of Korea arrested my daughter. My grandchildren suddenly have become orphans and cry day and night. With what has happened, how can I feel comfortable?" He smiled desolately. My heart aches thinking this cannot be happening just to his family. As I could do nothing to help him, it seemed as if it might have been better if I hadn't known.

October 26, 1950.

As I was told the car taking Taeksik *koon* to his new post would leave at eight o'clock from the front of the Weapons Management Office downtown, I came out early and got a ride. It's the first time for me to cross the Han River since 6. 25. There was a floating bridge at Mapo. Although we were supposed to cross that bridge in the car, American soldiers forced us to get out of the car and cross the river in a ferry boat. There was a checkpoint on the riverbank and ferry passenger inspection was intense. However, I was told that anybody worried about the inspection could give American soldiers money or buy women for them in order to cross the river openly in an American soldier's car.

Driving south, we saw all the bridges were destroyed, and makeshift bridges were being built everywhere. The cars needed to cross small streams on numerous occasions, but luckily it was relatively easy because it was a dry season and there wasn't much water flowing. We stayed in Daejeon that night. The destruction of Daejeon was much more severe than I'd imagined. We spent the night on a bench in a hospital that was almost like an open space as its windows were all blown out. As I looked at the cold moonlight shining upon the ruined streets, I could only think sadly that this is our fate after all.

October 27, 1950.

What struck me yesterday and today, as we were coming down from Seoul, was that there were many disabled (*Soviet*) tanks alongside the streets. Along the Seoul-Busan railway, broken tanks numbered in the hundreds. As there must be more of them along the Central Train Line as well, I could only guess that our soldiers and the American soldiers were not only fighting against the People's Army but also against the Soviet Union.

Along the road, it was high time for harvesting. The Northern Army had pushed down up to this point but retreated before the harvest. It was comforting to think, although many war victims may have lost their homes and belongings, at least they would not die of hunger this winter.

We stayed the night in Daegu. It was rather amazing that Daegu was relatively intact compared to the wretched destruction we had seen along the way.

October 28, 1950.

It had been a long while, but I could finally kneel[145] in front of my father. It seemed as if I'd gone to a foreign country far away, been through life-threatening experiences and somehow salvaged my life to come back. My old father shed tears profusely as he caressed my wrists. How much did he worry about his one son[146] all this time? He had been taken to sickbed because of the worry.

I told him, "You know there was a story of a father who was told his son was seen boarding a ship that later capsized. He wouldn't accept it at all, saying his son could not have died so. Please be strong as he was and even if there is another war, please do not worry." He simply kept shedding tears.

How would my father have felt when he heard these rumors?:

---

145 In Korea in the past, young people knelt in front of their elders. Many homes didn't have chairs, and people sat on floors. When one comes home after a long absence, he/she first kneel-bow to the parents and sit kneeling in front of them. Then the parents would give permission to relax and he/she would shift to a half-kneel position. One was not to sit Buddha-style in front of elders. This kneeling tradition is changing slowly now, but the respect for elders remain.

146 Prof. Kim was the only son with four much older sisters. Some older nephews mentioned in the diary were only ten years or so younger than him. As the only male child born very late, he was the hope of the family. His parents adored and were proud of him as the only educated one in the family.

- 'Donam-dong[147] had become a total ruin and even though there were sacks of rice on the streetcar lines, there was nobody to pick up and eat them.'

- 'Almost everybody has been taken away or shot. In particular, there were no university professors left.'

At sunset, I went up to my mother's grave and wept heartily as if to weep was the only means I had to tell her that I had survived the war.

October 29, 1950.

The People's Army did not enter our home village, but with the threat of their arrival, everybody was forced to move out. People here used the words, 'we were made to move out,' instead of 'we moved out.' The military and the police pressured them so much that they had to move to a place about six to seven miles away and returned home only after ten days or so. In the meantime, everything had been taken, including food, firewood, blankets, clothes, soy sauce, bean paste and whatever. The only things they had left were what they had on their backs when they left. Thus, everybody became like beggars.

When I asked who took all of the possessions if it was not the enemy, they said, "Who else but the ones who re-

---

147 Donam-dong (or Donam-jung) is where Prof. Kim used to live before the war and is close to Jungreung-ri.

mained in the village? The military, the police, their associates, and a few who were able to remain thanks to some connections they had." I didn't want to believe my ears. Then I remembered the words of a certain congressman who did *namha*, "Whenever there is retreat, the military and the police benefit."

I am sure not all the military and police are like that. There may be some bad elements. *Is there no way to punish them? Is the administrative power of the Republic of Korea so incapacitated?*

October 30, 1950.

I went out to visit relatives. I saw many darkened stones along the river and when I asked about them, they said that people from many towns north of here came down in the summer and stayed in this valley. They numbered forty to fifty thousand people and the riverbed was where they cooked their rice.

None of them had enough to eat. When the harsh sun shone down or when it rained, there was no place for them to find shelter. When it became unbearable, they could seek a bit of shelter in kitchens or under the eaves of local houses, but they could not all be accommodated. People fell sick and there was no medical care. Amid this, some women delivered babies and some older people collected their last breaths. It was a living hell.

A youth of the town said, "During this, there were pawns of the CIC[148] who took young girls under the false accusation of being secret agents and raped them. There were also soldiers who threatened ignorant refugee farmers, and forcefully took their cows away. They claimed they were paying for the cows, but they paid less than one-tenth of the market price. And then there were wicked men who followed those soldiers to buy the cows and sell them elsewhere. You'd never guess how many farmers had carried their belongings on their cows only to have those cows taken away and then were left weeping. When I look at these things and think about the future of our nation, all I see is darkness." I could not find the words to console this young man.

October 31, 1950.

There is a big pond in the village. They say it is about five miles around. It is quite big. It is a reservoir managed by the Water Co-op which irrigates the Keumho Plain. The plain is the lifeline of several tens of thousands of farmers.

Two drunken policemen were catching fish with hand grenades when they accidentally destroyed the sluice gate yesterday. Water from the reservoir was now gushing out. Fortunately, youths and firefighters from nearby towns were quickly called upon, and they redirected the water flow to minimize water damage. But the reservoir water will empty in a few days. They say that next year's harvest is already

---

148 Central Intelligence Corps of the 24th Corps of the US Army

ruined. Even with heavy spring rain, it will not fill half or even one-third of the water capacity.

Grenades are for fighting against commando groups, not for fishing. Pitiful are the people who rely on these policemen who get drunk in the daytime and play these dangerous games. But the real problem is the Republic of Korea which doesn't punish these recklessly irresponsible individuals.

An enormous amount of money, called the Situation Preparation Fund, had been available for poor farmers. Farmers who were bold enough to speak out complained that it was distributed only to benefit those policemen who became drunk and lawless in the daytime. I want to believe this is not true.

November 1950

November 1, 1950.

I went out to meet Kim Sangjuk *koon*. At the time of the October 1st Incident (*1946*) when he was a leading member of the local police, somebody attacked his face with a knife and he almost died. I heard he has an emotional aversion against the leftists, but I doubt that it is solely due to this incident. He had been a teacher in middle school. He had a close connection to the party[149] and had actively taken part in party affairs during the War.

His younger twin brother Kim Sangsool *koon* must be in the North by now. When they were young, people called both of them prodigies. About twenty years ago, the two young boys came to Daegu from a mountain village, Chungsong, after finishing primary school to attend a teachers' school. It was hard to distinguish one from the other. They were widely known for their brotherly love for each other at that time. They are now citizens of different countries, as they followed different ideologies. It is nothing new to see the tragedy of the separation of fathers from sons or brothers from brothers in this land but seeing Sangjuk *koon* now triggered my feelings anew.

---

149 It was possibly the Korea Peoples Party (Daehankookmindang), the major democratic party in ROK.

November 2, 1950.

I met Mr. Park Woodong in Daegu. He marveled that I had survived the war.

"As I had only been a powerless teacher, I survived the war with no big calamity. I had not been a big enemy of the People's Republic from the beginning. Nevertheless, they told me to come to the school every day in the sweltering summer. Our house is far from the school and streetcars had stopped working. Because I suffer from the heat more than others, and there was not much to eat, my original lazy nature came out. So, they fired me. But when the Republic of Korea came back, it was to my benefit that I had been fired during the People's Republic." I said.

"Still, I was told that almost everybody had been taken away, or went through severe hardship, hiding underground."

"You know, I don't belong to any groups of people of any importance. What would the People's Republic do with those who have no political inclination? I heard rumors later that many people were taken and shot to death. I was terrified and didn't show my face even in my village, but it turned out to be a baseless concern. Up until the end, nobody came to take me. However, one thing I learned through this experience is that the best way to survive in any precarious situation during a war is not to resort to some ingenious hideouts, but to keep good relations with the people of the village and to make no enemies in the world."

"As you were a citizen of the People's Republic, even if only for a few months, what do you think about it?" he inquired.

"I just breathed the air of the People's Republic, but I had no contact with it in reality. As I was hiding in the house for those three months, what could I have seen or heard? After a while, I expect to have opportunity to talk to the people who personally interacted with it. In any case, the People's Republic is no longer a puzzle to us anymore. Its naked, self-exposed identity is directly in front of us. Their organization and training were excellent. Many soldiers had wonderful qualities. I was happy to witness some solid evidence indicating that, depending on what we do, neither our society nor military have to be corrupted. On the other hand, I truly lost any sympathy toward it because of its cruelty - which was not treating people as human beings - and because of its politics which was comprised of, most of the time, false propaganda.

"At any rate, looking at the trends, many conscientious citizens in the North had longed for the Republic of Korea and came South while idealists in the South went to the North with absolute hope in the People's Republic. I now imagine both groups of people are harboring enormous disappointment. However, as there is no other place to go anymore, they may have fallen into a spiritual dilemma. If there is a way to open a door for both groups of people, I would work for it even with my life...."

November 3, 1950.

I saw Um *sunsaeng*. She is the wife of Kang Kyungsuk *koon*. She was hoping to hear any news from me about her son, Moonkoo, if not her husband, but I didn't have any since he had gone to the North. She was separated from her husband, came to Daegu alone, and got a teaching job at an elementary school when she couldn't endure her domineering mother-in-law's nagging anymore. Her mother-in-law had been a widow since a young age. Um *sunsaeng* had been hoping to be united with her husband and son. But the unexpected War banished her husband and son to another country with no prospect of getting reunited with them ever again.

"That young thing, could he have walked hundreds of miles safely under the threat of artillery shells and bombs? How could this be? Until now, it didn't matter whether he was with his father or mother. But if they were going to take the road of suffering, they could have at least left Moonkoo with me.....

"When I see children of Moonkoo's age at the school, his image keeps appearing in my eyes and I wipe away tears several times a day. Until now, I had hope of seeing him someday, but the thought of not being able to see him ever...

"Really, he was too young to be on a journey.... Could he have ever made it?" Bloody tears formed in her eyes. Listening to her story, I could not help but crying myself. There weren't many comforting words I could offer. How she could survive now with nothing to hang on to... I feel quite desolate myself even though this is not my affair.

"Moonkoo was not alone as he went with his father and grandmother and most likely he will be all right. The North is a place where people live just like here, so he can grow up with his father with little hardship. And when there is unification of the two countries, he will come and visit you. However, please try not think about your husband and son all the time... Find a good hobby or get interested in learning." I wondered how these hollow words which sound empty even to me could assuage her troubled mind.

Kang Kyungsuk *koon* has been one of my closest friends since youth. Our friendship has allowed us to spend twenty years as if they were a single day. I've always had respect for his exceptionally conscientious approach. But after the Liberation, we didn't get to see each other often and he turned to the left. Whether a leftist or a rightist, I still regard him as my friend. Now he had become a citizen of a country against which we are fighting.

This might have been my fault in a way, and I can't help but wonder if his reaction against me had contributed to his turning to the left. Thinking about it, I cannot help but feel a pang of remorse, even now.

After the Liberation, he'd taken the trouble to visit me in Choongchung-do from Daegu. For several days and nights, we discussed what we wanted to do together. Our chief topic was for us to build a small school and educate youths properly. He was very ardent about it, and I felt the same to a certain extent. In the daytime, we walked in a pine field talking and we continued the discussion into the night while in our beds. Sometimes we were excited by new hope and at other times we despaired when we saw obstacles.

But then, there appeared to be a bit of a difference between us regarding the method of execution and its timing and we decided to study it further. Then sudden changes in our surrounding conditions stopped us from pursuing it any further. Even when we got together in Seoul later, he showed a deep interest in politics with a pure and ardent heart for the people and the country while I was occupied with my work at the university. Since we did not walk in the same direction anymore, this inevitably created a bit of a separation between us.

However, he was not the type that would go away and do things alone once he found a pathway he believed to be right. There had been a couple of times we could have discussed the matter again; but I was not a person to follow such a political path by then.

We therefore became separated.... But I didn't know we would be separated this far. Life is after all a sorrow as I look back on it now.

November 4, 1950.

I saw Kim Yoojin *koon* on the street. I asked him about Kim Choongsup *koon*'s whereabouts, but he said he had no idea.

It was the summer of 1941 about ten years ago. I had spent that summer at the Dongwha Temple in Palgong Mountains[150]. There were three students who came there to study and prepare for the entrance examination to Daegu

---

150 It was the practice of aspiring students to room and board in quiet Buddhist temples in remote mountainous areas and spend summers when school was closed. They isolated themselves from society and focused on studying. The translator did the same during a couple of high school summers for a few weeks each. Although he did not study as much as he had planned, it was a valuable time for him, being alone in the mountains.

High School[151]. Even in a quiet place in the middle of the mountains, there wasn't much contact among the students. All three were such hard-working students that they barely acknowledged each other's presence until September when it was almost time for them to leave. They exchanged names: Kim Choongsup, Kwon Sewhan, Yoon Joongki. I firmly believed these three would eventually become hard and conscientious workers of our country.

I didn't have any news about them after that until a few years ago when Kim Choongsup *koon* became a student at the Arts and Science College as a student of history. I then became close to him. I heard that Kwon *koon* is now working underground actively and Yoon *koon* is at home suffering from a nervous breakdown. We laughed saying Kim Choongsup *koon* now should take on the study load of study three people.

At first, I wondered what Kim *koon*'s ideology was. As time went by, I realized he was a pure liberalist. However, his mind was genuinely too pure and beautiful to paint some thick ideological colors upon it.

Then he said to me after June 25th, "A representative who stayed in the North relayed this to me. He once visited a farming village in the North to see the current state of affairs. He liked that everyone treated him in a friendly manner saying, 'comrade representative, comrade representative,' and every household in the village had a radio, a phonograph, and a fine chest for clothes. It sounded truly like

---

151 A high school in Daegu. Prof. Kim attended this school before being expelled in 1928. There were nationwide competitive, sometimes very competitive, entrance examinations to middle schools, high schools and colleges.

the realization of the ideal society that we had been dreaming of. The North must be a really good place to live!" I could read on his face the fervent expectation of an idealist. He must have gone to the North with this expectation and longing.

How much would he then be disappointed if he should see the villages that Myung Daemok described to me after seeing them with his own eyes, "In the villages, the only modern convenience was lightbulbs. People have only one pair of clothes for the summer and another for the winter. It was rare to see anybody wearing shoes and windows were pasted over with newspaper."

November 5, 1950.

Coming south, I was lucky to bum a ride in the car taking Taeksik *koon* to his new post, but now I don't have any idea how to return to Seoul. People with money can have roads opened for them and men with power can travel comfortably, but a naive academic like me has nothing to fall back on. In Daegu, I anxiously searched for three days but nothing seemed to be available.

I went to the train station very early and waited with patience today. Luckily, there was a train heading north. I elbowed my way forward and got a space. But as there was only one carriage allocated to passengers, everybody was packed in or dangled precariously from the storage space on the roof. One may call it 'train hell'. I was still young, and I stuffed decorum into my pocket and squeezed inside.

Inside the carriage, most people were those who had taken shelter in Busan. There were women with malnourished faces in rag-like clothes, with dirty children clinging to them. Among them, there was a young mother whose husband was recruited as a soldier during the war. With no news concerning her husband and with her children clinging to her, she sighed desolately that she didn't know what to do, all the while getting irritated with her hungry children.

Inside was like packed bean sprouts with no room even to wiggle. It made me anxious being squeezed in between so many people. My head ached from the fetid smell of sweat. Children urinated and defecated where they were, making the air inside unbearable. The windows were open, but they were not enough to help cope with the smell inside. The smell was like a cesspool in the middle of a sweltering summer.

While the car was moving, it was bearable, but this car stopped much longer than it moved. The situation became unbearably miserable when our train stopped at an insignificant station for many hours with no one bothering to let us know how long it was going to take before we were again on our way. The only thing we could do was crawl out of and crawl back through the windows whenever it stopped. In this manner, we covered about twenty-five miles in twenty-four hours, from Daegu to Goomi. To get to Seoul, it may take a week or ten days, and people were already deadly tired. The color of urine is not yellow anymore. It was turning red. With my strength fading, I didn't think I could make it to Seoul.

November 6, 1950.

The car that arrived in Goomi that night would not leave in the morning. As I couldn't wait anymore, I went inside the station office only to find the train operator and the fire stokers were sleeping there. When I scolded them about leaving all the passengers by themselves, they said that the line was blocked ahead of us so the train could not move. When I suggested they should have let the passengers know, they answered that it was not a passenger car. People just boarded on their own, so it's not their responsibility to care about them. It's true that the railway does not yet accept passengers. Everybody got on board because they needed to. *Could they still say things like this and get away with it?*

As I couldn't stand the carriage anymore, I got off with my bag. Not that there was a better way, but I was afraid of getting ill if I stayed there any longer. My body is not yet trained enough to suffer through the nation's hardships. It shouldn't be like this…perhaps I would be better off walking to Seoul[152]?

I was enjoying the fresh autumn morning air and resting my tired head on the platform when an express train came rushing in with full force. A station worker said it's a military train for British soldiers only. I explained my situation to an elderly-looking soldier at the door, but he didn't seem to have any power and was perplexed about what to do. In the meantime, when the train started moving, I simply jumped in. We reached Kimchun in a dash. If I'd remained in the earlier train, it would have taken another day.

---

152 Some 170 miles away.

On the way to Kimchun, I had a good time chatting with the soldiers and sharing food. I felt closer to them when they said they were Irish. But when we stopped at Kimchun, an officer came to tell me to get off. I tried to carefully explain my plight, but he said this car doesn't allow anybody other than soldiers, especially not Koreans. Hearing this, I felt insulted and hurried off.

I went to the front of the station to inquire and was told there were many trucks going to Seoul, and some will take passengers for 10,000 won. Unfortunately, I didn't have 10,000 won. On the way here, I saw military policemen controlling truck traffic at the bank of the river coming into Kimchun. I went there but realized there wouldn't be any among them that could take me.

As I sat there by the bridge for half a day, a military policeman asked me who I was. As I explained my situation, he laughed and said they were there controlling car traffic but not helping pedestrians get a ride. This friendly MP finally directed me toward a decent truck. In this way, I made it to Daejun.

November 7, 1950.

From the car, I could see that all the houses along the street were destroyed and burnt. But the houses a little removed from the street looked relatively untouched.

In a way, our country is like a house along the street of the world.

November 8, 1950.

When I got home, I was told that Mrs. Ko, the wife of Chul *koon*, had been there. I couldn't listen to her story without tears, the story of the pregnant woman who followed her husband hurriedly on a path for more than a hundred miles with a young child on her back and carrying a heavy sack. She'd hit a point where she could no longer continue, was separated from her husband and then turned back. Trekking on mountain roads day and night, the temperament of Mrs. Ko became uneven. Meanwhile, scared of gun/cannon sounds, the child could not sleep well and would wake up in the night and cry without end, making everyone around them miserable. Wife related this story to me through her own tears.

Mrs. Ko is calm and wades through most things in life unperturbed. If she were not so, she would have gone mad. May God protect her and her daughter.

November 9, 1950.

Our town leader, Mr. Sung Yoonkil, was taken into custody. I know very well that while he may not have been very knowledgeable, he is a very capable and sincere person. In managing town affairs, his actions were based on a sense of justice, without falling into obstinacy.... And he always had room to think about the future.

After June 25th, he was stripped of the town-leader job and was sometimes seen working in the fields with an A-frame[153]. Just before September 28th, he was the one who told us, "The UN soldiers have already captured downtown Seoul. It will be a mere day or two before Jungreung-ri will be restored, so do not worry." I was quite surprised he was arrested for being an enemy helper.

It is really a pity to lose such a capable person based on a totally baseless accusation when our town already suffers a severe shortage of talented people. There must have been somebody who wanted to become a town leader himself. It is really deplorable that a government investigative organization was part of such a nonsensical business.

November 10, 1950.

Mr. Kang Daeryang came to see me in the morning quite unexpectedly. He used to be an assistant professor. He went to his hometown a week prior to June 25th, and there has been no news from him since then. His wife visited his friends and organizations to get food and his salary from the Department of Education revealing over and over that Mr. Kang had been a party member for a long time. She said he had been a guerrilla member and Kim Jaeryong, who was captured and killed by the ROK Navy a while ago, was actually Mr. Kang's subordinate. When she revealed all these facts, people became aware of who and what he had been in

---

153 A simple structure made of wooden poles to carry loads on one's back. From the back, it looks like a letter 'A' and from the side, it looks like an 'small y'. It has shoulder straps on either side.

truth. He had been known to be a dedicated student who had received absolute confidence from the chair professor, Lee Byungdo.

I had known for a year that he was a leftist. Mr. Lee Byungdo had secretly told me he had contacted Mr. Yoon Bosun[154] for Mr. Kang's release from the military police and from potential harsh treatment there. I also heard that, when Lee Bonryung *koon* was taken to the Mapo Police Station, some policeman asked him about a 'bad boy' by the name of Kang Daeryang. But nobody else in the world knew until his wife publicized it.

Therefore, I thought he was a person who could not come back to Seoul. He looked emaciated. He came to Seoul without realizing that his identity was blown. As he now cannot cross the Han River, he is living the life of a refugee. He cannot rest his mind as there are many students who would recognize his face. With a grave expression on his face, he said, "What disappointed me more than anything was not that my identity was blown or that the People's Republic Army was defeated and ran away, but that the People's Republic lost the hearts of the people through and through. I see that citizens of Seoul now abominate North Koreans from the depth of their heart. That's why I do not have a place to stand here and now. Kim *sunsaengnim*, you are a fair-minded person. How do you see this?"

I asked him at the end of our discussion, "How do you assess the current situation of the war?"

He said, "As I have no contact with the North now, I have no basis to judge the situation. But when the cold weather

---

154 Mr. Yoon would become the president of ROK in 1960.

comes, I suppose there might be some changes.[155]" These are truly scary people.

There was an opening ceremony of the Arts and Science College at Sungkyoonkwan University[156].

November 12, 1950.

A story by a friend from my hometown:

"In the summer, countless refugees had crowded along the river by the time we were retreating from the Nakdonggang front. But crossing the river was very tricky and challenging. If it was delayed too much, American bombers might drop bombs at any minute. In this confusion, there was a young couple with an old father and a baby. They realized, however they tried, they could not save both their father and baby at the same time. So, they threw their baby into the water, and everybody admired their filial loyalty."

It was a commendable act. However, from this event I have also come to agree with the criticism that Korean people do not look forward, but only look back. I don't think it is our God-given nature. It is a long-cherished habit influenced by Confucianism.

---

155 He seems to indicate the North may somehow not be completely defeated.
156 Buildings of the Seoul National University were occupied by the military.

November 13, 1950.

On a road in the hills, I saw Son Woosung *sunsaeng*. His face was swollen and he had difficulty walking. When asked what happened, he said a patrolling policeman was conducting a routine questioning around the middle of last month. It was found that his briefcase happened to contain a certificate of food distribution that had been issued by the People's Republic. He was immediately taken to the Sungbook police station and suffered for some twenty days. He was released only yesterday.

At the beginning of the People's Republic, they advertised generously but groundlessly that there would be a special distribution of food to public servants. I had prepared an application form myself at the Self-Governing Committee. They said the format was incorrect every time I submitted it. I had to rewrite the form three or four times over. It was a four-page long document requiring detailed information about family members. There was no food distribution after all. I heard later that party members and their agents shared the booty after kicking us out.

I might also have that kind of paper in my briefcase. I could not understand how they could take a national university professor for such a minor infraction, keep him for over twenty days, and then release him in that shape? All I can do is to cry for the Republic of Korea.

November 14, 1950.

There is a rumor that our ROK soldiers have become an immense disappointment for the people of the North as the soldiers went into Pyungyang and other areas in the North while committing brutalities, such as plundering villages and raping women recklessly. It is a heart-wrenching rumor. I pray and hope the rumor is not true.

I recall how the hearts of the people of Seoul had been turned in favor of the Republic of Korea over the three months. Then their hearts were seriously scarred by the violent behavior of some military men and police since September 28th. I worry deeply that pure hearts of the people in the North who have waited for five years[157] might have been similarly crushed by these reckless actions.

November 15, 1950.

It has become severely cold with temperatures dropping as low as 5 degrees Fahrenheit. There was opening ceremony of the Law College at the Dongkook College. Into the auditorium, which was left without a single pane of windows, piercing North winds blew in as if foretelling upcoming challenges we will face in education.

Nevertheless, I made a firm promise in my mind to overcome whatever challenges we may face. On my frozen cheeks tears were flowing for no reason.

---

157 People who had democratic inclinations but were trapped in communist North Korea after liberation from Japan in 1945.

November 16, 1950.

On the issue of administration in the restored areas of the North, there seem to be different opinions between ROK and UN. One side (*ROK*) wants to send Southern officials and the other side (*UN*) wants to use people from the North. It may be difficult for the Republic of Korea to accept the UN's proposal as it had already named ghost heads[158] of the five Northern provinces a long time ago and has since been waiting to recover the North. However, we would like to support the UN's opinion.

Let's suppose that we follow what the South insists and send some low-quality administrative officials from the South. They may be easily swayed by emotions, oppress or insult the people of the North, or monopolize their own profits and treat the North as the South's colony. An impassable chasm could form between the people of the North and the South, creating and solidifying a psychological 38th parallel firmly in our minds. This could never be the best policy for the long-term future of all Korean people.

We should now abandon seeking such small benefits as 'preserving the honor of the Republic of Korea'. For the long-term future of our people, I believe we should follow the UN's desire to leave the North to the people of the North.

---

158 Before the war, ROK had selected ghost heads of provinces in the North so they could assume the job when one day the ROK would take over DPRK. Their titles were in name only.

November 17, 1950.

At the Euljiro Bangsan Primary School building, I gave the first lecture since the war. Only two students came. The cold classroom was even more miserable, but I gave an inspirational lecture with new ideals and passion.

Come to think of it, I may have already lost my qualification as a teacher. Although I never actively misled the young people who followed me, I didn't show them a clear path to follow, either. My heart ached at the thought that this may be the reason why some died and others are struggling in this unfamiliar world.

"But this still should be my God-given occupation. Even if I didn't guide them explicitly concerning the North and the South, wouldn't it still be my job to educate and let them decide for themselves what their proper path in life is?" I felt more confident about this long-held conviction of mine and was able to deliver a more enthusiastic lecture than ever before.

November 18, 1950.

There is a person called Jin Seungrok. He taught at Bosung College for a long time and was the dean of the Law College of the University at the time of the War. He was taken by the students he had taught and sent North only to be saved by another student of his. The sorrows and joys of a teacher may exist in such events.

I also heard a story like this: The head monk of Kyungkook-sa temple was taken to the Sungbook police station. When there was an air-raid alarm and the station was in confusion, an unknown boy led him to escape. As he was leaving, he said to a sentry, "Good work." Mistaking him to be a person who was allowed to leave, the sentry said, "Goodbye." One could say the monk was under Buddha's benevolent protection.

November 19, 1950.

Immediately after June 25th, there were posters (*posted by North Koreans*) in the streets that proclaimed, "The president of America declared it would keep its hands off of Korea," but we found out later that the American Army, Navy and Air Force all had orders to mobilize by that time.

Immediately after September 28th, there were posters (*posted by South Koreans*) that said, "China has decided not to intervene in the Korean War." Both sides spread similarly false propaganda and it soon became hard to tell which one was worse than the other.

The dispute about whether China would intervene became an undeniable fact[159] when MacArthur lodged a complaint with the UN Security Council about it on November 6th.

Mr. Sung Yoonkil said when he was released, "Kim *sunsaeng*, let's take refuge quickly, perhaps into the mountains of Choongchung Province." I hadn't realized until then the situation was that urgent. According to Jungyong, they

---

159 China intervened in the Korean War and crossed the Yalu River (the border between China and Korea, North of Pyungyang) on Oct 19th.

were digging trenches around Seoul and putting up barbed wire fences. *What is happening here? I thought the front line is at the Yalu River. There was a rumor that tens of thousands of People's Army soldiers are still in Kangwon Province*[160]*. Could that be the reason?* Anxiety is pushing my heart down like a heavy lead block.

I had a job offer to work for the War History Publishing Committee.[161]

November 20, 1950.

These days, articles written by people of cultures from all corners of society appear under the title 'Defeat of Communism,' in Seoul newspapers every day. They all proclaim, "Communism is a group that should never be accepted in the world, hence it needs to be destroyed completely." Even people we have never suspected are writing such valiant articles. None of these articles show any hint of being written against the author's will and accordingly they all appeal to our sense of reality…. The articles all touch our hearts. One might call this a change in the world.

---

160 A mountainous region, south of the 38th parallel, east of Seoul.
161 Prof. Kim would later take the job as a refugee in Busan.

November 21, 1950.

It was my understanding that the collision of the cold Liman Current flowing from the North along the eastern coastline of Korea, with the warm Black Current from the South, is resulting in an abundant fish population and thus large catches of fish. This should be comparable to the situation on land where American and Soviet powers collided and consequently drew a line, the 38th parallel.

While fish in the East Sea make good use of the collision of north and south currents to increase their own population, how on can earth people on land fail to make use of this crossing of American and Soviet powers for a better purpose but instead continue the tragedy of fratricidal war? Is it because people are dumber than fish?

November 22, 1950.

My mood was black all day as I heard that the sons[162] of Park Jonghong *sunsaengnim* were selling cigarettes on the streets. Wife also grieved with a sigh, "How can we guarantee our children won't do the same?"

---

162 Park sunsaengnim had seven children. Woochang was 15 years old, Kyoochang was 12 and the last daughter (Yekyung) was perhaps one year old at the time. The fourth child, Yoonchang, was of the translator's age (5) and became his very good friend after the war. He is now retired from his position as a chemistry professor at Sungkyoonkwan University.

Park *sunsaengnim* is the sincerest scholar I know, and Mrs. Park is one of the most devoted housewives in the world. Their children are also upright and diligent middle school students. He isn't rich, but not poor either. But now Woochangand Kyoochang do not go to school and instead sell cigarettes on the streets. If we feel terrible and frustrated hearing this, how must *sunsaengnim* and Mrs. Park feel?

It was easy to imagine the tragedy of fratricide would bring countless hardships to our people. Mistreatment of scholars doesn't seem to be confined to the People's Republic. Could there be any future for our country, when broken into worthless shards like this?

November 23, 1950.

I think it was last autumn... only about three miles from my hometown, mountain people (in my hometown, we call guerillas mountain people or mountain guests) came down to the town of Kyungsan-koon, Wachon-myun, and Paksa-dong, and burned about ninety houses, and killed about forty people and injured many more. The people who died were mostly young men between the ages of twenty and forty. They were not simply killed with guns. They were butchered with knives, stabbed by spears, or bludgeoned to death with clubs. The unimaginable cruelty was very hard to witness, I was told. The townspeople took complete leave of their senses, shaken by the scale of loss not knowing what to do after losing their homes, property, husbands, and sons.

I wondered what kind of hatred had filled their minds to lead to the massacre defenseless people in such a brutal fashion. They say it was because one town person alerted the police to their hiding place. I wonder if this was one of their 'merciless struggles', one of the catch phrases of the Northern communists? People in nearby towns shuddered at this abominable cruelty.

Lee *koon* from Kyungsan happened to visit Pyungyang where he saw posters on the street referring to 'A heroic uprising by farmers in Kyungsan'. Upon reading further, he realized they were referring to the very same incident in Waryong-*myun*. The posters proclaimed, "Unable to suffer through the Southern puppet regime's tyranny, farmers revolted and killed hundreds of counter-revolutionaries."

November 24, 1950.

Mr. Kim Namsoo was a well-known and important leader of the Communist Party during Japanese rule, who died in jail. A Communist Party member at that time was not necessarily a through-and-through Bolshevik. At the time, the young generation was mostly impassioned about the liberation of our people. Considering the world situation at the time, they thought the Soviet Union was the only country that could help us, and they joined the communist movement. I am not necessarily saying he was such a person, but....

Mr. Kim's two sons grew up and were living in Seoul with their mother. When the war broke out, both of them said, "Now is the time to avenge our father," and volunteered to the Volunteer Army. I don't know whether they are alive, but now Mr. Kim's aging wife, with her daughters-in-law and grandchildren, leads a hard life. *When the children grow up, what will they think about their grandfather and fathers?* I can see already that communism in our country is following bloodlines. When I recall that 'the Power Struggles of Four Factions[163]' during the Chosun Dynasty was intermingled with bloodshed, I realized that familial succession of philosophies among disputing factions is one very important cause of prolonged struggles. We need to watch out for that.

November 25, 1950.

There was a faculty meeting at the school today. There was a heated argument, primarily between Mr. Kim Sunkee and I, on how to resolve the issue of a substitute student whose acceptance to the school had been denied just prior to June 25th.

Mr. Kim argued that Dean Son Jintae, under pressure from a higher-up, had reversed the previous no-acceptance action. He said, "Now that Mr. Son has died, we don't want to disgrace him, so let's not bring this issue up." I countered that a person is a person, and an organization is an organization—one cannot sacrifice an organization for the sake of one person. I also pointed out that this cannot be allowed when we consider the authority and dignity of the faculty decision.

---

163 A very prolonged political power struggle in the Chosun Dynasty that lasted generations. It had devastating effects on the country Chosun.

As a formal acceptance letter was already sent, he and some others argued we should handle any blame within the school, and the student's acceptance should not be cancelled. I strongly argued that a privilege obtained through a faulty decision based on impropriety can and should be annulled.

November 26, 1950.

There was news that General MacArthur urged soldiers on the front line to take Sineuijoo within the month to stop the potential loss of UN soldiers' lives, and that he went to the frontline himself. This gave me the same jolt as the one I felt last August 15th when General Kim Ilsung stated that the month of August should be proclaimed 'The Liberation Month'.

November 27, 1950.

[*A portion of the original content is lost*]

I told him that people who had volunteered for the Volunteer Army should turn themselves in and then the government should let those people go free. I urged him to go to the police, but he seemed quite scared, saying, "I lose my nerve and my heart trembles at the sight of even a police uniform." I dragged him to the Joongboo police station and quite unexpectedly found that the head of the investigation there was Jung Kiyup *koon* from the same hometown. Everything was taken care of smoothly. There are really some strange coincidences in the world.

November 28, 1950.

"We were taken from areas around Daegu to be trained in Japan as UN soldiers during the summer. We were all given the same amount of food as the American soldiers, but only the Korean people were always hungry and looking for more food. Sometimes there were occasions when shameful incidents occurred," a student told me. I understood what he said as follows:

A reason for their hunger could be that the UN forces had taken anybody available in Korea as soldiers, many of them uncultured. I can also think of two other reasons why Koreans cannot be indifferent to food: one is physiological, and the other psychological.

The physiological reason is that all Koreans have dilated stomachs. To produce a certain amount of energy, one has to take in a certain number of calories. To obtain a given number of calories from plain/meager diets, one needs large quantities, resulting in dilated stomachs. With dilated stomachs, we therefore cannot be indifferent to food.

Psychologically, suppose I have a bowl of rice in front of me. If I am assured that I can eat rice tomorrow and the day after tomorrow, I can look at this bowl somewhat indifferently. But if I don't expect that I can eat the same food tomorrow and it could be even worse the day after tomorrow, I would look at that bowl of rice very differently. For generations, we were never sure of having food the next day. One can see this dismal aspect of life, especially in our most recent history. As a result, anxiety about food has become a kind of hereditary trait. Given this history, a constant psychological hunger for food is understandable.

Koreans often like to point out and criticize their own ugly habits as if they are talking about somebody else's affair. But we should first reflect on how and from where these national shortcomings have come and, after that, think seriously about how we could overcome those shortcomings.

November 29, 1950.

They say Mr. Chang Myun became the prime minister and Mr. Kim Joonyun and Mr. Kong Jinhang became cabinet members. As Mr. Kong is from our town, there are numerous posters in street alleys that exclaim, 'Hooray for His Excellency Kong Jinhang'. There must be other and more urgent matters the Korea Youth Organization could address.

There is a saying, "When a country is going downhill, only personnel changes become matters of concern." The only wind blowing in Korea these days is the wind seeking government positions. But the positions will not last long anyway. Can a capable administration be formed with all these comings and goings of people in numerous positions? One good thing from these quick rotations may be it allows everybody who wants to wear a hat to do so at least once.

There was a theory that a parliamentary cabinet system would not work well because instability would ensue, but I wonder how stable we are now with our presidential system of government.

November 30, 1950.

I bought a Boston Bag[164] at Arirang Hill. I remember, just prior to September 28th, officers of the People's Republic Army, with a help from the Women's League, were going around looking for a Boston Bag in exchange for a sack of rice.

I was told today that a huge Chinese Army unit crossed the Yalu River. I am now buying a Boston bag using most of the money I have with the same intention.

---

164 A travelling bag or a general utility bag.

December 1950

December 1, 1950

I gave my third lecture today. There were only two students at the beginning, but the numbers grew gradually, and the classroom now looks respectable. Having students from more than ten schools study in one place is an unavoidable measure because of the war, but it is also quite an interesting phenomenon. If it is properly done, the efficiency of education may even be greater. Although there are many female students, the number of male students is not too far behind. Considering that military summons may be given to them at any minute, I feel boundless gratitude for the minds of those who are coming out to study like this.

I gave the lecture in a classroom with no heat in bitterly cold weather - with the temperature around 14 degrees Fahrenheit.

Although chattering and rattling on, I may be better off than the students. They must have felt the cold even more, sitting still. The ink was frozen, and their hands were frozen numb as well. I could not ask them to write anything down. Talking away as I please, I naturally broached the issues of the present day along with issues regarding the future of our people. At times, both speaker and listeners felt the upward swell of emotion in the chests.

These lecture days induce in me a feeling of worth amid deep sadness.

December 2, 1950.

During these long, sleepless winter nights, life seems like a charade. Close friends of ten years, close colleagues with whom I could discuss everything, students who frequented my study--all have left for another country far away and I am left alone in a devastated city.

Will there be a time when we can work hand-in-hand towards the unification of our mother country? Although my body is alive, I feel as if my world is already gone. How much time will have to pass before I can shake this feeling of emptiness and I can regain the desire for life with new friends?

Kang Kyungsuk, Lee Chul, Hong Seungkee, Lee Bonryung, Kim Ilchool, Jung Heejoon, Kim Deukjoong, Jung Chanyung, Chae Hikook, Kim Hongki, Choi Bongrae, Lee Seungryun, Lee Wonjo, Kim Byungje, Lee Jongak, Jo Wonje, Kim Choongsup, Kim Suksun, Park Joonkyoo, Kim Janghi, Yoo Yul, Park Chanhyung.... Please, may good health be with you all always.

December 3, 1950.

They say one can only survive in this world with three "whether-or-nots." I didn't know what they meant. They told me, one can only survive: (1) in a town too difficult to tell from the outside whether or not it exists; (2) with a house too difficult to tell whether or not it is a house; and (3) by acting in such a way that they don't know whether or not one is a person. It's a lesson for people in a country riddled with the ruthless fighting of left against right.

December 4, 1950.

Since it was known that a large contingent of Chinese army is now taking part in the war, and the retreat of UN troops from Pyungyang is no longer a rumor, the discussion of whether atomic bombs should or should not be used has become the talk of the city. The *Seoul Daily* adamantly advocates the use of atomic bombs as soon as possible.

As no one in the world would pay any attention to these newspapers anyway, they may have been saying whatever they felt like saying. But pleading - 'Please use atomic bombs made by somebody else on our land' - cannot be the approach taken by a prominent newspaper of a country. However urgent the situation is, this is not too far from insanity, carrying the matter of fratricide to the extreme.

It must be our priority never to use such things as atomic bombs to kill people. It is very hard to understand their reason for advocating the use of a fratricidal weapon on our land, of all places.

December 5, 1950.

There are rampant rumors in the streets that the Japanese military has landed. Common sense tells us this cannot be true, but people truly believe it. Perhaps they are fooled by Communist propaganda. There actually are people who claim they saw with their own eyes Japanese troops asking for directions speaking in Japanese. I doubt America could be in such a dire situation to ask for the help of its previous enemy...

There are two groups of opinions about Japanese participation.

"I never want to hear sounds of Japanese wooden sandals," is one side, while another says, "Japanese troops or whoever, even those who are worse than the Japanese should come and help us."

December 6, 1950

The streets were quite noisy and confused over the last few days. Officers in the army are moving their families and belongings to the south. People with money are following them. Hiring a truck to Daegu would cost 120,000 *won*. I think fleeing for safety is solely the prerogative of people with money or power.

December 7, 1950

People say the Chinese Communist '*Orangkae*' are coming. The Korean word *orangkae* was originally used to generally indicate 'different tribes, or *eejok*' because there used to be a foreign tribe that was a branch of the Yujin tribe, located near us in the north just outside the Dooman River, called '*orangkae*'. The word is now used with a certain amount of disdain implied.

If the word *orangkae* is used to describe the Chinese Communists in order to mean a different tribe, *eejok*, that is understandable; but if it were to somehow mean eejuk[165] as Chinese people use the word, that is not right. Justifiably or not, Chinese Communists are descendants of Joongwha and according to them, we are one of four barbarian tribes called the Dong-ee (*Eastern bowmen*) tribes. If we use the word, *orangkae*, in a derogative sense, it will become an example of the proverbial saying, 'spitting at the sky'[166]. I am not saying this because I am an obsequious person to China.

December 8, 1950.

I went to give a lecture today, but the school had declared a vacation day and things were being packed. It looked like

---

165 Chinese people called themselves Joongwha people. The word Joongwha means the center of the universe. They called people of its surrounding countries as follows: 'Eastern bow(ee)men', 'Insect-infested South', 'Western spearmen' and 'Wolf (juk)-infested North'. On the whole, these words were used to mean 'barbarians with no culture'. Together, these four words are condensed into 'eejuk'.

166 The spit would fall back onto your own face. Or, if one insults somebody, the insult will come back to you. Prof. Kim didn't want Koreans to get involved with such meaningless exchanges of insults.

preparation for another departure. I did not complain because what I had prepared was rendered useless, I was simply dispirited.

December 9, 1950.

Even the government has announced it is okay for the elderly and children to leave Seoul. The reason given is not that the Chinese Communists are surging into the country, but that Seoul has not secured enough food and coal for the winter.

Whether it was in fact an official recommendation for evacuation or not, but it was a tacit approval at least, so it came as a big jolt to the citizens. I told my brother-in-law to go down to Daegu and Kim Jongok (*Mansoo*) *koon* to go to his hometown. He came back to Seoul a month ago to study, but as the school had not yet been restored, he has been studying at home. I remember forcing him to go down on June 27th.

December 10, 1950.

I had told Wife to butcher a goat. But when I came home, she conveyed that she was distraught when a young man in military uniform from the neighborhood came and asked for the meat. He identified himself as a member of the Communist Guerilla Defeat Corps. It had been very active, working underground during the summer and had been awarded an official commendation by the military. I may have seen an article about it a few days ago.

While I was listening to her story, a newspaper arrived that had an article about the wholesale arrest of members of the Communist Guerilla Defeat Corps. The newspaper said they actually were communists with false masks. Some northern party members, who were not able to escape to the North during the September 28th period, had recruited roughnecks and organized themselves with the respectable-sounding name of Communist Guerilla Defeat Corps. Wearing military uniforms and carrying arms, they infested the towns of Soongin-myun and Sindo-myun at the edges of the Samkak Mountains and committed many evil acts - including homicide, plunder, rape, illegal imprisonment and recruitment.

The world is too complex to understand for those of us with simple minds. Reading this article, a friend questioned, "What happened to the office that had awarded a commendation to these people just a few days ago? Who knows for sure if the principal members of the unit are indeed communists or not?"

December 11, 1950.

While packing for escape to the south, every organization is still occupied with investigations, suspensions, and firings. If there still remains a sleeper agent, that's another matter. But it was believed that all of the sleeper agents had disappeared already by September 28th. The people who remained had been abandoned by the government and were left helpless while an overpowering force had thrown the country upside-down. They had to pretend to be people of the new country to survive.

If those who are now punishing these people were in the same situation, they themselves could not have done anything differently. These were the very people who told others not to worry and stay put, claiming things were well in order, while they themselves cowardly did *namha,* or they were the irresponsible people who did not obey government orders to keep and secure offices but ran away south, or they were the people who did not enjoy the glorious *namha* themselves for some reason but were somehow able to hide underground.

They may be forgiven if they said something like: "How harrowing and painful was it to be harassed and have your lives threatened for three months? We are ashamed that we alone somehow avoided hardship." Instead, they were very high-handed and spent too much energy and time punishing people, stating, "We are the only true patriots, and we know there are none of you who didn't help the enemy. It is only a matter of degree."

If the people who were investigated and punished for helping the North were anything like or sympathetic to the Bolsheviks, that's another matter. But all of them were pure nationalists and most of them were proficient in their own work. Furthermore, their personalities were sincere and generous. That's one reason why the People's Republic had tried hard to recruit and use them.

I carefully thought about the true intentions of these persecutors. I realized the following: Even though they fully understood what had really happened to these people during those harsh times, they have other hidden objectives. They may be supervisors wanting to remove not-so-easily manageable subordinates and replace them with their own people, same-level people wanting to push out capable people to eliminate competition, or they may be lower-level people wanting to take coveted positions. Sometimes, all three of these parties present a unified front leaving the people who stayed in the People's Republic to be unfairly punished.

I have always said the Republic of Korea, which is already suffering from the paucity of talented people, has lost so many more of them during the war. The malicious intention of those who try to get rid of the few remaining people this way, without good reason, is unforgivable. For an organization, it causes work delays, and, for the country, it turns into the stupidest act of deliberately pushing excellent mid-level individuals to the enemy's direction. I sometimes cannot suppress my violent anger at the government for playing for so many months this kind of game which I can only characterize as the suicide of our country.

There may occasionally be some bad enemy informants. But aren't there already enough investigative organizations out there to deal with them? Perhaps somebody would say self-regulation is preferable. But once someone tries self-regulation, he would soon find it to be very harmful indeed. It is sad that all the public institutions are spending all their energy on this issue at this busy time. The results would only generate suicidal tragedy ….

On top of this, so many military or police organizations are acting recklessly, and their malignant effects are too absurd to list. Either way, the pure hearts of Seoul's citizens of the time of September 28th are being trampled on repeatedly.

December 12, 1950.

The number of trucks running on frozen roads, loaded with large groups of runaway people, is increasing daily. Citizens without such means just look mournfully out of the corner of their eyes at the back of the trucks with leaden hearts and worried faces.

Standing on the streets of Seoul at twilight, feeling the north wind of winter, I have never felt more keenly the helplessness of a scholar. I never felt envious of old friends who got high positions and drove luxurious cars, but believing they can now move their children to a safe place with little effort... I feel envy for such magical powers this evening.

December 13, 1950.

We packed our own refugee baggage.

We know neither where to go nor there would even be a place in which we can settle. Even if there is such a place to settle down, we can't be sure whether the Chinese Communists, after rolling over Seoul, would leave Busan alone[167]. But we can't stay here with the children where intense fighting in the streets will undoubtedly ensue. As everybody says they are leaving, we also feel agitated. But more than that, if there actually comes an order to vacate,

---

167 Losing Busan means ROK would cease to exist.

we wouldn't be able to do anything in the confusion. We need to move the children away from these streets in a hurry.

December 14, 1950.

We moved to Mr. Lee Keunmoo's Namsan-dong house (*closer to the downtown Seoul*) first. Mr. Lee has already left, but an old relative was keeping watch on the house. We thought we might have a better chance here for an easier access to downtown. In the north Jungreung-ri corner of the city, we may miss an opportunity to escape even if one came along.

Leaving the house and plots, to which we'd become attached for several years, made our hearts sink. Many books were left in my study. They were the collection of thirty years of blood, sweat and tears. I'd even skipped lunch during student years to buy these books one-by-one. I had wrestled with these well-thumbed books, page-by-page, during long winter nights. My thoughts had hovered over those pages. My pencil made lines on them. They were books, but they were also almost like a part of my body. I am throwing them away now so I can be on my way to an unknown place.

December 15, 1950.

Everybody seems to be feeling relief at President Truman's announcement that the UN troops will not leave Korea under any circumstance. I think I could drink barrels of wine and put my head into an ice hole to die because of the ugliness in this country. The ugliness that started a fratricidal war, that brought foreign forces in and that wishes to keep the foreign troops here forever while being worried to death that they might leave.

December 16, 1950.

A news agency report of the use of an atomic bomb, that is seconded by wall posters issued by responsible organizations, agitated people for a while. The Attlee-Truman meeting[168] was just a few days old and the resulting communiqué did not indicate the use of atomic bombs at all for now and made people skeptical at the news. Just as they had expected, there was a news article later regarding its falsehood.

It shames me to think how foreigners would view these reports. They may be sneering at us for hoping so much for the use of atomic bombs that this type of nonsensical news could sweep the city.

We missed the trains, and a car I had hoped for did not materialize. It has now been several days since I came out to Namsan-dong, but I still do not see any way out. It has been extremely uncomfortable ever since we left our house. Expenses keep piling up despite dwindling funds. It is also

---

168 The communiqué issued by President Truman and UK Prime Minister Attlee on how US and Europe would respond soon to stop expansion of communism in the world.

hard to watch Wife going through hardship. It's like unbundling a bag of bowls in the morning and packing it again at night. Mr. Su Kyungsuk brothers and Hyunok[169] had followed us, hoping to get some help, and I was truly sorry to see them all go back.

I myself roamed the streets of Jinsooryung Hill in a snowstorm with indescribably fretful thoughts, but I still do not see any light at the end of the tunnel.

December 17, 1950.

As I couldn't find any leads in Namsan-dong anyway, I moved to Myungryoon-dong to see if I could get any help from Mr. Lee Yonghi. However, the discomfort of being guests in somebody's house is the same. Wife is talking about going back to our house. Suppose we did that; we would then lose any opportunity of leaving Seoul for good.

When Bong-a suddenly said, "What would the goat eat?", we remembered what we had left behind. There was a goat that had a kid twenty days ago. We couldn't kill it because of its pitiful kid, but eating the kid was not something we could do either. We just left some food for it and left. We were too occupied with starting our journey to think about them. When Bong-a reminded us of the poor things, pity overwhelmed us.

---

169 Prof. Kim's sister-in-law.

December 18, 1950.

We could finally leave in the late afternoon today. It happened to snow in large flakes. We were so anxious we couldn't leave Seoul fast enough, but sitting on a truck bed and looking at the streets of Seoul disappearing into a snowstorm, I felt deep emotion surging within me. It was a mixture of emotions filled with relief and sorrow.... *Goodbye, Seoul.*

By the time we crossed the floating bridge of Han River, it was already dusk. Passing by an airport and heading toward Yungdeungpo, only the bright moonlight shone in a boundless silver world. The single line of the headlights of cars, as if strung together, was quite a sight. *No one could say it was poetic.* Korean people are now too tired to be poetic.

December 19, 1950.

We slept overnight on the floor of a shabby café in Suwon. We are again driving on the snowy Kyungboo Highway[170] today. We were relieved to be able to squeeze the children into the compartment of a Jeep, but we were sitting atop belongings packed high upon the truck bed, attempting to block the snowstorm with our heavy coats. This was still much better than people who were loaded fully on the top of trains:

---

170 The main road connecting Seoul to Busan.

- A mother on the top of a train had tied her children to herself, but when she fell asleep, she fell killing herself and the children.

- A woman gave birth to a baby on top of a train while others held up blankets to shield them from the wind. But how fiercely cold must it have been on top of a running train in this cold winter. The new mother picked up the baby and threw it under the train before she crumpled and lost consciousness.

- A young woman with a baby on her back was trying to climb to the top of a train with all of her might, but as her hands were frozen, she could not protect the baby much. After a while, when she tried to feed her baby, the baby was already dead from the cold. The young mother went mad right there.

Any of these horrible stories would make listeners' hearts break, but nowadays there are so many stories of a similar kind that our senses have become too dull to feel any shock even when we hear them. The lives of Koreans have become comparable to those of worms.

We stayed in Jochiwon today. I met Kwon Yunghee *koon*. As he watched the trains and trucks full of refugees going south, he said it was hard to continue working. I could understand him.

He asked, "How do you see the war?" I couldn't say anything because I didn't know. In fact, no Korean would know. Korea is now moving with absolutely no volition of its own. The only lifeline comes from the prolonged stationing of foreign troops. I am not saying it is not right. I just feel bad that we continue to do nothing while becoming more corrupted.

December 20, 1950.

The day is cloudless, but the entire world has been turned silver. The road is quite slippery with packed snow. One doesn't know what would happen if the tires slipped. There are some instances where cars have been overturned, causing people to die or to get injured. We saw one such accident. We urged the driver to please drive slowly and carefully even if we consequently arrived there late.

We slept in Yungdong at night at a so-called lodging house that was built with cinder blocks on a completely burned-out, empty space. We couldn't sleep because the snowstorm disturbed our slumber. Realizing this will be the fate of our people, I have no place to turn to and complain.

December 21, 1950.

We reached Daegu. News that my father is ill weighs heavily on my heart.

I need to go and see him…. My public and private duty is to bring this group of people safely to Busan. I could not sleep again. The farther I go; the more onerous burdens seem to await me.

December 22, 1950.

Kim Sanggee *sunsaeng* left for Suwon in a military police car because his wife had left 300,000 *won* in Suwon on the way down. My responsibility of transporting this group became heavier thereafter.

We left Daegu late and went only as far as Kyungjoo today. We passed Yungchun in the night. It was such a bright night. On this side of Choopoongryung (*a pass connecting Chungchung Province and Kyungsang Province*), there was no trace of snow. Looking at the dim mountains of my hometown from the bed of a running truck, I can only fight back tears.

I remember a similar moment under a bright moon, at dawn on a day during Japanese rule when I was fifteen. I got arrested[171] and was taken to the Yungchun police station and passed by this very hill. One may regard that the past half of my life as checkered. It was. The future half of it will not be smooth either, I am sure.

December 23, 1950.

We reached Busan—the southern end of Korea where one can see the ocean.

With frozen hands and dirt-covered faces carrying refugee bundles, we landed in the middle of Busan, but there was no place to spend the night. Dragging the car along, we

---

171 See Appendix B: My Parents.

roamed unfamiliar streets until late only to find there was no inn with room available. As our arrival was so late, all the rooms were already taken. And there still will be many more people from Seoul heading this way….

Mr. Shin, who accompanied us, uttered some unreasonable complaints, and then took off by himself to go to the house of someone he knew, leaving me to struggle by myself with ten women and children. Furthermore, I am on pins and needles as the Jeep with our children hasn't arrived yet. My family and the family of Mr. Lee for whom I am responsible for are all riding in the Jeep.

In the end, I took the ten women and children to Lee Suk-tae *koon*'s parents' house in Danggam-dong and there unloaded baggage close to curfew.

December 24, 1950

My biggest worry was set to rest as the Jeep arrived with a tale of a car trouble[172] in Yangsan where guerrillas have appeared frequently. It was quite fortunate the children were all in good spirits even after suffering a two-hundred-and-fifty-mile journey.

I was quite worried as we saw many refugees from Seoul staying under the eaves of other people's houses in this cold weather without being able to secure a room. But I breathed

---

172 The translator, 5 years old at the time, vaguely remembers riding with the Jeep's window cracked.

a sigh of relief when Mr. Park Yunghee[173] welcomed us just like old times and obtained a room for us next door in a company house of the Head of the Grain Department of the Union. Trustworthy people can be trusted in whatever the situation. I was quite relieved, as if I had come across an oasis in a desert.

December 25, 1950.

When I went to Danggam-dong to pick up the luggage I'd left, there was a telegram informing me of my father's critical illness. I got on the road again in a hurry. I got a ride on a fish truck heading to Daegu, but we lost the sunlight when it had car trouble on the hillside of Oolsan. Driving in moonlight, we reached Yungchun late around 11:00pm. My mind was racing, but I couldn't go further because a curfew was in place. I went to the Yungchun police station and through the goodwill of strangers, spent an uncomfortable night in a night-duty room.

December 26, 1950.

Upon hearing the chime indicating it was six o'clock, I ran seven miles home in the dark. I came across a well-

---

173 A close friend at Chosun Financial Union in which Prof. Kim had worked before he became a university professor.

dressed person with a hat who said he lived in Sinduk-dong. I asked if there was any news of illness from Wonchon-dong. I relaxed a bit when he said he hadn't heard any special news during the last few days.

It was ten minutes before eight when I arrived at home. My father's condition was grave as his heart had been weakened by a bout of severe coughing. He was our father, aged and exhausted from taking care of us. I tried to find something I could do, but all I could do was worry. He was kept alive by daily injections.

December 27, 1950.

The doctor said he may recover, but I didn't feel at ease as his symptoms were very grave. As the doctor said, smoking is bad, and when he smokes, there will be coughing spasms. We insisted he not smoke, but it was such a long habit of his. It was hard to see him seeking cigarettes even while losing consciousness. I hid away all his cigarettes and their accessories. Being unable to offer him the cigarettes he wanted so badly and feeling guilty about smoking outside, I myself made a decision to stop smoking that day.

December 28, 1950.

Some American soldiers who had retreated from Heungnam[174] moved into town and are creating an atmosphere of uneasiness. There were incidents of rape in Booheung-dong and Chiil-dong. In a town near us, there was a shooting of an innocent person because he wouldn't release a woman to them. All young women are taking refuge in the mountains.

A note from Hijoon had arrived at daytime saying there were American soldiers at his house and so I went there. Drunken soldiers had brought a bucket of rice wine and were goading my cousin's sister-in-law to drink. When I got there, they asked me to drink. I made a show of drinking a bit and told them I could not drink anymore because it was too cold and they must leave as this was a respectable house. One of them said, "You must be a People's Republic Army soldier. I should kill you." He pointed a gun at my chest and noisily loaded bullets. My heart skipped a beat at his drunken, tongue-twisted voice and the sound of his gun loading. But I told him calmly, "I am not such a person. I am a professor at a national university." Then the other soldier took the gun away and they left.

The Republic of Korea is now in a state where it needs to beg and cry for even these kinds of soldiers to stay here for

---

174 As unstoppably large Chinese troops came down, a large-scale shipboard evacuation of US forces, ROK forces and civilians from Heungnam, an East coast port city in North Korea, to Busan, took place from Dec 15 through Dec. 24. The operation was called 'Christmas Cargo' during the operation and was subsequently called 'Christmas Miracle'.

a very long time. The People's Republic have brought forth the situation whereby this would happen. *Ahh, where can we go and find our real motherland?*

December 29, 1950

The government rounded up all eligible candidates for soldiers from the Kyunggi, Kangwon and Chungchung Provinces, named them 'recruit trainees', and sent them south for training. The daily number of people passing our town is tens of thousands. They must be dog-tired, walking ten days or so during these coldest days of snowy winter. But when I see spirit and energy in their eyes, I think I can keep a hope for the future of this country.

Every house has been allocated ten or more of the recruit trainees to feed and house. Watching them drag their feet into the house late at night, gobble down rice bowls, fall down to sleep anywhere they could, and then in the morning, gulp down meals at dawn before marching away, I wonder how worried their parents must be.

On the other hand, I can see that the administration's policy is an effort to preserve the country's youth, even with these drastic measures. They had escaped the Volunteer Army recruitment during the three-month communist period, within the areas that had fallen to the North. I thought if the People's Republic had made them suffer less, they would not have come *en masse* like this when the Republic of Korea called them. Politics seems to involve getting paid back with its own coin when things are turned around.

December 30, 1950.

Facing an unprecedented national crisis, it's true my mind would sometimes become gloomy. But I believe at the same time that our nation's power and will to survive is strong.

Although accounts from early history are not very clear, after Kokooryu[175] collapsed, the hegemony of Balhae[176] was controlled by migrant Kokooryu people. After the middle period of Koryo[177], its border was pushed down by the Mongolian power below Jabiryung and Chulsan[178]. Many Koreans moved to Manchuria beyond the Yalu River, making the area of Simyang[179] a major region in which our people lived since. During the late Chosun dynasty, while a border marker was not being settled by international politics, the

---

175 One of old three kingdoms in the Korean peninsula. BC 37 through AD 668.
176 Balhae (698-926) was a large country established by Koreans in some northern parts of Korea and a large part of Manchuria.
177 Koryo (918-1392) followed Shilla (57 BC-935) and was succeeded by Chosun (1392-1897). Chosun changed its name to Daehan Jekook (1897-1910). These four successive kingdoms governed Korea for nearly two thousand years continuously, but Daehan Jekook was absorbed into Japan in 1910.
178 Places South of Yalu River, the boundary between Korea and China.
179 A major Chinese city about 130 miles north of Yalu River where many Koreans have lived for a long period.

land of Bookgando[180] had already become the de facto place of our people's settlement.

Under the harsh exploitation and oppression by the Japanese colonial regime, hundreds of thousands of Korean people crossed the East Sea to live in Japan while a million went north to settle in the plains of Manchuria. Of course, they were forced by Japanese oppression into these oppressive or extremely inhospitable living conditions of other countries. However, Korean people did not collapse but instead expanded their foothold within their respective regions using their tremendous survival powers.

Whatever hardships and struggles arise in our nation's future, we will overcome them all with our power of sheer survival ....

December 31, 1950.

Heavy winds blew during the night, but despite that, it is warmer today. I spent the long night dozing and waking while taking care of my father. I then fell into a deep sleep at dawn dreaming of Seoul. Seoul has become a place I can see only in a dream.

I was dreaming about new shoots that would arise from dahlia bulbs at the foot of the south-facing window. I was worried the new shoots would not survive under the heavy burden of soil unless I moved them to the field soon, but I

---

180 An area north of Dooman River, the other river that separates Korea and China.

realized I could not reach them with my hands. I woke up to the sound of my father's coughing.

Without fail, fresh shoots will arise from dahlia bulbs when spring comes. While under the frozen soil, as if holding their breath during these long and interminable winter nights, there is a force of life within them that will prepare them for the new spring. When the time comes, new shoots will arise and strong stems will grow. Then fragrant flowers will blossom gracefully and elegantly.

When will we be able to go back to Seoul?[181]

[*There is a gap in the diary until Mar 1. Getting a job and surviving in Busan with all other refugees from the north must have been challenging for him to continue writing the diary. – the translator*]

---

181 He would never return to Seoul.

Life in Busan

March 1951

March 1, 1951.

The 1st of March[182] has arrived once again, but our surroundings remain gloomy. Listening to the expected congratulatory speeches, I do not feel any emotion. *Is it because my senses have become dull? Or is it because my mind is now twisted?* The cut I had on my face when I was shaving last Sunday has flared up and my face is quite swollen. When on my way to the hospital, passing the Choongmooro rotary, I saw a plaza full of manly youths. There were endless lines of students coming into the plaza with fluttering flags, banging drums, and blowing horns. There were lines and lines…. Watching this mass of people, I felt as if I was possessed by something. I forgot to go to the hospital and turned my car around towards home feeling something like pride fill my chest.

I am happy to pick up a pen again after abandoning it for the last couple of months as a refugee.

---

182 A national holiday celebrating the nationwide peaceful demonstration against Japanese rule in 1919.

March 2, 1951.

As my face was too swollen to open my eyes, I visited Dr. Park, a dermatologist. He said the skin inflammation seemed to have reached a peak and would subside even if left untouched. With reluctance, he gave me a shot of calcium.

As he was writing in my chart, I told him my name. He looked up at me again and asked me which high school I had attended. When I told him I had attended the Daegu High School for a while, he grasped my hands and told me his name is Park Doosik. I could vaguely remember his old face.

Twenty-five years. Compared to the history of mankind, it is just a blink. But a young boy who is now a middle-aged doctor untangles my dim memory. It is a trite remark, but I cannot but feel ephemerality of life.

How then can I explain this tragedy of mankind unfolding in this ephemeral life?

March 3, 1951. Clear.

Last night's rain gave the trees in the yard a shine of a bluish-tinted sheen. The wind in this port city becomes intermittently fierce and cold, but the new season is here, without fail.

The children's spontaneous and inadvertent comments about the peach blossoms back at home induce the futile longings of a refugee.

I was so happy to see my books intact when in a dream I returned home. Wife just laughed it off saying that dreams are the opposite of reality. My mind is now fully awake but filled infinitely with frustration and sadness.

March 4, 1951. Clear.

I enjoyed the sunshine in the morning, and I went to the law school[183] in the afternoon to give a lecture with my still-swollen face. As it was the first lecture after coming south, I didn't allow myself to skip it just because I was not well. We used a rented room in Mr. Byun's law office in front of the court. About twenty students were overflowing the room and a small adjoining floor space. There was even a baby sleeping in a corner of our room.

I told them, "During these harsh times, we are so lucky to have this kind of atmosphere which is filled with the desire and will to learn. No matter how bitter the current circumstances are, we should not allow ourselves to buckle under the force of harsh realities. We should endeavor to maintain the pride of young students and thus see the realities with rational mind and eyes." I may have gone a bit overboard in conveying the harsh circumstances and bitter times because the students, from one corner to another, began to sob. I also had a lump in my throat.

---

183 The school also moved down to Busan.

March 5, 1951.

Perhaps I worked too hard yesterday. I developed a fever overnight and suffered throughout the day.

Lee Byungdo *sunsaeng*, along with Mr. Jun Haejong, visited me in the daytime to inquire after my illness. We lost track of time while talking about lost books and buried manuscripts.

He said, "Although we vacated Seoul, we didn't realize how the 38th parallel would so easily fall and Seoul would be captured again."

I said, "I thought, if Seoul falls, Busan will also fall, so bringing those books and manuscripts would just be a burden in the end." Together with Mr. Jun, we smiled sad smiles.

March 6, 1951. Rain.

In the morning rain, Wife helped the house owner with their bean paste preparation. As the wife of a household, I wondered how she would feel that she cannot even think about preparing our own bean paste at this time of the year while she is helping others. I decided to overlook any of her irritation today.

Mr. Lee Kanghoo, who used to work with me at Daechi, came to visit me. We enjoyed meeting again after ten years. He brought his whole savings of 1,000,000 *won* and trusted me to keep it for him. His trust overwhelmed me. But at the same time, holding this large sum of money makes me agitated and nervous because we are dismally pressed for money these days.

Hyub-a was weaned from breast milk recently and cannot eat much more than rice water these days. His countenance deteriorates every day. It's heart-wrenching, but there is not much we can do.

I have been in my sickbed and all food tastes badly like a tree bark. "I wish we could get a sheet of *gheem* (*salted and dried seaweed sheets*)," said Wife. I told her, "Oh, don't think about *gheem*. I feel guilty even for being able to eat some rice grains these days." But there is no mistaking that I also feel pains of hunger. Bong-a and Mok-a don't complain too much about food, but their less-than-enthusiastic attitude towards meals is so pitiable.

What if I take 10,000 won from what Mr. Lee left in my care, visit a hospital, buy a few days of food for the children and before he comes back, I could replace the amount. Wouldn't that be okay? Even if I couldn't replace the amount by that time and told him the story, he would say what I did was right, wouldn't he? These thoughts occur once or twice every day and I consider the effort I make to suppress them must be a trial God is giving me.

March 7, 1951.

Busan children tease Seoul children, "Seoul *naegi, damanaegi*, tasty *gorin aegi*." Seoul children counter,

"*Ggolddigi, ggolddigi, sigolddigi.*[184]" A sliver of refugee life.

March 8, 1951.

700 *won* for an apple!

When my father heard an apple cost 15 *won* in Manchuria a while ago, he was shocked and wondered how those people could live with such high prices. He is gone now, but this was only about five or six years ago. To exceed that, it was 100 *won* only three months ago. One can only guess at the speed of inflation.

Hyub-a has just been weaned from his mothers' milk, but we can't buy proper food for him. He has been fretful, but all we can do is watch the quickly-rising food prices. After having had no income for the past week, Wife's complaints multiply, and I can find no words to placate her.

March 9, 1951.

Bong-a has become quite good at counting these days.

---

184 These are teasing words against each other, juxtaposed with sounds (naegi, aegi, and ddigi) and meanings. Their meanings can be roughly explained as follows, "Seoul kid, onion, tasty smelly baby" against "octopus, octopus, country bumpkin." One can see endings of words rhyme.

Counting good things to do every day, he made it to forty-two. Happy with himself, he tries hard to count all those things with his tiny fingers. At his side, Mok-a tries to copy what's being recited:

5. Don't fight with Mok-a.

6. Be affectionate to Hyub-a.

12. Don't covet my brothers' cookies.

21. Be good at paper folding.

25. Be good at reading clocks.

30. Wash hands before meals.

20. Eat *dried cabbage* without complaint. These were given to us by other families.

The best one is # 18... Never go next door before mealtime like a beggar[185].

March 10, 1951.

We went to Park s*unsaeng*'s in Koejungree with the children.

We were resting in front of a hut at the top of a mountain when a passing young Chinese man showed me his ID card. We both laughed heartily as he mistook me for a roadside inspector. I thought those inspectors were only on the city streets, but now I see they are even on a backward mountain road like this one. They are checking passersby one-by-one

---

185 Because, at Mr. Park's house, he would be given something to eat more often than not.

to find secret agents without papers of citizenship or province residency, or youths who have evaded their military duties. This is another of our country's peculiar sights these days. But these measures probably do little. Any capable special agent can forge citizenship papers these days. It is also commonly known that sending children to the army happens only because their fathers and brothers are too poor and incapable to support them.

We forced ourselves to march home through Gamchun and Songdo in the afternoon. As the children all had aching legs, I carried them on my back or held them in my arms and arrived home late.

March 11, 1951.

Mr. Park told me I can study at his house. His entire family always shows us such kindness. I could never express enough gratitude for all the kindness I have encountered in this bleak refugee life.

I had a law school lecture in the afternoon.

Although Korean people now live in the most underdeveloped country in the world and possess many inferior characteristics, it is also true they have superb and hidden potential capabilities. Excellence in physical strength and endurance has been clearly demonstrated by repeated victories in marathons[186]. Outstanding intellectual strength, originality and creativity is amply demonstrated in creating

---

186 First and third place in the 1936 Berlin Olympics and first

Hangeul[187]. Even if our current situation is dire and seemingly hopeless, we should not therefore lose our national hope. I said with emphasis: "However unbearable our current situation is, we can project an unbounded hope to our future."

I dropped by the temporary University office on the way home and discussed the subject of my history class. A corner of a shabby, tin-roof barrack by the streetcar rails is being used as a classroom, but the 'best university in the Republic of Korea' may have to pack its belongings again soon as we will be kicked out even from there.

---

place in Boston Marathon in 1947.

187 In 1443, the Korean alphabet, Hangeul, was developed by a group of scholars under the direction of King Sejong. Hangeul is by now well-recognized and has been voted by world linguists several times in recent years to be the clearest and most efficient alphabet in the world. It has been adopted by many small countries without alphabets. An example of praise: "It is really impossible to withhold admiration for this conception of a shape-function relationship and for the way it was carried out. But for those shapes themselves to be rationalized on the basis of the speech organs associated with their sounds – that is unparalleled grammatological luxury! The Korean phonologists were skillful indeed, but they were not lacking in creative imagination either." G. Ledyard, Columbia University.

March 12, 1951.

I struggled hard to come up with 26,000 *won* so as not to miss the opportunity of receiving a sack of flour that was being distributed. It is an ignominious life but, with children with voracious appetites, I cannot keep insisting on living on sparse provisions.

Wife brought a unit of cloth for a skirt and a pair of men's trousers to the market. This is after ten days of suffering through all kinds of hardship, with no income. With a small bit of cash, we can get some food for the malnourished children. When we get some of the rice distribution, we can bring some rice back to market to sell in order to pay off urgent debts.

Poverty is cutting to the bone these days.

March 13, 1951.

Lee Heeseung *sunsaeng* dropped by to say goodbye as he is leaving for Jinhae[188]. Most people around me are being sucked into the military in one way or another. War holds such immense and scary power.

After parting with the *sunsaengnim,* I watched a piece of cloud floating at the edge of the sky with blankness in my heart.

---

188 A nearby city where the Korean Navy is headquartered.

April 1951

April 6, 1951.

"Bird, bird, bird/In morning wind, cold wind — That flying wild goose, crying — What is it going to do there — To hatch chicks — How many — Three chicks — You have one — I have one — Stew and eat them — Roast and eat them — *jang ggen bbo* (*paper-scissors-stone*)."

This is a favorite song of the children while playing. When one-year-old Hyub-a hears this song, he gets excited and mimics dancing. I don't know who wrote this song, but how can they think about eating baby chicks of wild geese, of all things, 'either stewed or roasted'? It would be painfully sad if there was something in this song that reflects our national characteristics.

April 7, 1951.

"*Over and over the corpses of comrades/forward and forward,*" Bong-a and Mok-a raise their pitch on this military song. I don't know where they picked it up.

I agree entirely with Wife when she comments, "Do they have to use the word 'corpses'? Can't they use the word, 'fallen comrades' instead?"

In the refrain of the song somewhere is a phrase, '*Ahh, Korea, Korea—Korea of righteousness*'. Whenever I hear this part, there is something that does not feel quite right in the corner of my mind. Everybody talks about the corruption of the Republic of Korea. All of them are members of the Republic of Korea, but nobody seems to have any clear idea of what to do about it.

April 8, 1951. *(March 3rd in the lunar calendar).*

Flowers blossom and fall in the fierce winds of the port.

The refugees greeted the spring amid their weary existence.

Discussed with Wife what to do in the future. We should endeavor to read and translate books about children while we pick up our own pens to write a book that can be handed down for posterity. A book which is comparable to *The School of Love* by Amicis[189].

** *The diary ends here. Prof. Kim would die six months later.*

---

189 The original Italian name of the book is Cuore by Edmondo de Amicis. It tells stories of young happy children in a school setting who are cared for with love. At least, that is how the translator remembers.

Appendix A: A Short History of the Korean War

Mostly From Wikipedia, April 2014 and January 2020

The Korean War (25 June 1950 – 27 July 1953) was a war between the Republic of Korea (South Korea), supported by the United Nations, and the Democratic People's Republic of Korea (North Korea), supported by China and the Soviet Union.

After the surrender of Japan at the end of World War II on 15 August 1945, Korea was divided at the 38th parallel into two zones of occupation. The Soviet Union administered the northern half and the United States administered the southern half.

The Korean people were in a state of confusion with regard to choosing the right political system for the liberated country between communism and democracy. There were movements of families from one side to the other depending on their political preferences. Political leaders and intellectual elites were divided, and tensions were built among them.

As a result of Cold War tensions, primarily between the United States and the Soviet Union, the occupation zones became two sovereign states in 1948. A socialist state was established in the north under the totalitarian leadership of Kim Il-sung and a capitalist state in the south under the authoritarian leadership of Rhee Syngman. Both governments of the two new Korean states claimed to be the sole legitimate government of all Korea, and neither accepted the border as permanent.

Although reunification negotiations continued during the months preceding the war, tensions intensified. Cross-border skirmishes and raids at the 38th Parallel persisted. Finally, the situation escalated into open warfare when North Korean military (Korean People's Army, KPA) forces invaded South Korea on 25 June 1950. The United Nations (UN) Security Council passed a resolution allowing military intervention in Korea to repel what they recognized as a North Korean invasion. Twenty-one countries of the United Nations contributed to the UN force, with the United States providing around 90% of the military personnel.

After the first two months of the war, the South Korean Army (Republic of Korea Army, ROKA) and the UN forces were on the point of defeat. As a result, the ROKA and the UN troops retreated to a small area behind a defensive line known as the Pusan (*or Busan*) Perimeter.

In September 1950, an amphibious UN counter-offensive was launched at Incheon cutting off many KPA troops in South Korea. Those who escaped envelopment and capture were forced to retreat back to the north. The UN and ROK forces moved into North Korea in October 1950 and moved rapidly towards the Yalu River—the border with China.

On 19 October 1950, Chinese forces of the People's Volunteer Army (PVA) crossed the Yalu and entered the war. The surprise Chinese intervention triggered a retreat of UN forces back below the 38th Parallel by late December. While not directly committing forces to the conflict, the Soviet Union provided material aid to both the North Korean and Chinese armies.

In these and later battles, Seoul changed hands four times and the last two years of fighting became a war of attrition with the front line near the 38th Parallel. The war in the air, however, was never a stalemate. North Korea was subject to a massive and ruthless U.S. bombing campaign. Jet fighters confronted each other in air-to-air combat for the first time in history and Soviet pilots covertly flew in defense of their communist allies. North Korea became among the most heavily bombed countries in history.

The fighting ended on 27 July 1953 when the Korean Armistice Agreement was signed. The agreement created the Korean Demilitarized Zone (DMZ) to separate North and South Korea and allowed the return of prisoners. However, no peace treaty was ever signed, and the two Koreas are technically still at war and engaged in a frozen and endless conflict.

The Korean War was among the most destructive conflicts of the modern era with about 3 million war fatalities and a larger proportional civilian death toll than World War II or the Vietnam War. About 1,000,000 DPRK soldiers and civilians, 1,200,000 ROK soldiers and civilians, 600,000 Chinese soldiers and 36,000 American soldiers perished during the War. The country was completely leveled.

Appendix B: My Parents

Kibong Kim, son and translator

Some details of this Appendix are obtained from: A revised '*Yuksa Apesu* (Facing History) with a bibliographical essay by Chung Byungjoon, 2009

My Father, Kim Sungchil

To many adolescent sons, their father is a giant. Our father, Kim Sungchil, still is a giant to me, even though I am an old man in my seventies now. Not that I remember him very well as he died when I was only six. But it is because I have since learned what he had done and who he was as a person. By the time he died at the relatively young age of 38, he had done many things only a giant could do.

There were several notable events that marked him. In 1928, at the age of 15, he was arrested as one of the leaders of a school strike and as a founding member of a high school reading group that studied communism as a possible way for Korea to become capable of self-governing after it would hopefully be liberated from Japan. For this, he was arrested, kicked out of school, and held in prison for a year.

He stayed home for three years and helped at his family's rice farm in the small Southern town of Yungchun near Daegu. By himself, he studied poetry, agriculture, and history. He tried a new strain of rice from Japan and when it was successful, he reported this success to the *Dong-A Ilbo* (a major newspaper and one of the very few media outlets at the time). There were many inquiries from farmers from all over the country afterwards.

In 1932, when the same newspaper ran a contest for ideas to define a national policy concerning how best to vitalize Korean farming communities, his treatise won first place. I was told later that, at the award ceremony, people were shocked to discover a 19-year-old boy walking in to claim it. With the prize money, he could finally go to Japan and finish high school at the late age of 22.

In 1935, he won another national contest by the same newspaper on the topic of 'The Relationship between Cities and Farm Villages'. Afterwards, he worked as a board member in a local branch office of the Chosun Financial Union (which was the predecessor to the Agriculture Bank). He continued his search for better village-scale as well as national-scale farming management methods and submitted his research results often to various magazines and newspapers.

He gradually turned his attention toward Korean language and Korean history. He enrolled himself at the Kyungsung Law College in the History Department in 1935-1937. He continued working at the Financial Union headquarters before enrolling at the Kyungsung National University in the History department (1942-1946). In 1946, he started working as a full-time lecturer in the same department and a year later became an assistant professor.

One of his professional accomplishments was the publication of the book, *Chosun Yuksa* (Korean History), in February 1946. Korea was liberated from Japan in August 1945 when the United States defeated Japan. He immediately recognized an urgent need to re-educate Korean people about their history, differently from how it was intentionally mistaught by Japan.

He authored the history book for the Korean people who had never learned the proper history of their own country. The resulting lucid and readable book became very popular. Even now, I meet people living in the United States who tell me the book was one of the most influential books in their lives.

From 1946 through 1950, he seemed to have devoted himself fully to research and education. An entry appears in his diary on April 16, 1946: "I will lie hidden for a few years pouring all of my efforts into my studies.' In those four or five years, which amounted to almost all of his entire scholastic professional career, he authored five Korean or East Asian history books, translated five Chinese, Japanese or English books. He also authored numerous newspaper articles and magazine articles.

What I admire beyond these obvious events and accomplishments is that he was a very caring and diligent person with a firm purpose in life. His purpose was almost evangelical in a way. It was helping the people of his country, Korea. The people had been oppressed by the Japanese, had very few possessions and were suffering from the hardships of a suddenly liberated country with little resources. There was also confusion about where the country was politically heading. This confusion about whether the country should become a socialist/communist country, or a democratic country, was the seed of a reason why the Korean War would happen later.

He cared for people around him. He cared for his family, relatives, friends, fellow workers, and others. As shown in the diary, he gave his full attention to people and his actions towards them were always thoughtful. His thoughts and decisions were moderate. He saw both sides of conflicts. He worked hard to be in the middle when the middle was forbidden.

He cared for the country and its people. He researched old Korean words buried in the names of old towns, hills, brooks, etc. to study the origin of the Korean language. He published books on Korean history and translated foreign books (such as *The Good Earth* by Pearl Buck) to educate people. He devoted his life to the study of Korean identity and to the education of its people.

The country and its people were the objects of his devotion. That he mentions the word 'people' continually in the diary belies this. Even the very last line of his diary (April 8, 1951) speaks of how to better educate young Korean children.

Whenever I pick up my father's diary, I am reminded how lucky we are to be small people in a peaceful society, thanks entirely to the deeds of many unheralded giants like him during troubled times.

He was killed by a thug in October 1951.

Prof Kim's Publication Record

Books

- *Chosun Yuksa* (Korean History, 조선 역사), Chosun Financial Union, 1946
- *Dongyang Yuksa* (Eastern Asia History, 동양사), Jungeumsa, 1947
- *Shin Dongyangsa* (New Eastern Asia History, 신동양사), with Kim Sanggee, Kim Ilchool, Dongjisa, 1948
- *Life and History of Neighboring Countries* (이웃 나라의 생활 역사, with Kim Sanggee and Kim Ilchool, Dongjisa, 1949
- *Oorinara Yuksa* (History of Our Country, 우리나라 역사), Jungeumsa, 1950
- *Joongdeung Kookuh* (Mid-Level Korean Language, 중등 국어), Section 5: *Shilla Culture,* Kyohakdosu Ltd., 1951
- *Kooksa Tongron* (National History Overview, 국사통론), Gangdamsa, 1951
- *Facing History* (역사 앞에서), Changbisa, 1993

Translations

- *The Good Earth* (대지), Pearl Buck, Inmoonsa, 1940, from English
- *Chosun Nongchondam* (Korean Farm Village Stories, 조선 농촌담), Shigematsu Shoushu, Inmoonsa, 1941, from Japanese
- *Yongbiochunga* (용비어천가), 15th Century Chosun Government, Chosun Financial Union, 1948, from classic Chinese
- *The Grass Roof* (초당), Kang Younghill, Kemryongdosu, 1948, from English

- *Yulha Ilgee* (열하 일기), 5 volumes, Park Jiwon, Jungeumsa, 1949-50, from Chinese

Newspaper articles, 1928 – 1935

28 articles, mostly on 'Farm Village Relief Plan' and 'Relationship between Cities and Farm Villages'.

My Mother, Lee[190] Namduk

My mother was born in 1920 in Gongjoo, Choongchung Province. Her father ran away to a Northern part of Korea after he participated in an anti-Japanese movement. She did not attend high school because her father did not think it was a good idea for a girl to be educated. She self-studied at home in a city near Hamheung (a North Korean city on the East Coast). She passed a college qualification examination, came to Seoul by herself and enrolled at Ewha Women's University in the Korean Language department.

Before the Korean liberation in 1945, she transferred to the Korean Language/Literature Department at Kyungsung Imperial University. She met my father there.

It was a time when Japan forced Koreans to change their names to new Japanese names and tried hard to suppress the usage of Korean language in Korea. Written/spoken Korean language was banned, and Korean scholars were taken to jail while Korean newspapers were closed. She was the only student in the department, and there was only one Japanese professor.

After marriage, she stayed home, gave birth to us, and suffered through the war with all of us. When our father passed away, she started her career by teaching Korean language at a local girls' high school in Busan. After we returned to Seoul in 1955, she became a professor at Ehwa Women's University in the Korean Language and Literature Department.

---

190 In Korea, wives keep their family names after marriage.

She devoted her research life to the etymology (study of linguistic origin and historical changes) of the Korean language. She also specialized in comparative Ural Altai language group studies. For example, she compared similar indigenous words in the Korean and Japanese languages to identify similarities, differences and historical changes, ultimately to discover the origination and evolution of these indigenous words. One major conclusion of the study was her theory that both the Korean and Japanese languages came from one origin. To be precise, based on the similarities and variations of about two hundred corresponding indigenous words of both countries, her theory was the Japanese language was developed after the Korean language.

Her ultimate accomplishment was a large, four-volume treatise, *Study of the Origin of Korean Language*, published in 1985-1986 just prior to her retirement from the University. She published a book in Japanese on the comparative statistical study of the origins of the Korean and Japanese languages in 1988.

She also co-translated her husband's diary into Japanese in 1996. The name of the book was, *People's Army in Seoul*.

She had always told us, "Your father was my husband and teacher."

Epilogue

This diary, plus an earlier diary of the period of 1945-1946 and January 1950, was published for the first time in 1993. It was 40 years after the armistice between North Korea and the United Nations. The reason why its publication was so delayed was because of my father's neutral views during the war. My mother feared that after the devastation and suffering from the war, most South Koreans might not take to his neutral views kindly.

My mother kept her husband's diary hidden until the national hostile sentiment mellowed and its publication became possible. The diary is one of a few documents in Korea that recorded events of the Korean War from a personal viewpoint.

In 1987, my mother gave the diary to her third son, Kim Kihyub who appears in the diary as Hyub-a. Kihyub, who is a historian and writer himself, edited the diary and the result was the book, *Facing History (Yuksa Apesu,* 역사 앞에서, 1993*)*. The book became an instant national bestseller in Korea.

I found an interesting anecdote while flipping through a copy of the original manuscript. An unpublished one-sentence passage appears in January 1951. It was just before Hyub-a's first birthday, when my father had paused writing the diary for a few weeks. It says, "I am inserting this sentence because Hyub-a keeps pointing to the manuscript and urging me to write something in it." That Hyub-a would become the editor of the published book 42 years later.

In 2009, Chung Byungjoon published a revised '*Yuksa Apesu (Facing History)* with a comprehensive bibliographical essay. The book was a go-to reference for this translation.

A portion of the diary prior to June 25th, 1950 describes life after the liberation from Japan, until the war. In this English version, I omitted that part to focus on the Korean War.

Having been 5 years old at the time of the war, I do not remember much of its harshness. What I remember, however, is the warmth of the people around me who cared for each other. While preparing and translating this book, I had the feeling I was once again in my parents' arms.

I started translating the diary about five years ago. As a non-native English speaker, it was laborious work. My original goal was to teach our children and their children about from where they came, and there was no better way to do so than their reading the diary.

However, as I have read and re-read the diary many times during the course of translation and editing, I have come to see there is more of the diary that I wanted to share with the world: what Korea is like, who Koreans are, and how one Korean person lived.

There is one family picture. It was taken a few days before my father's death in October 1951. My guess is that it was taken on the fourth birthday of Kimok (Mok-a, who retired as a professor of statistics at Koryo University), who is sitting next to my father. Hyub-a, in my mother's arms, was one at the time. I was six. My mother was 31 and my father was 38. My father never met his daughter with gentle and beautiful eyes, Moonyung, who would be born six months later.

I wish to thank the people who made this book possible: my father, my mother, Hyub-a, my wife, and the people who made it better: Chung Byungjoon, Yoon Yeo Ick, Mira Park, and my daughter – Sonia Rapko.

Kibong Kim

The first page (June 25, 1950) of the original manuscript.

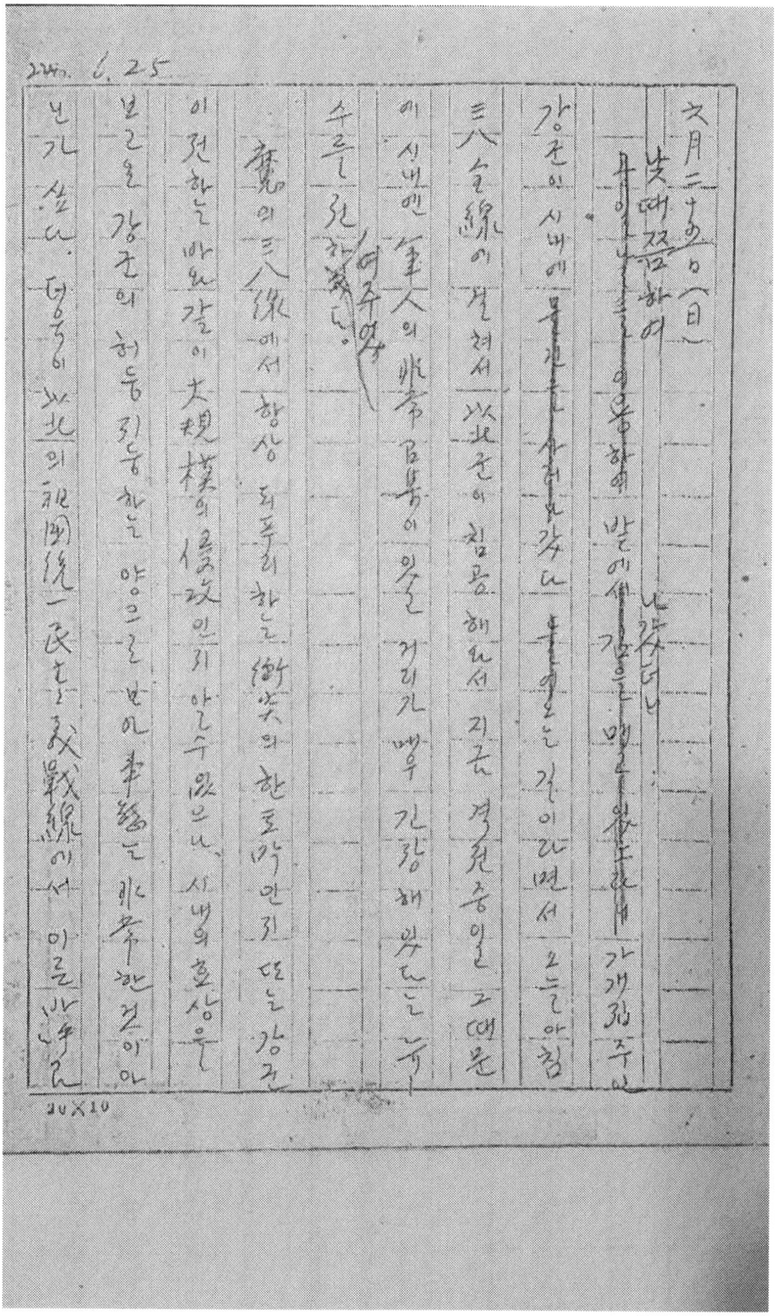

Printed in Great Britain
by Amazon